CARL MENGER

INVESTIGATIONS INTO THE METHOD OF THE SOCIAL SCIENCES WITH SPECIAL REFERENCE TO ECONOMICS

Formerly published under the title:
PROBLEMS OF ECONOMICS AND SOCIOLOGY

(Untersuchungen über die Methode der Socialwissenschaften und der Politischen Oekonomie insbesondere)

WITH A NEW INTRODUCTION
BY LAWRENCE H. WHITE

EDITED BY LOUIS SCHNEIDER

TRANSLATED BY FRANCIS J. NOCK

The Ludwig von Mises Institute
Auburn, Alabama 2009

Library of Congress Cataloging in Publication Data

Menger, Karl, 1840–1921.
Investigations into the method of the social sciences, with special reference to economics—formerly published under title, Problems of economics and sociology.

(The Institute for Humane Studies series in economic theory)
Translation of: Untersuchungen über die Methode der Socialwissenschaften, und der politischen Oekonomie insbesondere.
Bibliography: p.
1. Economics. 2. Economic policy. 3. Social sciences. I. Schneider, Louis, 1915–
II. Title. III. Title: Problems of economics and sociology. IV. Series: Studies in economic theory.
HB175.M48153 1985 330′.072 85-8918
ISBN 0-8147-5396-5 (alk. paper)
ISBN 0-8147-5397-3 (pbk. : alk. paper)

Mises Institute, Auburn, Alabama 2009

Clothbound editions of New York University Press books are Smyth-sewn and printed on permanent and durable acid-free paper.

Manufactured in the United States of America

INVESTIGATIONS INTO THE METHOD OF THE SOCIAL SCIENCES WITH SPECIAL REFERENCE TO ECONOMICS

TABLE OF CONTENTS

INTRODUCTION TO THE NEW YORK UNIVERSITY PRESS EDITION

It is a rare book in economics that deserves to be translated into English as much as eighty years after its initial publication. The book that actually receives such attention after so many years almost *ipso facto* qualifies as a classic.[1] Carl Menger's *Untersuchungen uber die Methode der Socialwissenschaften und der Politischen Oekonomie Insbesondere* of 1883 clearly merited the translation that it finally received in 1963 (under the title *Problems of Economics and Sociology*[2]), for there is no doubt about its preeminence as a treatment of vital methodological issues in economics. When this translation fell out of print in recent years, the Institute for Humane Studies and the New York University Press became naturally eager to reissue it as part of their series of Studies in Economic Theory. This series includes the 1981 edition of Menger's only other book-length work, *Principles of Economics*, which was first published in 1871. Thus the *Investigations* takes its well-deserved place alongside the *Principles* as a classic of economic thought enjoying a second century of life in a new language.

The republication of the *Investigations* today is especially appropriate in light of the interest that economists have recently been taking in this work, in the writings of Carl Menger generally, and (still

[1] Beside the present work the only examples that come to mind of works translated into English after eighty years are both classics: Richard Cantillon, *Essai sur la Nature du Commerce en General* (1752) in 1933, and Hermann Heinrich Gossen, *Entwickelung der Gesetze des Menschlichen Verkehrs* (1845) in 1983.

Menger's own *Grundsatze der Volkswirthschaftlehre* (1871) also a classic, went 79 years before an English translation appeared.

[2] Carl Menger, *Problems of Economics and Sociology* (Urbana: University of Illinois Press, 1963). The present title attempts to render literally the wording of the original German title.

more generally) in the ideas of the Austrian School of Economics he founded. In his introduction to the 1963 edition of this work Louis Schneider wrote (p. 3): "Neither economists nor sociologists working in the English language have paid any notable attention to the *Untersuchungen.*" Since that edition appeared the situation has noticeably changed. The *Investigations* has been garnering numerous citations each year by authors in major economics journals, at a rate only slightly slower than that of the *Principles*. Citations to these and to Menger's other works are by no means found exclusively in articles concerned with the history of economic thought.[3]

Much more evidence of Mengerian scholarship appears outside the narrow confines of the journals, in recent books and monographs by members and critics of the modern Austrian School. The direct influence of Menger's *Investigations* on F. A. Hayek, noted by Schneider (pp. 12, 16) with particular regard to *The Constitution of Liberty,* continues to be evident in Hayek's more recent *Law, Legislation, and Liberty,* particularly the first volume of this triology. In criticizing the view that such social institutions as law, language, money, and markets were deliberately designed or rationally constructed, Hayek comments that the *Investigations* "contains still the best earlier treatment of these problems."[4]

Menger's insight into the spontaneous character of economic and social orders has also had an unmistakable importance for other "Austrian" economists. Ludwig M. Lachmann, the second prominent elder statesman of the Austrian School, has pointed out the impact of the *Investigations* on the thought of the great sociologist Max Weber, whose views on institutions Lachmann endeavors to develop in *The Legacy of Max Weber.*[5] The younger economists Gerald P. O'Driscoll, Jr. and Mario J. Rizzo, in a very recent restatement and extension of Austrian economics, enunciate a research program derived in part explicitly from the *Investigations*. Menger (p. 146) considered it "perhaps the most noteworthy . . . problem of the social sciences" to ask: "How can it be that institutions which serve the

[3]For specific evidence consult the *Social Science Citation Index* for various recent years. A brief selected bibliography of the doctrine-historical literature on Menger up to 1981, compiled by Richard Ebeling, appears in Carl Menger, *Principles of Economics* (New York: New York University Press, 1981), p. 10.

[4]Friedrich A. Hayek, *Law, Legislation and Liberty,* volume 1, *Rules and Order* (Chicago: University of Chicago Press, 1973), p. 147 n. 5. The index of this volume lists six references to Menger; all of them are to the *Investigations.*

[5]L. M. Lachmann, *The Legacy of Max Weber* (Berkeley: The Glendessary Press, 1971), esp. pp. 55–60. In these pages Lachmann also criticizes the deterministic arguments made by Menger in the *Investigations*. We return to this below.

common welfare and are extremely significant for its development come into being without a common will directed toward establishing them?" Menger and his heirs have, of course, offered answers that describe ways in which individual self-seeking actions can coalesce. In light of this O'Driscoll and Rizzo rephrase the question a bit more programatically: "More precisely, our self-imposed question is: *How can individuals acting in the world of everyday life unintentionally produce existing institutions or, more generally, the overall pattern of social interactions?*"[6] Thus Menger's research agenda, put forth in the *Investigations*, lives on.

The *Investigations* has clearly had direct and important bearing, and an indirect influence conveyed through the writings of Hayek and Lachmann, on the writings of the Austrian School of today. Yet in many respects the School has outgrown or rejected Menger's methodological outlook, and it cannot be said that current Austrian methodological views derive predominantly from Carl Menger. Much of Menger's argument has been filtered out, as it were, particularly by the writings of Ludwig von Mises in the midtwentieth century. It is noteworthy that the early chapters of Mises's influential treatise *Human Action*, which discuss methodology, contain not a single reference to Menger's *Investigations*.[7] Hayek could say of the Austrian School in 1934 that, with respect to theoretical analysis, "its fundamental ideas belong fully and wholly to Carl Menger."[8] No one could say the same today with respect to methodology.

The distinctness of the Austrian tradition in economics is correctly attributed to the consistency with which members of the school have employed a common method of analysis, namely one rooted in subjectivism. Yet the defense of this method—the explicit methodology of the school's members—has rarely been alike from one writer to the next.[9] It should therefore not be surprising that from a modern

[6]Gerald P. O'Driscoll and Mario J. Rizzo, *The Economics of Time and Ignorance* (Oxford: Basil Blackwell, 1985), p. 20.

[7]Ludwig von Mises, *Human Action*, 3rd rev. ed. (Chicago: Henry Regnery, 1966), pp. 1–117. Ludwig M. Lachmann, "Ludwig von Mises and the Extension of Subjectivism," in Israel M. Kirzner, ed., *Method, Process, and Austrian Economics: Essays in Honor of Ludwig von Mises* (Lexington, MA: Lexington Books, 1982), p. 32, states that Mises "saw in Menger's distinction between 'exact laws' and empirical regularities the pivot of Austrian methodology," but unfortunately provides no reference to textual evidence of this. I could not find in Mises's writings any comment on this aspect of the *Investigations*.

[8]F. A. Hayek, "Carl Menger," reprinted as the introduction to the 1981 edition of Menger, *Principles of Economics*, p. 12.

[9]There is no need to relate here the doctrinal history of Austrian methodology generally. I have tried to do that elsewhere: Lawrence H. White, *The Methodology of the Austrian School Economists* (Auburn: Ludwig von Mises Institute of Auburn University, 1984).

Austrian standpoint the *Investigations* receives a somewhat mixed review.

It may seem somewhat unfair to subject a century-old book in economics to criticism from a modern perspective. For works in economic theory it indeed is generally unfair (though it may well be instructive). A methodological work in economics, however, is closer to being an exercise in applied philosophy (in fact it *is* philosophy of science if properly done) than in economic theory. Philosophers are continually offering exegesis and criticism of important works of the past from present-day standpoints. In that spirit it seems not unfair to comment on the value of various aspects of the *Investigations* for present-day research in economics.

As Menger indicates in his Preface, the *Investigations* was originally written for the sake of German economists of the late nineteenth century. It was intended to be a methodological house-cleaning, to clear away in particular the antitheoretical attitudes of the dominant Historical School.[10] For this reason three of four sections ("Books") of the work have "Historical" in their titles and focus on the proper role of history in economic studies. Books Two and Four are particularly oriented in such a then-topical way that the modern reader will naturally take greater interest in Menger's more sweeping statements than in the details of his argument against particular historicist doctrines. In the present state of economics antitheoretical historicism is an annoyance occasionally encountered rather than a reigning orthodoxy demanding to be overthrown.[11] This state of affairs is of course due to the success of the "neoclassical" tradition in theoretical economics which Menger's own *Principles* helped to launch. Nonetheless it is the rare page of the present work that does not have several sentences worth underlining today. It is a measure of Menger's stature as a social scientist that what might have been solely a tract for his times holds so many passages of enduring importance.

Among the most pertinent themes of the book is the delineation of distinct and complementary roles for theory and history in economics. Here Menger is somewhat more generous in bestowing the title of theory upon certain types of knowledge than seems warranted. In particular he includes within the realm of economic theory the deter-

[10] A rather detailed account of the debate that ensued—the famed *Methodenstreit*—is offered by Samuel Bostaph, "The Methodological Debate Between Carl Menger and the German Historicists," *Atlantic Economic Journal* 6 (September 1978): 3–16.

[11] But for an argument against what the author sees as an antitheoretical streak in some recent writers see George A. Selgin, "Praxeology and Understanding," unpublished ms. (New York University, 1983).

mination of empirical regularities, apparently to be achieved through induction from a large number of cases. Such research is better categorized as a form of economic history. We are today all too aware of the pitfalls of elevating to the level of theory such "empirical laws," as Menger (p. 105) would presumably call them, as the original Phillips trade-off between inflation and unemployment rates or "Okun's Law" relating changes in the unemployment rate to the magnitude of real GNP growth. Menger may have unconsciously sought to sell historicists on the value of economic theory by convincing them that some of what they were already doing was a form of theory. No such strategic concern need influence us today.

Fortunately, Menger draws and even emphasizes a suitable distinction between the "realist-empirical orientation of theoretical research" and the "exact" orientation (p. 59). The search for so-called "exact laws" alone is more appropriately considered the task of purely theoretical research in economics. We can make sense of "exact laws" as theoretical propositions which (necessarily) take an "if-then" form: *if* conditions A and B hold, *then* condition C must also obtain. Menger rightly insists (pp. 70, 215) that realist-empirical generalizations (e.g., A and B are usually accompanied by C) can by their nature never attain the strictness that necessarily characterizes logical implications. The two sorts of "laws" are on different epistemological planes. So without too much dissent from Menger's thought we may divide economic theory from economic history where he divided strict theory from what he considered an empirical sort of theory. What is empirical is really historical, and this accounts for its different status from what is deductive.

Such a redivision yields a methodological outlook on the respective roles of economic theory and history closer to that of Mises, but by no means yet identical. Menger does not claim, as Mises later would, that pure economic theory is axiomatic, deducing theorems from premises a priori to empirical investigation of causal linkages. Indeed he rather plainly rejects such a vision of economic theory (p. 37 n. 4). Instead he sees (p. 60) a "partially empirical-realistic analysis" entering into the selection of ideal-type theoretical assumptions, and empirical observation entering into the ascertainment of causal linkages *between ideal types:* "Phenomena A and B *must* under the same conditions always be followed by the strictly typical phenomenon C in so far as A and B are thought of as strictly typical and the succession of phenomena under discussion here has been observed even in only a single case." It is not at all clear how Menger thinks even a single sequence of *purely ideal* (strictly typical) phenomena can ever be observed in the real world, particularly when he is ready (p. 214) to "admit quite unreservedly that *real* human phenomena are not strictly typical."

Menger nonetheless anticipates Mises's argument that the validity of rigorous theoretical reasoning cannot be tested by historical-empirical methods. Menger puts it wonderfully (p. 70): "To want to test the pure theory of economy by experience in its full reality is a process analogous to that of the mathematician who wants to correct the principles of geometry by measuring real objects. . . ." In order not to misinterpret such a statement it is necessary to keep in mind that the (logical) *validity* of a economic theorem is distinct from its (empirical) *applicability* in any specific case. Neither Menger nor Mises argues that historical-empirical evidence is irrelevant when considering whether a particular pure economic theory actually pertains to a specified concrete event.[12]

A second theme running through the *Investigations*, important from a modern perspective, concerns the similarities and contrasts between the social sciences (economics in particular) and the natural sciences. The decades since Menger wrote have seen the rise to dominance of a positivist methodology, now losing ground but by no means dislodged, that upholds the supposedly "hard" natural sciences as a model for economics to emulate.[13] In one very perceptive passage (p. 142 n. 51) Menger contrasts the subjectivism possible in the social sciences to the objectivism necessary in the natural sciences. The economic theorist has immediate familiarity with the constitutive element of economic phenomena, namely planned human action. Physicists looking for the ultimate building blocks of matter and physical phenomena must deal at the frontier with elementary "particles" (Menger calls them "atoms") and forces of a hypothetical nature. The natural scientist, then, stands ouside the object of study and knows the complex whole more immediately than the elements, whereas the social scientist has an inside perspective and apprehends the elements more immediately than the patterns or structures they comprise. Both Mises and Hayek have elaborated this Mengerian theme.[14]

[12] For a neo-Austrian statement on the role of modern empirical methods see Mario J. Rizzo, "Praxeology and Econometrics: A Critique of Positivist Economics," in Louis M. Spadaro, ed., *New Directions in Austrian Economics* (Kansas City: Sheed Andrews and McMeel, 1978), pp. 51–52.

[13] See Bruce Caldwell, *Beyond Positivism: Economic Methodology in the Twentieth Century* (Boston: Allen & Unwin, 1982).

[14] Mises, *Human Action*, p. 355; Hayek, *The Counter-Revolution of Science* (Glencoe, IL: The Free Press, 1952), pp. 38–39. These passages are juxtaposed with Menger's in White, *The Methodology of the Austrian School Economists*, pp. 19–24.

Menger does not draw from this insight the conclusion reached by Mises and Hayek that a basic distinction exists between the methods of inquiry and validation appropriate to social science and those appropriate to natural science.[15] But this is not because, like some economists,[16] he sees empiricism or positivism or falsificationism as the only proper method for both social science and natural science. Instead he argues (p. 59 n. 18) that both the search for empirical regularities and the formulation of *non*-empirical, *non*-falsifiable ("exact") theories are methods common to both economics and such natural-science fields as chemistry. In viewing theoretical research in every field as having a non-empirical proposition at its core, Menger's position bears some resemblance to that of modern philosophers of science.[17]

With regard to the specific *content* of the core proposition of economics, however, Menger's view is not nearly so modern. In claiming (p. 88) that economic theory is limited to the realm of "the efforts of economic humans aimed at the provision of their material needs," Menger seems wedded to a late Classical, or at any rate

[15] This has been usefully pointed out by T. W. Hutchison, *The Politics and Philosophy of Economics: Marxians, Keynesians and Austrians* (New York: New York University Press, 1981), pp. 187–189. Hutchison evidently considers methodological monism to Menger's credit, as he labels "rather pretentious" Menger's claim that social scientists have an advantage in apprehending ultimate elements. Hutchison devotes a chapter (an earlier version of which appeared in J. R. Hicks and W. Weber, *Carl Menger and the Austrian School of Economics* (Oxford: Oxford University Press, 1973) to a critical exegesis of the *Investigations*. He offers evaluations of the book's strengths and weaknesses opposite in many respects to those offered by the present introduction.

[16] E.g., Mark Blaug, *The Methodology of Economics* (Cambridge: Cambridge University Press, 1980), pp. 46–49. Blaug, unlike Menger, clearly distinguishes between techniques of investigation (here natural and social sciences obviously differ, e.g., in the use of laboratory experiments) and standards of theory acceptance (here the methodological monist says they should not differ).

[17] In particular, Imre Lakatos has written: "All scientific research programmes may be characterized by their '*hard core*'. . . . This 'core' is 'irrefutable' by the methodological decision of its protagonists: anomalies must lead to changes only in the 'protective' belt of auxiliary, 'observational' hypothesis and initial conditions." Lakatos, "Falsification and the Methodology of Scientific Research Programmes," in Imre Lakatos and Alan Musgrave, eds., *Criticism and the Growth of Knowledge* (London: Cambridge University Press, 1970), p. 133. Lakatos (ibid, pp. 128–130) gives an example from chemistry that fits neatly Menger's conception of exact theory prevailing over attempted refutation by observation of actual (non-pure) elements. For a comparison of Lakatos with Mises see Mario J. Rizzo, "Mises and Lakatos: A Reformulation of Austrian Methodology," in Israel M. Kirzner, ed., *Method, Process, and Austrian Economics: Essays in Honor of Ludwig von Mises* (Lexington, MA: D.C. Heath, 1982), pp. 53–73. Mises, as noted already, held that the core propositions of economics are not falsifiable.

needlessly narrow, view of the scope and method of economics.[18] On a properly broad view of economics as the study of ends-seeking activity of all sorts, it becomes clear that the "Pure Logic of Choice," as Hayek has called the core of economic theory, does not need to ascribe a "definite volitional orientation," i.e., a special set of concrete ends, to the agents it studies. Still less does pure economic analysis rest, as Menger believes it does (p. 216), on the assumption that "the *ultimate* goal of all human economy is . . . to cover our direct material needs" or in other words that economic behavior is physiologically determined.[19] Without this idea Menger's distinction between "economic" and "other" sources of human action breaks down. Yet we should not too harshly criticize Menger for what amounts to a failure to see all the implications of the subjective approach to economics he himself pioneered. We who intellectually stand on the shoulders of those who stood on his shoulders quite naturally see a wider horizon for economics.

Menger fortunately advances a positive research program which is commendably free of pseudo-natural-scientific approaches to economic subjects. Indeed, his insights into proper and fruitful methods—distinctly social-scientific methods—reward a careful reading today. He enunciates a compelling case for methodological individualism and the compositive method (pp. 93–94, 198–199, 195–196) as necessary means for arriving at any satisfying explanation of complex economic events. Because "to know is to know through causes," any satisfying explanation of aggregate-level economic phenomena must begin with individuals as planning units ("singular economies") and "investigate the laws by which the former are built up from the latter." It is widely accepted today (at last) that macro- and monetary economics must have "microfoundations." So too must the economics of the firm, the state, price adjustment, growth, and any number

[18] See Ludwig von Mises, *Epistemological Problems of Economics* (New York: New York University Press, 1981), p. 124 n. 5, for the statement that Menger's *Investigations* defends classical rather than modern economics. This is cited and endorsed by Ludwig M. Lachmann, "The Significance of the Austrian School of Economics in the History of Ideas," in *Capital, Expectations, and the Market Process,* ed. Walter E. Grinder (Kansas City: Sheed Andrews and McMeel, 1977), p. 48. It was Lionel Robbins's *The Nature and Significance of Economic Science* [2nd ed. (London: Macmillan, 1935)] which, borrowing from Mises and other Austrians, decisively broadened modern economists' conception of their discipline from that of a science of material welfare to that of a science of allocative behavior generally. On this see Israel M. Kirzner, *The Economic Point of View,* 2nd. ed. (Kansas City: Sheed and Ward, 1976), ch. 6. Kirzner (ibid., ch. 7) points out that Mises's conception of economics as a science of human action is broader still.

[19] Mises has criticized Menger's views on this in detailed fashion in *Epistemological Problems of Economics,* pp. 171–174.

of other topics which are often treated with *ad hoc* holistic assumptions. Menger's blast against the holism of the classical economists and the German historicists remains pertinent today: "But how foolish to want to simplify the science in contrast to the nature of things by an inadmissible fiction, to want to view a complex of economies as a large individual economy. How foolish to do this, instead of examining the real phenomena of human economy in their actual complication, i.e., instead of reducing them to their factors of individual economy and the striving for understanding of them—an understanding which, to be sure, is not easy."

We see in this passage just quoted an "essentialist" outlook quite contrary to the "instrumentalist" outlook officially more popular among neoclassical economists today, which says that the falsity of assumptions does not matter. (Significantly, instrumentalism is particularly preferred by those who espouse a hard-natural-science model for economics.) The ultimate goal of science for the instrumentalist is prediction,[20] which enables control. Menger recognizes prediction-and-control as one goal of economic science (p. 36), but not as the exclusive goal: "Theoretical economics has the task of presenting not merely the *'laws'* of economic phenomena to us, but also their *'general nature.'* (p. 198) Menger later, in a letter to Leon Walras, defended nonmathematical methods of economic theorizing as the only way to study "the *nature* of economic phenomena . . . (e.g., the nature of value, rent, profit, the division of labor, bimetallism, etc.)."[21] An emphasis on essentialist understanding and explanation through verbal methods has been characteristic of the Austrian School from Menger down to the present.[22] With respect to essentialism Menger's methodological views are very much alive in modern Austrian economics.

The theme from the *Investigations* most often celebrated by recent writers, and understandably so, is Menger's elucidation of the concept of spontaneous order, i.e., his insight into how useful social institutions "come about as the unintended result of individual human efforts (pursuing *individual interests*) without a *common will* directed

[20]The *locus classicus* here is Milton Friedman, "The Methodology of Positive Economics," in *Essays in Positive Economics* (Chicago: University of Chicago Press, 1953), esp. pp. 7, 41.

[21]Quoted in William Jaffé, "Unpublished Papers and Letters of Leon Walras," *Journal of Political Economy* 43 (April 1935), p. 200.

[22]For a recent reconstruction of the methodological case for this approach see Don Lavoie, "The Interpretative Dimension of Economics: Science, Hermeneutics, and Praxeology," Center for the Study of Market Processes Working Paper 1985–15.

toward their establishment." (p. 133) Louis Schneider not only embroiders on this theme in his introduction to the 1963 edition of the *Investigations,* but suggests that it was wholly responsible for his interest, as a sociologist, in making a translation of the work available to an English-language audience. We have already noted the crucial importance of this theme to Hayek, Lachmann, and O'Driscoll and Rizzo.

The concept of spontaneous order was not original with Menger, but he is unquestionably one of its major developers and expositors. The "tradition of spontaneous order" in social thought, as Norman Barry has shown, is both long and rich.[23] Yet if one name from each of the last three centuries could be chosen to exemplify the tradition, the names would be: Adam Smith, Carl Menger, and Friedrich A. Hayek. Before Smith there were noteworthy contributions to nonintentionalist social theory by Bernard Mandeville, David Hume, and Adam Ferguson. Smith is well known today for his simile likening spontaneous social ordering forces to an "invisible hand," of course, and for his explanation of how the division of labor is promoted by market forces stemming from the pursuit of self-interest. Between Smith and Menger valuable applications or extensions of the spontaneous-order concept were made by the French *economistes* Frederic Bastiat and Gustave de Molinari, by the British free banking advocates Thomas Hodgskin and Samuel Bailey, and by the sociologist Herbert Spencer.[24]

Menger expresses an indebtedness to none of these earlier writers, however, not even Smith. On the contrary, he actually accuses Adam Smith "and his closest followers" of holding the opinion "that the institutions of economy are always the intended product of the common will of society as such, results of expressed agreement of members of society or of positive legislation," and of holding this opinion so closely that "the broad realm of unintentionally created social structures remains closed to their theoretical comprehension." (p. 172) Accounting for this unsympathetic interpretation if not monumental misunderstanding of Smith is difficult. Given that Menger goes on to praise the teachings of Edmund Burke as against the "one-sided rationalism and pragmatism of the Anglo-French Age of Enlightenment," it would make more sense for Menger's target to be Jeremy

[23] Norman Barry, "The Tradition of Spontaneous Order," *Literature of Liberty* 5 (Summer 1982), pp. 7–58.

[24] On Hodgskin and Bailey see Lawrence H. White, *Free Banking in Britain* (Cambridge: Cambridge University Press, 1984). On the rest see Norman Barry, op cit.

Bentham than Adam Smith.[25] Perhaps the key lies with Menger's apparent affinity in policy matters for Burkean conservatism rather than the "one-sided rationalistic liberalism, the not infrequently impetuous effort to do away with what exists" that he associates with Smith and his followers (p. 177).

To exemplify the concept of a spontaneously evolved social institution Menger restates his own theory of the origin of money (pp. 152–155). This marvelous theory shows that the use of certain goods as money is not originally invented by the state or adopted by a conscious social agreement, but is arrived at through a natural convergence of self-seeking actions in a market setting.[26] The same approach can be extended to explain the origins of advanced monetary institutions such as coinage, banknotes, checks, and clearinghouses.[27] Menger identifies several other major institutions as undesigned or "organic" in origin: language, law, morals, trade customs, professionalism, cities, and tribes (or primitive "states"). He does *not* fall into the error of regarding *all* existing institutions as undesigned, however. He recognizes quite explicitly (p. 157) that "legislative compulsion not infrequently encroaches upon [an institution's] 'organic' developmental process and thus accelerates or modifies the results," and points to modern monetary, market, legal, and state systems as the results of mixtures of "organic" and "positive" forces.[28]

The Mengerian research program, then, calls upon social scientists, and economists in particular, to unravel the "pragmatic" or designed-order strands in current institutions from the "organic" or spontaneous-order strands. The ways in which legislative compulsion

[25] On Adam Smith and Edmund Bruke as like-thinking "antirationalist" individualists see F. A. Hayek, "Individualism: True and False," in *Individualism and Economic Order* (Chicago: Gateway Edition, 1972), pp. 4–13.

[26] Philosopher Robert Nozick offers Menger's theory (as retold by Mises) as a paradigmatic example of what he calls an "invisible-hand explanation": Nozick, *Anarchy, State, and Utopia* (New York: Basic Books, 1974), p. 18. Nozick points out that such explanations are satisfying because they economize on the knowledge that must be attributed to the mind of any agent in the theory.

[27] Lawrence H. White, "Competitive Payments Systems and the Unit of Account," *American Economic Review* 74 (September 1984), pp. 703–706. Menger's theory continues to have the greatest relevance because of the prevalence of "one-sided rationalism and pragmatism" among economists spinning out visions of ideal monetary systems without inquiring into the problem of having the public adopt a new means of payment.

[28] Menger's discussion of the primitive state as sometimes organically formed, and of "the modern state" as partly the result of organic factors indicates that he does not use "organic" to mean "free of coercive influences" but rather "not the result of one deliberate overall plan." Still less does he signal an approval of all organic institutions and a condemnation of all pragmatic ones. The present-day term "spontaneous" is sometimes ambiguous between these two meanings, and often carries a favorable connotation.

modifies institutions require especially sensitive study, as the actual results of intervention are typically not those ostensibly intended. Piecemeal interventions often fail to achieve their stated aims, and give rise to more encompassing measures. The attempt to legislate an overall design for an institution usually creates unforeseen incentive structures such that the pursuit of individual purposes generates an outcome not attributable purely to the lawmakers' intention.[29] Modern monetary institutions, particularly central banks, may again serve as a case in point. It would be just as naive to regard the actual functioning of the Federal Reserve System as having been comprehensively designed as it would be to regard the system as the spontaneous outgrowth of free market forces.

Arriving at a satisfactory understanding of such an institution requires that economics first build up, from the essential features of individual human action, theoretical structures adequate to explain the relevant institutional features of both market behavior and political behavior. Then the various forms of interplay between market and state agents and institutions must be studied theoretically. Finally the theory must be sensitively applied to singular historical events. This is all quite a challenge and requires that some researchers have a broad field of vision. But then Menger set high standards for economists as social scientists. For this reason too, the *Investigations* richly deserves a place on the bookshelves of today's economists.

Lawrence H. White
New York University

[29]The relevant literature here is vast, but includes Friedrich A. Hayek, *The Road to Serfdom* (Chicago: University of Chicago Press, 1944); Ludwig von Mises, *Planning for Freedom*, 3rd ed. (South Holland, IL: Libertarian Press, 1974), chs. 1–2; and Murray N. Rothbard, *Power and Market* (Menlo Park, CA: Institute for Humane Studies, 1970), chs. 3–5.

TRANSLATOR'S PREFACE

Thirteen years ago there appeared a translation of Carl Menger's *Grundsätze der Volkswirthschaftslehre* done by James Dingwall and Bert F. Hoselitz.[1] The translators' preface could almost be repeated here verbatim, for the causes of their complaints are largely to be found also in the original of the present volume, entitled *Untersuchungen über die Methode der Socialwissenschaften und der Politischen Oekonomie insbesondere*.

Dingwall and Hoselitz state that Menger's book "is more than normally difficult to translate." This is so mild that it is almost an understatement. To anyone who is at home in German, Menger's meaning is nearly always clear. In fact, because of the repetitiousness of his style and his insistence on leaving nothing to the reader's imagination, his meaning is unusually clear considering what may in all honesty be called the atrocity of his style of writing.

He had all the features usually associated with the verbose and involved style of the last century. One example may suffice. One paragraph in the *Untersuchungen* consists of thirty-eight printed lines. It also consists of only two sentences, one of twenty lines and one of eighteen. Because of grammatical features of the German language, such as agreement in grammatical gender, case forms, agreement of verb forms with subject forms, and so on, such long sentences are understandable. The translator, however, is faced with the problem of breaking up these monstrous units into smaller ones. At the same time he must keep the connections and relationships clear in a language which can do this only by position in the sentence, not by grammatical forms.

Another feature that is hard for the translator to handle is the use of

[1] Carl Menger, *Principles of Economics* (Glencoe, Ill.: The Free Press, 1950), translated and edited by James Dingwall and Bert F. Hoselitz, with an introduction by Frank H. Knight.

certain particles in German to express slight variations in emphasis, mood, and connection. English expresses all this in a different way. The translator is thus compelled to render the force of the German statement at times without using words to do this as the original does.

Menger uses a number of words with a variation of connotation in various places. He also makes rather fine distinctions by using two different words. For example, *Verkennung* ordinarily would be rendered into English with "misunderstanding," in the sense of a "misunderstanding" of the situation. However, Menger uses *Missverständnis* upon many occasions with an obvious shade of difference. I have therefore, in spite of its slight awkwardness, usually translated the former word with the quite correct meaning "failure to recognize."

This matter is further complicated by Menger's use of words of Latin or Greek origin side by side with native German ones. It does not offer a great problem when he uses *Erscheinung* and *Phänomen* interchangeably and then also uses the former to mean "(putting in) an appearance." He regularly seems to use *Volkswirthschaftslehre* (to keep his spelling) and *Nationalökonomie* interchangeably. For instance, in the first paragraph of Appendix IV he writes "Theoretische Volkswirthschaftslehre (theoretische Nationalökonomie)." Consequently I have translated both words with "economics." Yet I cannot avoid the feeling that he may have had a slight shade of difference in mind when he switched from one to the other, although I can recall no instance where he uses them side by side to indicate a difference.

But with *Politische Oekonomie* (again keeping his spelling) he obviously means something else. It embraces, as he states many times, "economics," "economic policy," and "science of finance." I have kept his distinction by rendering this with "political economy." The 1910 edition of *Meyers Konversations-Lexikon,* which I happened to have at hand, gives a long discussion of *Volkswirtschaftslehre,* and for *Politische Ökonomie* and *Nationalökonomie* simply refers the reader to the article on *Volkswirtschaftslehre.* Thus Menger makes a distinction which more modern German does not make, and which the English translations do not make.

Volkswirthschaft I have translated with "economy," except in those instances where a distinction had to be made clear. In a few places Menger wrote of *Wirthschaft* and of *Volkswirthschaft.* Then I used "economy" and "national economy" for these.

Certain words that Menger used have English translations which have, however, changed to a greater or lesser extent. To translate *Wissenschaft* with "field of knowledge" or "branch of knowledge" was hopelessly unwieldy, considering how often Menger used it. "Discipline" was not very satisfactory in most places. I finally gave up and used the English word "science." Similarly, though fortunately not so frequently, I was confronted with *Politik* and *Politiker*. For these I used "politics" and, upon occasion, "politician." "Political scientist," which I could use for the student of the science of government, did not apply to the person practicing the science or art of government.

I quickly recognized that all these things, and others, meant that the translator would have to fight his way through this forest of difficulties and arrive at a fairly faithful translation, simply trying to do this in English reasonably acceptable to a reader of this age. Or else he would have to do a complete paraphrase, simply giving Menger's ideas in his own language. Two things made me avoid the second alternative. For one thing, I have seen too many paraphrases in which not only the author's language was changed, but his ideas were, too. It is too dangerous a procedure. Tying in with this is the second consideration. To do such a paraphrase the person must be thoroughly at home in the field, not just in the language. As I am not an economist, I did not feel remotely justified in trying it.

One last item. After some debate with myself I decided to keep Menger's references as he gave them, with all his inconsistencies (but some concessions have had to be made to current printing conventions). I translated, of course, whenever possible, except for titles. In connection with the titles I decided to keep Menger's archaic spellings, for actually most, if not all, of the works are so listed in catalogs and the like.

My thanks are due to my colleague Professor Louis Schneider. He first suggested that the work should be done. He has aided me repeatedly on the technical vocabulary, and has also read the whole manuscript critically. The translation is basically my work, but because of circumstances that neither of us could help it was necessary for him to put finishing touches on it.

For this translation I used the first and sole edition of the work, published in 1883 by Duncker and Humblot in Leipzig. As Professor Schneider indicates in his Introduction, the London School of Economics issue of the *Untersuchungen* in 1933 was simply a reprint.

FRANCIS J. NOCK

University of Illinois

INTRODUCTION

The name of the Austrian economist, Carl Menger, is familiar even to many with but rudimentary knowledge of the history of economics. Menger is repeatedly referred to in the treatises dealing with the development of economic doctrine as one of the independent formulators of the principle of marginal utility, and he is thereby conventionally linked with such men as Jevons, Walras, and John Bates Clark. He is also remembered for the acrimonious "battle of methods" (*Methodenstreit*) in German-Austrian economics, which, indeed, the volume herewith translated may be said to have initiated.

Evaluations of Menger's work tend to be decidedly favorable. Not all economists would go so far as Zuckerkandl, who terminates an exposition of Menger with the assertion that among the men who, at the beginning of the sixties of the last century, broke from classical economics and laid the foundations for fruitful new developments Menger performed the most comprehensive and most significant services.[1] But the generally favorable tone of comment on Menger is unmistakable. A high opinion of him was expectably entertained by Friedrich Wieser, who makes it quite plain, even if we did not know this from other sources, that Menger's work in its time had very considerable significance for some able young Austrian economists.[2] Nor is it surprising that Eugen von Böhm-Bawerk has been referred to as "completely the enthusiastic disciple of Menger."[3] Schumpeter, who so describes Böhm-Bawerk, himself regarded Menger's work as "masterly," and if he added that it was "'simply a descendant from Davanzati's" he had previously asserted of Menger that "he was a careful thinker who rarely slipped, if ever, and

[1] See Robert Zuckerkandl, "Karl Menger," in *Zeitschrift für Volkswirtschaft, Sozialpolitik und Verwaltung,* XIX (1910), pp. 251-264.

[2] Friedrich Wieser, "Karl Menger," in *Neue Oesterreichische Biographie* (Vienna: Wiener Drucke, 1923), pp. 84-92.

[3] Joseph A. Schumpeter, *History of Economic Analysis* (New York: Oxford University Press, 1954), p. 845.

his genius stands out only the more impressively because he lacked the appropriate mathematical tools."[4] Should comment from those of Central European provenience seem likely to be overfavorable to Menger, there are judgments like Frank Knight's, to the effect that "Carl Menger's place at the very top among the creators in the development of modern economic thought is secure."[5] Praise is not unqualified. The economists appear well enough agreed that Menger's work as a pioneering endeavor exhibited numerous crudities, and indeed crudities not always evident in the work of other and comparable pioneers. But the generally friendly tone of comment on Menger which I have noted remains.

Yet it is also noteworthy that this kind of favorable evaluation of Menger is made largely in the light of the work of his youth, the *Grundsätze der Volkswirthschaftslehre,* translated into English as *Principles of Economics* in 1950[6] but originally published in 1871, when Menger was thirty-one years old. In 1883, a dozen years after the *Grundsätze,* Menger published his *Untersuchungen über die Methode der Socialwissenschaften und der Politischen Oekonomie insbesondere,* now translated as *Problems of Economics and Sociology.* It is not that commentary has been lacking on this latter work. Schumpeter, again, if with some reservations, characterized it as "one of the significant performances in its field."[7] Friedrich Hayek, who has been greatly influenced by Menger's thought as set out in the *Untersuchungen,*[8] has commented that "the *Untersuchungen* are hardly less an achievement than the *Grundsätze.*"[9] Another sympathetic student has gone so far as to say

[4] *Ibid.*, pp. 1085-86, 827.

[5] Frank H. Knight, in "Introduction" to Carl Menger, *Principles of Economics* (Glencoe, Ill.: The Free Press, 1950), translated and edited by James Dingwall and Bert F. Hoselitz, p. 10.

[6] See footnote 5.

[7] *Op. cit.*, p. 814. n. 11.

[8] See especially F. A. Hayek, *The Constitution of Liberty* (Chicago: University of Chicago Press, 1959), *passim.*

[9] See Hayek's article, "Carl Menger," in *Economica,* n.s., No. 4 (1934), pp. 393-420, at p. 405. This article affords a treatment of Menger and his work that was written as an introduction to the London School of Economics reprint of Menger's *Grundsätze* (London School of Economics and Political Science, Series of Reprints of Scarce Tracts in Economics and Political Science, No. 17) in 1934. I have referred to the article in *Economica* rather than to the introduction with which it is identical simply as a matter of convenience. (I am, incidentally, indebted to the article for a number of useful bibliographic references.) It is also convenient to note here that the London School reprinted Menger's collected works over the years 1933 to 1936: the *Grundsätze,* as I have just indicated, as No. 17 in the series named (and as Vol. I of the collected works) in 1934; the *Untersuchungen* as No. 18 in the series (and Vol. II of the collected works) in 1933; *Kleinere Schriften zur Methode und Geschichte der Volkswirthschaftslehre* as No. 19 in the series (and Vol. III of the collected works) in 1935; and *Schriften über Geldtheorie*

with regard to the *Untersuchungen* that it is a contribution of Menger's "which entitles him to a rank among the greatest minds in the social sciences at large."[10] This may well overstate the case. But more noteworthy is the circumstance that the statement appears at all in an English-language medium. For English-speaking economists, certainly, the *Grundsätze* or *Principles* has been the more important work by far, and it has now been available in translation for over a dozen years. Neither economists nor sociologists working in the English language have paid any notable attention to the *Untersuchungen.*[11] When Hayek wrote on the reverse of the title page of the 1933 London School of Economics reprint of the *Untersuchungen* that the book "has profoundly affected all the social sciences," he could hardly have been thinking at any rate of *direct* influence on the social sciences in the English-speaking world. I am convinced that the book is well worth presenting in English dress. After a lapse of eighty years it merits the chance of a more direct impact on social science in the English-speaking world than it has hitherto had.

Hayek, once again in his evaluation of Menger which I have previously referred to, has given a commentary on the *Untersuchungen* worth reproducing for the purposes of the present introduction:

> In their way the *Untersuchungen* are hardly less an achievement than the *Grundsätze.* As a polemic against the claims of the Historical School to an exclusive right to treat economic problems the book can hardly be surpassed. Whether the merits of its positive exposition of the nature of theoretical analysis can be rated as high is, perhaps, not quite certain. If this were, indeed, its main title to fame there might be something in the suggestion occasionally heard among Menger's admirers that it was unfortunate that he

und Währungspolitik as No. 20 in the series (and Vol. IV of the collected works) in 1936. Volume III, *Kleinere Schriften,* contains as its first item the incisive *Irrthümer des Historismus in der Deutschen Nationalökonomie,* which continues discussion of issues broached in the present volume. A bibliography of Menger's work is afforded in *Schriften über Geldtheorie,* pp. 324-332.

[10] Henri-Simon Bloch, "Carl Menger: The Founder of the Austrian School," *Journal of Political Economy,* 48 (June, 1940), p. 433.

[11] Albion W. Small is an exception to this assertion. Small's *Origins of Sociology* (Chicago: University of Chicago Press, 1924), shows keen and detailed interest in German historical, economic, and sociological thought. It affords a translation of Menger's preface to the *Grundsätze* (*Origins,* pp. 168-171), gives a synopsis of the first chapter of that book (pp. 173-175), and renders a few additional passages from the book into English (pp. 177-180). Small also translated the preface to the *Untersuchungen* (pp. 180-189; note, however, the qualifications Small states in the last sentence of the footnote on p. 180, referring as he does to "one or two omissions and a few condensations"), rendered chapter, appendix titles, and other passages of this volume into English (pp. 189, 190), and afforded a digest of material from its Book III (pp. 205-219, 307-314). The present translation, however, was done in entire independence of Small's early translation.

was drawn away from his work on the concrete problems of economics. This is not to mean that what he said on the character of the theoretical or abstract method is not of very great importance or that it had not very great influence. Probably it did more than any other single book to make clear the peculiar character of the scientific method in the social sciences, and it had a very considerable effect on professional "methodologists" among German philosophers. But to me, at any rate, its main interest to the economist in our days seems to lie in the extraordinary insight which is revealed incidentally in the discussion of problems mentioned to exemplify different methods of approach, and in the light shed by his discussion of the development of the concepts with which the social sciences have to work. Discussion of somewhat obsolete views, as that of the organic or perhaps better physiological interpretation of social phenomena, gives him an opportunity for an elucidation of the origin and character of social institutions which might, with advantage, be read by present-day economists and sociologists.[12]

In this passage Hayek clearly discriminates three major elements in the content of Menger's *Untersuchungen.* On the first two of these I shall have little to say, but the third is the element that afforded me the motivation to bring out the present edition of Menger's book, and about this I shall have much more to say.

The first element is, of course, that aspect of the *Untersuchungen* which constitutes "a polemic against the claims of the Historical School to an exclusive right to treat economic problems." Menger's argument against the historical school appears to me to be on the whole well founded. Certainly, the numerous confusions he pointed to were well worth marking, and in principle it is now very difficult to see how anyone could contend for the scrapping of an analytical or theoretical apparatus in economics in favor of purely historical approaches. Where the historical bias went as far as this, Menger obviously had every right to be extremely critical of it. I am wary in the matter of making a judgment about the actual extent to which the historical bias among German economists went in this direction, and I would rather leave the matter to the treatment of competent historians of economic thought. Schumpeter has averred that the history of the literature bearing on the "battle of methods" (*Methodenstreit*) heavily involving Menger and Gustav Schmoller is "substantially a history of wasted energies."[13] The judgment seems to me at least too sweeping and too harsh, simply on the evidence of the *Untersuchungen,* which, if it does nothing else in regard to the historical school, makes some challenging and incisive statements about it. The reader has only to turn the pages of the present volume to find such statements in some quantity.

[12] Hayek, "Carl Menger," pp. 405-406.
[13] *Op. cit.,* p. 814.

The second element in the volume which Hayek discriminates is Menger's "positive exposition of the nature of theoretical analysis." To the present-day reader, at any rate—whatever impact Menger's exposition may have had in its time on economists and philosophers concerned with "methodology"—in respect of this element of his work, Menger must appear rather wordy. Why expend so much space in a comparatively short volume on the distinction between the individual and the general? Why make so much of the abstracting character of scientific analysis and point out so insistently what is after all rather obvious, namely, that particular sciences choose for analysis selected aspects of "reality" about which they make statements that must be understood as representing an effort to create special theoretical structures whose merit lies precisely in the circumstance that they do *not* constitute "reproductions" or "pictures" of empirical phenomena as they exist in full-blown actuality? But, again, it may well be that Menger sensed correctly that he could make a worthwhile pedagogic contribution by his long-winded treatment of these matters. Moreover, even today his distinction between, and exposition of, what he calls the "empirical-realistic" and the "exact" methods of economic investigation has, I venture to say, a certain sharpness and cogency that render it of genuine interest.

But on the third element in Menger's book that Hayek discriminates, I believe that the latter's judgment is extremely shrewd. Herein lies much that could be valuable now. When Menger discusses "the organic or perhaps better physiological interpretation of social phenomena" and elucidates "the origin and character of social institutions," he does indeed, as Hayek puts it, offer materials "which might, with advantage, be read by present-day economists and sociologists." Herein, too, the reader may find the justification for the change in title I have imposed on Menger's work, to make it read *Problems of Economics and Sociology*. And again, herein lies the main ground for my own concern, as a sociologist, with his work. That his work deals with "problems of economics" is perfectly obvious. But it deals, just as unequivocally, with a number of "problems of sociology." If the problems of sociology with which it deals also run through economics and perhaps, for that matter, still other social sciences, this scarcely reduces the general significance of those problems and hardly lessens their sociological significance in particular. The problems arise in connection with Menger's preoccupation with "the organic understanding of social phenomena" which he treats in Book III and to which he devotes the most considerable of his appendixes, that on "the organic origin of law and the exact understanding thereof" (Appendix VIII). It is significant that Hayek mentions that Menger desired to write "a comprehensive treatise on the character and methods of the social sciences in general" and that he was much concerned with philosophy, psychology, and ethnography. Hayek also notes interestingly that Menger's considerable library included not only material in economics but that "its collections on ethnography and philosophy were nearly as rich."[14] Given Menger's interest in the organic understanding of social phenomena, and the actual content of his treatment of what I may call organic social theory, it is very easy to believe that, had he managed to write his comprehensive treatise and drawn on his rich library resources for it, the treatise would have expanded considerably his ideas on organic theory. What may be called the organic theory of the origin of money (which I shall refer to below), even without the comprehensive treatise, was a favorite topic of Menger's.[15] His recurrence to this topic alone could easily induce one to think that the treatise that was never realized would have dealt with organic theory in detail.

When Menger takes up the organic understanding of social phenomena in Book III of the present volume, it is clear that he has an initial critical concern. He does not wish to be taken in by shallow analogies between biological and social phenomena. Nor is he willing to allow his understanding to be affected by the specious attractiveness or supposed explanatory value in social science of terms such as "organic," "original," "natural," and the like. If metaphors are to be employed, he plainly wants them understood as metaphors and their limitations kept in view. His critical interest is so plain that the reader may even, to begin with, get the impression that he is inclined toward an outright rejection of any work that leans in the direction of "organic" theory. But it is soon evident that this is not so.

Menger poses as "a noteworthy, perhaps the most noteworthy, problem of the social sciences" the problem put by the question: "How can it be that institutions which serve the common welfare and are extremely significant for its development come into being without a common will directed toward establishing them?"[16] This is certainly a central question not only for social science generally but for organic social theory in par-

[14] Hayek, "Carl Menger," pp. 415, 419.

[15] See his *Principles of Economics,* pp. 257-271, 315-320; pp. 152-155 of the present volume; and *Schriften über Geldtheorie und Währungspolitik,* in which the first lengthy article (on "money") presents an initial section (pp. 3-21) on the origin of generally employed media of exchange. Cf. also the essay "On the Origin of Money" by Menger in *The Economic Journal,* 2 (June, 1892), pp. 239-255.

[16] See p. 146. Note the slightly different translation given to this question of Menger's in F. A. Hayek, *The Counter-Revolution of Science* (Glencoe, Ill.: The Free Press, 1952), p. 83.

ticular. The question was not a novel one. Thus, the German economist Wilhelm Roscher, whose work was of much interest to Menger, had indicated, as a basic concern for political economy, the question of how one could account for the emergence and continuance of "functional" institutions (what Menger might well have called "institutions which serve the common welfare") which, despite their "functionality," had not been established on a basis of collectively or jointly agreed upon *purpose*—just as an analogous question regarding the "fitness" of organisms was a dominant one for biology.[17] The echo of the question is plainly audible in Menger's work. But Menger did not approach the question with some of the distinctive views that evidently handicapped Roscher, such as the "emanationist" view that constrained the latter to look upon the "wonderful harmony" between socially desirable consequences and individual actions in which those consequences were never contemplated as a more or less impenetrable mystery.[18] Indeed, it was Menger's deliberate design to penetrate the "mystery" as far as he was able to do so. Before looking at his efforts in this connection, it is well to obtain some general notion of organic social theory and of Menger's attitude toward this theory and some of its particulars.

Organic social theory is disposed to look upon human institutions as "fit" or "functional" or "serving the common welfare." When it is uncritical or politically biased or tendentious it moves toward an unqualified affirmation of the excellence of the institutions and powers that be and seeks to exploit analogies between institutions and biological organisms in which the "fitness" and "excellence" of organisms are exclusively stressed. The marvels of adaptation supposed to be found in nature are thus duplicated in society. Leaving aside for the moment the questions of political expediency or interest that this suggests, let it be noted that Menger approached organic theory with a *qualified* but genuine and, I may add, justified acceptance of its views and propositions. What does he accept? He accepts the notion that there are *some* social arrangements, institutions, structures, whatever we wish to call them, which "serve the common welfare" or are functional and which at the same time are organic growths, that is, have not been created by human intention but are spontaneous developments. The institution of money is certainly one such institution, in his view. He also accepts the allied notion, nourished by Savigny and Burke among others, that some historic institutions incorporate an unintended or unconscious "wisdom,"

[17] See Max Weber, *Gesammelte Aufsätze zur Wissenschaftslehre,* 2nd ed. (Tübingen: J. C. B. Mohr [Paul Siebeck], 1951), p. 29.

[18] *Ibid.,* pp. 33-37.

wisdom that has descended from the past, and he is accordingly willing to concede that there can be such a thing as hasty or thoughtless planning or reform effort that bungles its job just because of failure to recognize that there is sometimes built-in or implicit "wisdom" (in institutions) exceeding the wisdom that particular planners or reformers can bring to bear at a particular time. Here too there is an organic analogy in that the germ plasm of an organism may be said in a certain sense to carry the "wisdom" that forebears have bequeathed it—through "experiences" that wiped out some of those very forebears and occasioned survival on the part of others. As regards the social level, a writer on Savigny, who is well aware of the latter's significance as an opponent of a certain doctrinaire and mechanical rationalism that was one element in the Enlightenment, puts the thesis of the implicit wisdom present in some social arrangements succinctly by saying of Savigny: "'In the place of the reason that is the possession of the individual he put the reason that belongs to history.'"[19]

Menger, then, is quite willing to concede that there are points of validity, and significant ones, in organic social theory. But it is also quite evident that he has reservations. Thus, he insists that functional institutions *can* be the product of deliberate reflection and planning, and he writes accordingly of "pragmatic" explanation: explanation occasioned and justified by the existence of "a number of social phenomena which are products of the agreement of members of society, or of positive legislation, results of the purposeful common activity of society thought of as a separate active subject" (p. 145). He is also quite clear on the point that institutions may arise organically and spontaneously and yet be susceptible in the course of their later development to pragmatic modification that enhances their functionality. Given these qualifications, it is not surprising that he holds a resolutely rational outlook on institutions and refuses to accept the unqualifiedly "conservative" conclusions that emerge from the argument of some organic theorists. This last is worth some stress.

Menger notes (p. 91) of the German historical school of jurisprudence that it espoused the thesis that "law is something above the arbitrariness of the individual," that law is an "organic structure" not to be haphazardly shaped. He notes also that the school derived consequences of an "extremely practical" order from this thesis:

> It concluded that the desire for a reform of social and political conditions aroused in all Europe by the French Revolution really meant a failure to

[19] Eduard Müller, *Friedrich Karl von Savigny* (Leipzig: Wilhelm Weicher, 1906), p. 4.

recognize the nature of law, state and society and their "organic origin." It concluded that the "subconscious wisdom" which is manifested in the political institutions which come about organically stands high above meddlesome human wisdom. It concluded that the pioneers of reform ideas accordingly would do less well to trust their own insight and energy than to leave the re-shaping of society to the "historical process of development." And it espoused other such conservative basic principles highly useful to the ruling interests.[20]

As if to dispel all possible uncertainty about his own rational outlook on social institutions, Menger comments at the end of his appendix on the organic origin of law (p. 234) that the historical school of jurists had to afford us understanding of "the previously uncomprehended advantages of common law," yet he adds forthrightly: "But never, and this is the essential point in the matter under review, may science dispense with testing for their suitability those institutions which have come about 'organically.' It must, when careful analysis so requires, change and better them according to the measure of scientific insight and the practical experience at hand. No era may renounce this 'calling.' "

The above will serve as a set of indications of the character of organic social theory and of some of Menger's reactions to it. We are now in a better position to understand his struggle with the question of how it can

[20] The tone of this is of course unmistakably critical. That Menger had Savigny and his followers very much in mind when he wrote it there can be no doubt. It is of interest that, aside from Menger, others have been inclined to accept what they regard as valid insights of Savigny's into the organic character, or organic aspect, of law while rejecting the political conclusions he ostensibly drew therefrom. Thus, William Guthrie, a translator of Savigny (see Savigny's *A Treatise on the Conflict of Laws* [London: Stevens and Sons, 1880], tr. William Guthrie), is willing to say (or repeat after his authority, Rudorff) that Savigny's opponent, Anton F. J. Thibaut, in the famous Savigny-Thibaut controversy, was of "that philosophical school, fed on the theories of the eighteenth century, which believed that law can be produced, of the desired quality and at the shortest notice, on any soil." Guthrie's memoir of Savigny also contains the statement that the latter "pointed out, too, the source of the whole agitation for codes, the attempt to rectify the law from above and at one stroke, in the tendency of the time 'alles zu regieren, und immer mehr regieren zu wollen.' " Yet the memoir in which these statements, sympathetic to Savigny and opposed to Thibaut, appear takes Savigny to task specifically in point of his antidemocratic biases. See the "Memoir of Friedrich Carl von Savigny," in Savigny's *Treatise,* pp. 517-549, at pp. 528, 530, 542-543. Also pertinent in this whole connection, and still surprisingly readable, is Small's account of the Savigny-Thibaut controversy in *Origins of Sociology,* chap. 2. Small is not insensible of Savigny's contributions but remarks, with evident critical intent, that Savigny in effect contended that "because influences propagate themselves from generation to generation, and from age to age, therefore, trust in the dynamic power of inertia is the cardinal principle of a sane civic program" and, further, that Savigny's "refrain was, 'It must grow!' This was laissez faire applied to legislation." *Ibid.,* pp. 49, 55. Cf. also Roscoe Pound's critical remarks in "The Scope and Purpose of Sociological Jurisprudence," *Harvard Law Review,* 24 (June, 1911), pp. 598-604.

be the case that functional institutions arise "without a common will directed toward establishing them." What does he actually contribute to "the theoretical understanding of those social phenomena which are not a product of agreement or of positive legislation, but are unintended results of historical development?" (title of Book III, chap. 2). Let it be remarked first that Menger realized, in the very posing of his question and in the very utilization of a chapter title such as the one I have just repeated, perhaps as clearly as anyone had up to this time, that there are in simple fact "unanticipated consequences of purposive social action."[21] This may be said to be the starting point of his endeavor to explain unintended or unlegislated and at the same time functional institutions. Men act individually in a variety of contexts to achieve a variety of objects, and Menger as an economist is of course especially interested in their economic objects. "Self-interest" on the part of discrete individuals dictates a line or lines of action. As many individuals act, the effects of their action are seen to comprise elements that no single individual ever contemplated and that were never contemplated by individuals acting in concert since there was no concert to begin with. Mandeville and Adam Smith, among others, were already well aware of this. Menger was evidently intrigued by the emergence of unanticipated consequences of individual purposive actions in the sphere of trade and barter, as his preoccupation with the origin of money indicates.

Menger's view of the origin of money is based on the notions that where barter has come to prevail some commodities will emerge for which there is greater, more constant, more effective demand than for others; that economic agents recognize the advantage of getting to possess such commodities even if they are not the commodities they most immediately want for their own consumption purposes; that economic agents then, in fact, proceed to acquire such commodities and thereby increase their chances of obtaining the items they really desire for consumption purposes at "economic" prices, in virtue of their possession of the most highly salable commodities, which eventually become money. The path leads through cows and cowrie shells and other such items to money in the modern sense. An institution thus arises which no one contemplated, which is exceedingly "useful," and which, beyond certain historical points, looks inordinately complex and perhaps as if it could not possibly have been unplanned. Men do not begin by "wanting money." For Menger, that would be a ridiculous notion. They could not "want" what they could not even remotely conceive, nor could an in-

[21] See Robert K. Merton, "The Unanticipated Consequences of Purposive Social Action," *American Sociological Review*, I (1936), pp. 894-904.

stitution due to exist in the future cast back a desire for itself, in full-fledged form, into the past. What individual economic actors want is to do as well in the market as they can. Out of these elements of individual wants (the focus of the "exact" or "atomistic" orientation in economic analysis) the institution of money ultimately develops, unplanned and initially undreamt of.

In the sense that the above indicates, the institution of money is an organic growth. The same holds true of numerous other institutions. The appendix (pp. 223-234) which Menger devotes to law very plainly shows that he held there were ponderable organic elements in the growth of law also. And his brief discussion of the rise of "localities" or communities and states shows that he has an organic outlook on these as well. There is no special need here to discuss his views on these matters from the point of view of a realistic anthropology or history, for, no matter what anthropological or historical detail might reveal about "beginnings" in, say, money or law, such detail would not quite get at what he was concerned with when he considered "'origins," and it would not be central to his main objects in any case. Outright "beginnings" or "origins" of arrangements such as those involved in developed systems of money or law are notoriously difficult, if not impossible, to come to. (I pass over the numerous slippery issues that could easily arise here.) Although he was certainly aware of the relevance of ethnographic and historical evidence in his discussions of the rise of money, Menger was obviously mainly desirous of making a "reconstruction" of its rise that should fit well with what he knew of the workings of the self-interest of economic agents. His reconstruction is a very simple derivation from economic "motive" and economic interaction. It is in a special sense "prehistoric" or even nonhistoric.[22] Also, he is evidently much concerned to make his discussion of the rise of money serve as a kind of paradigm or "model" for the analysis of functional social phenomena that have arisen, not from purposive agreement or legislation, but as remote and uncontemplated outcomes of individual actions originally addressed to aims having nothing to do with the developed phenomena. Again, history and empirical anthropology are not necessarily irrelevant, but they could not provide quite what Menger was alert for.

It should be stressed very strongly that there is nothing in Menger's work to suggest that the unanticipated consequences of purposive action

[22] For a striking contemporary example of a reconstruction quite similar to Menger's in *method*, although concerned with very different subject matter, an example replete with both questionable and highly stimulating observations, see Leslie A. White, *The Evolution of Culture* (New York: McGraw-Hill Book Co., 1959), Chap. 4, "The Transition from Anthropoid Society to Human Society."

must move in the direction of what makes for "social welfare." They merely *may* move in that direction, and particular cases must be assessed according to particular evidence. It has already been noted that Menger was not receptive to sweeping "practical," "conservative" conclusions from organic social theory. If there are institutions that may in a sense be regarded as "storing" human wisdom (however unaware those who act out the terms of the institutions may be at some particular time of the freight of wisdom the latter carry), as organisms may be said to "store" a nonhuman, purely biological kind of wisdom, there is again nothing in Menger to suggest that there may not be institutions which "store" foolishness or inepitudes. And institutions may simultaneously be repositories of both wisdom and foolishness. It is the more necessary to say this because one might get from such a study as Hayek's recent *The Constitution of Liberty,* which profits greatly from the insights of Menger and from other currents in organic theory, rather too unqualified a reverence for what Hayek calls "that higher, superindividual wisdom which, in a certain sense, the products of spontaneous social growth may possess."[23]

Menger's whole treatment of organic theory, and his effort to answer the question he posed of how it can be that unplanned functional institutions emerge, may be regarded, and I for one would certainly so regard it, as a valuable pioneering effort. But it is in the end not very much more than a sketch. When Menger answers his question about the rise of unplanned functional institutions and points to the fact that out of the pursuit of individual interests "happy" social circumstances may arise, there is still much that he leaves untouched and with which one would have liked to see him concerned. In what follows, I wish to suggest a few lines of analysis that might have been pursued in his work and to indicate the really considerable significance of some of the issues he broached—often of larger significance than he could have known.

It is worth noting that Menger might have made his analysis of how unplanned functional institutions arise sharper and more cogent by giving it a wider context and introducing more sheer conceptual elaboration than he did.[24] He did not genuinely realize that his basic question about unplanned functional institutions could have had light thrown upon it by considering it within the general framework of the role of indirection and ignorance in the social and economic realms. There are pertinent hints on this line in his work, certainly, but nothing more.

[23] *The Constitution of Liberty*, p. 110.

[24] Some of the material that follows is drawn from a paper of mine, entitled "The Role of the Category of Ignorance in Sociological Theory: An Exploratory Statement," *American Sociological Review* (August, 1962), pp. 492-508.

The phenomenon of what I may call "gain through indirection" in human affairs is a broadly familiar one. It has been effectively noted in discussion of a variety of psychological matters. Philosophers have stressed the hedonistic paradox, the paradox that pleasure or happiness, when sought deliberately and directly, is elusive, but, when put aside as an aim while other goals are pursued, may be indirectly achieved. It is a standard psychiatric recommendation to the psychically impotent that they forget about sexual prowess and become immersed in object-love, on the presumption that desired prowess may come about indirectly by way of love. Students of insomnia[25] have developed approaches to sleep that depend heavily on indirection (as through muscle relaxation) and on the insomniac's "forgetting about" the goal of sleep. In economics, the effort of Böhm-Bowerk, Menger's disciple, to show the gain through indirection achieved by initial production of goods themselves to be used in further production comes readily to mind.[26] This simple example from economics could be bolstered by numerous others, and the psychological illustrations could be multiplied as well. I want only to add now that the same general phenomenon of gain through indirection forces itself on the attention also in numerous unequivocally "sociological" problems. Thus, gain through indirection is constantly suggested, at least implicitly and at least as a problem, in analysis of organizations, which have indirection built into their very structures. Do soldiers perform better when they are directly exhorted to combat an enemy whose undesirable traits or performances are "explained," or rather when reliance is placed on the additive effect for "victory" if each soldier of many is motivated singly to do his best in taking care of himself and his immediate "buddies?"[27]

Had it been possible for Menger to think on lines such as these, stressing the very pervasive nature of the problem of gain through indirection, he might have been prompted to go on and seek to tease out the elements of a very *general* representation of what occurs when individuals engaged in following out economic interests inadvertently also produce "beneficent" social results. Here, I can only indicate most cursorily that he might have provided some useful conceptual tools, involving stress on the already mentioned indirection, on intermediacy, on the attractiveness of intermediates, and on what I may call transmutation

[25] Notably Edmund Jacobson, in his *Progressive Relaxation* (Chicago: University of Chicago Press, 1929).

[26] See Böhm-Bowerk's *Positive Theory of Capital* (New York: G. E. Stechert and Co., 1923).

[27] See Samuel A. Stouffer *et al., The American Soldier* (Princeton: Princeton University Press, 1949), Vol. 2, Chap. 3.

mechanisms. Adumbrations of these several notions, perhaps even for the last of them, are already present in Menger's work.

I have referred to a "very general representation" just above. It is quite true that Menger afforded discussion not only of the rise of money but also of the rise of law and "localities" (communities) and states. However, his net *might* have been far more widely cast. Analysis of organizations, which could have offered him valuable material for his basic question, has developed only since his day, and I hardly mean to take him to task for not doing what he could not possibly have done. And as an economist he might have had little interest in religion, which also would have offered him pertinent material.[28] Yet, organizational analysis and certain kinds of sociological approaches to religion, not to mention other things, allow us to see, at least today, that there are possibilities in the way of tying together in a fashion bearing on Menger's basic question many more phenomena than he could imagine. As regards indirection, of course Menger saw that when economic agents, in ignorance of the fact that they were so doing, began to lay the foundations of the institution of money, they were beginning to build it in the only way they could—indirectly. But just how did they go about doing so? Again in the only way they could—intermediately. Indirection and intermediacy are substantially the same thing, looked at in somewhat different ways. When, in reading Menger's several disquisitions on the origin of money, we note that economic agents, as he portrays them, do not aim to produce the fully developed institution of money but instead far more limited ends coincident with individual economic interests and that the compassing of these ends is implicated in a process that ultimately leads to the developed institution, we mark the presence of indirection. But when we shift perspective slightly and direct attention to the way in which the individual actions "causally" construct or build the remote outcome of the developed institution of money, we may stress that the institution is built intermediately, precisely by way of building blocks of action on the basis of economic interest. The notion of intermediacy, too, is implicit in Menger.

We may add at once that the intermediates are intrinsically attractive. Perhaps Menger thought this so obvious that he felt no need to make it quite explicit. But the sheer utilization of a term such as "attractiveness of intermediates" appears helpful, especially for purposes of suggesting the comparability of a number of "economic" and "noneconomic" situations. To Menger it was clear that each individual in a barter situation could be usefully conceived ("usefully" in point of a certain kind of theo-

[28] See the article referred to in footnote 24.

rizing) to be aiming at objects attractive because they advanced his self-interest. The notion of attractiveness of intermediates may be allowed to alert us to the existence of quite analogous phenomena elsewhere. Among peoples who are unclear or ignorant on the point that sexual intercourse leads ultimately to reproduction, the theorist interested in reproduction of *the personnel of societies* may conceive of intercourse as an "attractive intermediate" which, more or less unbeknownst to participants in it (alert only to their "interest"), has a distinctive unintended effect. Durkheim's Australian primitives engaged in totemistic activity, individually absorbing and undertaken as a kind of "sacred" enterprise, not realizing that Durkheim would in effect construe the activity as both intrinsically, in some sense, "attractive" to them and as ultimately bringing about such results (unanticipated by them) as social integration or cohesion.[29] Workers in a factory may unwittingly, or at least with indifference, contribute to over-all factory production goals when these are jeopardized, say, by illness, because they are motivated to help the output of ailing fellow-workers: the chance to help a fellow-worker then appears, looking "back" from the over-all output goal, as an attractive intermediate which leads to the latter goal even if the goal is either outside the knowledge or beyond the concern of many of those who aid in achieving it. In all cases of this type the theorist may look "back" from the vantage point of a special outlook and assess the relative attractiveness of intermediates to agents who may not have even the slightest inkling that their action, for the theorist, falls into a kind of "chain" pattern in which they are providing indispensable "links."

A word should be added about transmutation mechanisms. This term is intended to point more specifically to *the precise ways* in which individual purposive actions addressed to limited objects can lead on to uncontemplated social effects. The words "lead on," as just used—however hard they or like words may be to avoid—indeed beg the questions that might be answered by close scrutiny of transmutation mechanisms. Just *how* do individual purposive actions "lead on"? Transmutation mechanisms operate in the area "between" individually realized goals and uncontemplated outcomes taken or defined as social effects (or, if one will, functional social institutions). Again I am concerned to point out the general character of the problem Menger, perhaps somewhat dimly, recognized in connection with transmutation mechanisms. In connection with the rise of money, Menger had to handle the processes by which individual interests "make" or build into an institution—or

[29] See Emile Durkheim, *The Elementary Forms of the Religious Life* (New York: Macmillan Company, 1926).

certain distinctive economic effects. As he posed the problem, the transmutation mechanisms involved were of a rather simple order. But there are cases in which transmutation mechanisms are even more rudimentary. Thus, where individual couples desire and have children but there is no contemplation of the "continuance of the personnel of the society" as a goal or desideratum, conversion from individually realized object to social outcome or effect is dependent on simple additivity. One female after another gives birth, a certain level of births is reached, and (other things equal) "continuance" is ensured by the sum of the individual births. On the market and in organizations, there are also transmutation mechanisms at work far more complex than those Menger had perhaps begun to discern. Again, he was not in a position to see the very pervasive character of the problem he had touched on in this sphere. Once we are aware of the great reach of transmutation mechanisms through ranges of social and economic phenomena, there is at least the chance that by shrewd and far-flung comparison we may begin to build the elements of a useful theory of such mechanisms.

Aside from these conceptual elaborations which I have suggested, and which, I conceive, might well achieve utility because of the suggestion they so easily carry that Menger's problems were general problems of social science transcending the specifically economic sphere, I should like at this point to make two comments about the whole matter of ignorance, on which Menger touched only very partially if interestingly. First, then, it should be quite clear by now that Menger did in fact and at least touch on ignorance as a problem in economy and society. The economic agents who lay the initial foundations of the institution of money, in Menger's representation, are plainly *unaware* that they are doing so. The indirection by which the institution is built up and the intermediacy involved in its building are not planned. A general blueprint of the institution is not aboriginally in anyone's "mind." No structure is deliberately built, with indirection, intermediacy, and "attractiveness of intermediates" purposively set up so that some agents "manipulate" others (however "benevolently") into making the institution. Ignorance that the building is indeed going up is initially universal. Menger was aware that there are situations in which ignorance (ignorance, that is, at least, of outcomes—such as the money institution—toward which action undertaken is due to lead) works more "effectively" toward certain ends than would knowledge of and planning toward those same ends. And his insight has been exploited, as by Hayek.[30] (It is clear, incidentally, that the insight is susceptible of indiscriminate exploitation

[30] See *The Constitution of Liberty, passim.*

in favor of rather uncritical laissez-faire biases.) But just when or under what circumstances has ignorance been functional in the past or is it functional in the present? It is not enough to *illustrate* by adducing particular cases where ignorance has been or is functional. We need a *theory* of ignorance in economy and society that will render a scheme of analysis enabling us to do more than illustrate the functional or dysfunctional character of ignorance in particular circumstances; that will, ideally, by way of example, allow us to say, given certain specific kinds of activity, whether ignorance or knowledge of prospective outcomes is likely to be functional—ignorance or knowledge *on whose part, in what measure, in what mixture,* and so on. A host of problems is suggested hereby which I shall not even mention. We are very far indeed, at least as yet, from a developed theory of the kind I suggest. And it would be merely silly to "criticize" Menger for not achieving such a theory. But this may again help to suggest that his questionings had even broader significance than he knew.[31]

The second comment on ignorance I should like to make is that the entire set of notions bearing on "ignorance"—and, for that matter, on "subconscious wisdom," and the like—needs careful rescrutiny. It is clear that when, in the vein of organic social theory, someone asserts, let us say, that some action based on traditional modes of acting is both "ignorant" and "wise," an interesting and significant perspective is suggested. This may be roughly represented as follows. As actors pursue their interest they apply such knowledge germane to the solution of their problems as they can discover. The knowledge becomes built into their activity. Its original background in problem-solving is often forgotten, and the behavior founded on knowledge is then passed on from one generation to another simply as *normative*. That is to say, one *must,* or is *required* to, do such and so, and either no explanation is needed or a perfectly adventitious "explanation" is afforded. As bits of "wisdom" are built into heritable biological modes of functioning, so bits of wisdom are analogously represented as built into social institutions. Ignorance and knowledge become mixed or compounded. Hayek again has said some very pertinent things about this mixture or compounding, though he does not so label it, and he has properly stressed that "the result of the experimentation of many generations may embody more experience than any one man possesses"; that under civilization "the individual benefits from more knowledge than he is aware of"; that in view of this

[31] There are of course numerous problems for a democracy posed by analysis of the role of ignorance in economic and social life, problems that cannot be touched upon here.

heritage of knowledge, built into the actions of individuals even if they themselves do not know that it is, the idea that "all useful institutions" must of necessity be "deliberate contrivances" becomes untenable.[32] Actors frequently do "better than they know" merely because they "know" better than they are aware of knowing. But the temptation to weave paradoxes around this kind of insight should be allowed only under careful control. All of this interesting matter, as I suggest, needs careful review. What is the precise value of organic analogies in these premises? Is it genuinely fruitful for social science purposes to construe the term "information" in a very broad sense and allow that both organisms and societies "store" it? What, if any, differentiations is it useful to make in regard to both the "storing" process and the "information"? The critical stance that Menger assumed eighty years ago toward the naïvetés of then current organic theories should certainly encourage us today to beware of facile metaphors, while of course we may remain open to significant efforts at generalizations that bind the organic and the social.

Menger's sketch of organic theory, sketch though it be, is suggestive in still other directions than those I have indicated. Brief allusion to two I have not referred to thus far may be allowed. At page 152, again in connection with the origin of money, Menger makes the following observation: "The problem which science has to solve here consists in the explanation of a *social* phenomenon, of a homogeneous way of acting on the part of the members of a community for which public motives are recognizable, but for which in the concrete case individual motives are hard to discern." Individual motives, on the line of economic self-interest, do not involve envisaging an institution which "serves the common welfare." Inevitably, the paradox that Mandeville among others had stressed is hereby suggested. Private economic "lusts" or "vices" lead to public "virtues." In referring to Mandeville's paradox, Weber had aptly written of "jene Kraft, 'die stets das Böse will und stets das Gute schafft.' "[33] Menger's individual agents, too, act on economic appetites, but unwittingly create the "good" institution of money.[34] This is

[32] *Ibid.*, pp. 62, 22, 21.

[33] *Op. cit.*, p. 33. Social theory is also well acquainted with the paradox in which there appears rather that power that constantly seeks the "good" and constantly achieves the "bad." A fine example is provided in Robert K. Merton's *Science, Technology and Society in Seventeenth Century England, Osiris* 4 (Bruges: Saint Catherine Press, Ltd., 1938), pp. 360-632.

[34] Once more, the basic notion involved is not necessarily limited to thought about the specifically economic sphere. Thus, in the course of a discussion of Turgot's historical views, Manuel writes: "If Providence was a source of goodness, why the long chronicle of wars and devastations, the spectacle of crimes and

another of the matters that it is easy to believe Menger might have treated in detail in the comprehensive treatise he never completed.

There is at least one other such matter. In the context of his discussion of law at page 228, Menger remarks: "What each individual experienced in himself and created from himself at the beginnings of civilization had thus in the opinion of the nation gradually become something *objective,* something divine standing above human wisdom and human interest." Unanticipated consequences of purposive individual actions can ultimately build into massive structures—"a world we never made" —whose "atomistic" origins and derivations, as Menger might say, are quite unknown to individual actors. Man faces the product (for a thinker like Marx, typically the "alienated" product) of his own work and fails to recognize his workmanship. The implications of this for social theory are significant. Menger was in an intellectual position to develop at least some of them. It is a pity he did not do so.

Menger's views, then, have their evident limitations. There were inevitably things he could not see in his time which are rather more easily seen today. His discussion of organic social theory does not leave us with specific enough resources for deciding in numerous particular cases whether some set of social desiderata is best attained "organically" or "pragmatically." Despite the limitations, his work after the lapse of eighty years remains extraordinarily stimulating, and it seems to me that there can be no doubt that he set out sharply and clearly a number of problems as important in our day as they were in his.

I must, for my part, say something about the present translation. Dr. Nock, as his preface indicates, did the basic work of translating. His manuscript was not in quite final form when he had to leave for an extended stay in Europe early in 1962. I then undertook a final revision. I may well have "meddled" more than I should have done, and if the reader is inclined to think that whatever merits the translation may have are attributable to Dr. Nock and whatever lapses it may show are due to me, I shall not object: the reader is likely enough to be right. At a number of points I have made the translation less literal than Dr. Nock's original. I sought to clarify several obscurities and may have taken more

barbarities perpetrated throughout the ages? The answer is common to most eighteenth-century philosophers of history—in this respect Turgot's concept is only one offshoot of a general theme. Without the impetus of the aggressive, evil passions, without the ambitions of individuals, the 'leading strings' of nature, there would have been no progress in the early stages of history and man would have been doomed to peace and mediocrity." Frank E. Manuel, *The Prophets of Paris* (Cambridge: Harvard University Press, 1962), pp. 46-47.

liberties with Menger's original than are warranted. Much as I have tried to remain within the framework of Dr. Nock's intentions as I understood them and much as I have tried to make changes in accord with the spirit of his work, I may not always have succeeded. As one instance of possible discrepancies, I note that Dr. Nock says that he translated "Volkswirthschaft" with "economy," except where a distinction had to be made clear. He adds that in a few places where Menger wrote of "Wirthschaft" and "Volkswirthschaft," he, Nock, used "economy" and national economy." In doing my work of revision, I may not invariably have preserved this practice. (I have not checked every case of possible discrepancy.) But if I have not, I do not believe there has been any real loss in clarity, and I may here and there have achieved a more concise phrasing. As an instance of deliberate change on my part, I have at points rendered as "theoretical" a German term that Dr. Nock correctly translated as "epistemological" because the former word appeared to me to fit the English version better.

Since it was constantly necessary for me, in revising, to recur to the German original, I feel constrained to add my lament to Dr. Nock's. I agree that Menger is *nearly* always clear—and even painfully so in that he does insist on "leaving nothing to the reader's imagination." But one has one's bad moments with him even in this matter of clarity. His work abounds in delightful combinations of words such as "without consideration of the above orientation of the same in respect to the above mentioned fact." Occasionally, at any rate, it is not altogether easy to discover what "the above" (a huge favorite with Menger) refers to. I have admired Dr. Nock's skill in hounding the interminable "the aboves" to their lairs. In the end, I believe, this translation is an accurate rendering of Menger's meaning. To have tried to convert it into an elegant or highly polished English version of Menger would, I feel with Dr. Nock, have been a mistake; and, even if it had not been a mistake, it would have confronted us with a virtually endless task.

In the original work, Menger's notes are numbered consecutively throughout the whole. His practice in this regard has been preserved. Dr. Nock made a number of notes (marked F.J.N.) which appear after Menger's. I have added some editorial notes of my own (marked L.S.). I have sought to keep these few and brief, and I can only hope that they will be of aid or interest to the reader on a number of points. (It has seemed convenient to indicate both Dr. Nock's notes and mine with letters of the alphabet.) The substance of what I have wanted to say about Menger appears in this introduction, and I have not sought to cram either incidentals or scholarly detail into my notes. This volume is not intended to be a bibliographer's delight. It is intended to convey to the reader of English what Menger wrote in German.

A grant from the University Research Board of the University of Illinois to cover costs of typing is gratefully acknowledged.

LOUIS SCHNEIDER

University of Illinois

PREFACE

Theoretical investigations in the field of political economy, particularly in Germany, have by no means progressed as yet to a true methodology of this science. Rather, the theoretical issues which occupy German economists, and to no small extent their non-German colleagues, revolve chiefly about the nature and the very concept of political economy and of its subdivisions, the nature of its truths, the matter of conceiving economic problems in such wise as to do justice to real conditions, and other such problems. They do not revolve about the intellectual roads to the goals of economic research, for the latter are themselves still in question.

To be sure, this phenomenon is of fairly recent date. The time is not so far back when the nature of political economy and the formal nature of its verities seemed established, and theoretical investigations in the field of our science were actually concerned with its true methodological problems. That political economy is "the science of the laws of national economy" was considered just as settled as sufficient, since the view of it as a mere technology had been overcome. Scientific discussion could go on to the investigation of the question of whether those laws had to be obtained speculatively or empirically, inductively or deductively, to the question of what particular form was suitable for these methods in the realm of social phenomena in general and of national economy in particular. It could go on to the investigation of other such questions of true methodology.

All this, of course, had to change as soon as one began to deal more thoroughly with methodological problems. Scholars in our science had to become aware that political economy exhibits in its theoretical and practical subdivisions knowledge of a completely different formal nature. Accordingly, we cannot speak of one method, *the method* of political economy, but only of its *methods*. Ways of attaining knowledge and the methods of research are oriented by the goals of research and by the formal nature of the truths of which we desire knowledge. The methods of theoretical economics and of the practical sciences of national economy cannot be the same. But even where this fundamental distinction was adhered to in treating methodological problems, or where only theoretical economics was thought of at first, upon closer investigation it necessarily became clear that even the concept of "laws of phenomena" was an ambiguous one comprising truths of very different formal nature. Therefore, the conception of political economy, or even of theoretical economics, as a science of the "laws of national economy" was inadequate.

The writers of the postclassical period had for the most part simply connected with the concept of economics the idea of a science of the laws of national economy, of the laws of the coexistence and succession of the phenomena of economics, somewhat in the fashion of laws of nature. They did this without becoming aware of the different nature of this knowledge and, with this, of the indefiniteness of the above concept. But, beside the concept of political economy as a science analogous to physics and chemistry the anatomical-physiological point of view soon made itself felt more clearly than had previously been suggested by individual workers in our science. The conception of the national economy as an organism and of its laws as analogous to those of anatomy and physiology confronted the physical conception; the biological point of view in research confronted the atomistic.

Scientific investigation did not stop at this complication of the methodological problem. It was pointed out that social phenomena in general and the phenomena of national economy in particular gained a special character through national individuality, through local conditions, and particularly in virtue of the developmental stage of society; they showed spatial and temporal differences which could not be without determinative influence on the laws that applied to them. The desire for universal and immutable laws of national economy independent of spatial and temporal conditions, and thus the desire for a science based on such laws, seemed from this point of view to be inadmissible and misconceived; it seemed to involve an undue abstraction from the "full empirical reality" of phenomena. The consideration of spatial and temporal differences of economic phenomena seemed to be an inevitable postulate of research not only in the field of "practical economics," but also in that of theoretical economics, the "science of the *laws* of economy."

Others went even a step farther by believing that they did not have to acknowledge any analogy at all between the laws of nature and those of national economy, and by characterizing the latter, rather, as laws of historical development (as parallelisms of economic history) and as laws of great numbers (as parallelisms of the statistics of national economy). The historical-philosophical and the statistical-theoretical orientations of research took their place beside the atomistic and the organic conception of the problems of our science and the desire to retain the national and the historical points of view in theoretical economics.

As if that were not enough, an orientation of research prevailed which even questioned the character of political economy as a "science of the *laws* of national economy." On the contrary, it characterized political economy, like historical jurisprudence and the science of language, as a specifically historical science, and historical understanding as the exclusively justified and attainable goal of research in the field of national economy. The conception of political economy as a specifically historical science was added to the multitude of views of the nature of economic laws, and accordingly of theoretical economics, which, indeed, was thought of as the essence of these laws.

The conflict of opinions was not limited to the formal nature of the truths of our science. While some characterized economics as the science of the laws of *"economic phenomena,"* others saw in this view an improper isolation of a special side of national life. The theory that the phenomena of national economy are to be treated in inseparable connection with the total social and political development of nations gained numerous adherents among economists. To the dispute about the formal nature of the truths of our science and the character of the latter itself was joined controversy about the extent and limits of the realm of phenomena that the science is to deal with. Indeed, it even appeared doubtful to many whether political economy in general is to be dealt with as an independent science and not rather as an organic part of a universal social science.

Discussion has now for almost half a century been revolving about the justification of all these orientations of research, which in part are contradictory and in part merge and complement each other. The remark is scarcely necessary that this state of the development of the methodology of our science could not be at all beneficial. How is investigation of the *ways* to the goals of research in the field of political economy (of true methodology!) to reach a satisfactory conclusion, how is even the interest of the scholarly world to turn seriously to the pertinent problems, if the goals themselves are so completely in question?

It is my intention for the present work, which developed from what I feel to be the immediate need of the present in the field of political economy, to serve this need first. This work, too, in conformity with the present-day standpoint of theoretical investigations, is primarily concerned with determining the nature of political economy, of its subdivisions, of its truths, in brief, with the goals of research in the field of our science. Methodology in the narrower sense of the word is chiefly to be reserved for future investigations, for which interest will of course be aroused immediately, as soon as some agreement has been reached concerning the basic problems treated here.

With such agreement attained, the solution of the second part of the problem characterized above will perhaps seem much easier than at first. After all, anyone who is to any extent familiar with the pertinent literature knows to what a high degree philosophical investigation has from the beginning turned to true methodological problems and how it has reached its most valuable results here. Let us just be quite clear about the goals of research in the field of national economy, and it may be hoped that it will not be too difficult for us to determine the paths to these goals if only all those who feel called upon to collaborate in establishing a methodology of political economy will endeavor to utilize the results of general theoretical investigations for the special problems of our science, to utilize them seriously—more seriously and intelligently than has, perhaps, been the case up to now.

Of course, we will look in vain in the writings of the logicians for enlightenment about the goals of research in the field of political economy. Insight into the nature of the truths of this field of knowledge can only be the result of comprehensive and competent consideration of the realm of phenomena to be examined by us and of the special demands life makes on our science. There can be no doubt that in the above respect we are not justified in expecting pretty much everything from the logicians, but that they are justified in expecting it from us. The desire to find enlightenment in the writings of prominent logicians on the goals of research in the field of our science has often been manifest recently among German economists. There can be no doubt that this must be regarded merely as a symptom of the extremely unsatisfactory state of this part of the theoretical structure of our science. However, I do, indeed, believe that general theoretical investigations will be highly beneficial to us as soon as we have reached assured results on the nature of the truths of political economy. They will be beneficial in examining the formal conditions for determining these truths and the intellectual paths to their attainment.

To be sure, even then only a comparatively slight amount will be accomplished for our science, which has remained far behind other disciplines. Indeed, I cannot really refrain from remarking that I am far from overrating the significance of methodology for research in general and in particular for research in the field of political economy. The most important scientific results have come from men who were far removed from methodological investigations, while the greatest methodologists have not infrequently proved to be extremely barren scholars in the field of those sciences whose methods they could expound with imposing clarity. Between the establishment of a methodology and the satisfactory development of a science there is an immeasurable gap which only the genius of its scholars can bridge over. Positive research talent has often enough created a science or changed it in an epoch-making fashion without developed methodology. But methodology without talent never has done this. Methodology, of incomparable importance for secondary achievements in the field of a science, is of lesser importance for those great problems reserved for genius to solve.

Only in one case, to be sure, do methodological investigations appear to be the most important, the most immediate and the most urgent thing that can be done for the development of a science. It may happen in a field of knowledge, for some reason or other, that accurate feeling for the goals of research coming from the nature of the subject matter has been lost. It may happen that an exaggerated or even decisive significance is attributed to secondary problems of the science. Erroneous methodological principles supported by powerful schools prevail completely and one-sidedness judges all efforts in a field of knowledge. In a word, the progress of a science is blocked because erroneous methodological principles prevail. In this case, to be sure, clarification of methodological problems is the condition of any further progress, and with this the time has come when even those are obligated to enter the quarrel about methods who otherwise would have preferred to apply their powers to the solution of the distinctive problems of their science.

But this seems to me now to be the presently prevailing state of research in the field of political economy in Germany. It is a state hardly intelligible to those who have not followed the development of this science in recent decades attentively.

The conflict of views about the nature of our science, its problems, and its limits, especially the effort to set new goals for research in the field of political economy, did not originally develop from the interest of economists in theoretical investigations. It begins with the recognition becoming more and more evident that the theory of economics as it left the hands of Adam Smith and his followers lacks any assured basis, that even its most elementary problems have found no solution, and that it is especially an insufficient basis for the practical sciences of national economy, and thus also of practice in this field. Even before the appearance of the historical school of German economists the conviction grew more and more that the previously prevailing belief in the perfection of our science was false and that, on the contrary, the science needed thorough revision.

Three ways were open for the reform of our science, as soon as this conviction had been reached. Either a reform of political economy had to be attempted on the basis of the previous views of its nature and problems and the doctrine founded by Adam Smith had to be perfected from the points of view from which it started, or else new paths had to be opened for research. The reform could be of previous practice, or it could be of the theory of research.

Aside from these two orientations of reform effort differing according to their nature and trend, one could also ultimately be adopted which in a certain higher sense combined the above two notions of reform. A reform of political economy could be striven for from the previous points of view and yet the way opened for new orientations. No single orientation of research encompasses all research problems. Rather, advancing cognition of the real world and its processes and increasing claims on theoretical and practical knowledge ceaselessly bring to light new orientations of the desire for knowledge. Justified in itself, the single orientation of research still seems inadequate in view of the totality of the problems which science has to solve. This is especially true of the theory of a science. Its perfection can only be found in the satisfactory development of all justified orientations of theoretical research and in the ordering of its results into one theoretical scheme, or into a system. It is thus in the theoretical natural sciences; it is thus in the theoretical social sciences in general and in the theoretical science of national economy in particular. The opening up of new branches of theoretical research can go hand in hand with the reform of the previous ones.

The first of the above ways to the reform of economics, although apparently the simplest and most obvious, nevertheless really presented quite unusual difficulties, for more than one reason. What the best minds of all nations had striven for in vain on the previous paths of research was now to be attained; what their genius ran aground on was now to be mastered. Not only was criticism to be practiced or some grand perspective opened, but something *positive* was to be created. The orientation to be adopted demanded of its representatives an originality capable of positive accomplishments. This was in a field of knowledge which, on account of its incomparable difficulties, makes the highest demands on the scholarly mind.

The efforts characterized here also offered little that was appealing for other reasons. Never is the reform of a science on previous paths of research more difficult and, at least at first, less rewarding than when outstanding minds have already undertaken it without success. For the pressure of their authority paralyzes the confidence of the individual who tries to follow, and at the same time it prevents acknowledgment of successes really attained. It paralyzes the energy of creative minds and the free judgment of receiving minds.

All these circumstances combined to cause a reform of our science, in the sense of the older view of it, to appear just as difficult as unalluring. The theory of economics, as the so-called classical school of English economists shaped it in the main, has not been able to solve the problem of a science of the laws of national economy satisfactorily. But the authority of its doctrine is a burden on us all and prevents progress on those paths on which the scholarly mind for centuries, long before the appearance of A. Smith, sought the solution of the great problem of establishing theoretical social sciences.

The other way to reform our science seemed much simpler and more rewarding. Its unsatisfactory state was not to be considered the result of a scholarly ability inadequate for the solution of its problems, but of an erroneous *orientation* of research, and a cure-all was to be expected from a *new* orientation. Whoever could establish such a new orientation would be considered a reformer of political economy, even if he did nothing worthy of mention in a factual way to deepen and justify it, even if he did not do anything directly for the solution of its problems. This would be so even if he was content, rather, to open up large perspectives or to work in fields of knowledge justified per se, but essentially different from political economy; even if he was content, for the rest, with a compilation, devoid of any unifying conception, of the results of just those previous orientations of research designated as erroneous and most emphatically criticized.

A variety of circumstances was added to further the above efforts. In the field of linguistic research, of political science, and of jurisprudence new orientations of research had come to prevail and had led to results which had not been valued according to merit by the scholarly world and public opinion, particularly in Germany, but had been considerably overestimated, at least temporarily. How obvious was the notion of applying these efforts to our field of knowledge! To become famous as a reformer of political economy there was scarcely need of anything more than a lively sense for the analogies of research. The reform of political economy in the previous conception of it was just as difficult as devoid of glory. The fame of a pioneer, a creator of new orientations of research, on the other hand, had come within reach with such a moderate expenditure of intellectual means. No wonder that among the truly scholarly economists of Germany the development of theory declined more and more. All those who were desirous of quick success struck out in new directions, particularly in those directions where any talent could assert itself usefully, even a lesser talent which was not sufficient for research into the great relationships of national economy and for the exact analysis of its phenomena.

To be sure, in doing this men overlooked the fundamental difference between the formal nature of political economy and of those sciences from which basic principles, even results of research, were borrowed more or less mechanically. They failed in particular to recognize the real trend of that scientific movement which had altered jurisprudence on a historical basis. Rare misunderstandings, as I will prove, have played a decisive part in the reform of political economy by its German reformers. The new orientations of research were to no small extent the result of misleading analogies and a failure to recognize the true problems of political economy.

However, even where a new orientation of research, justified per se, came to prevail, it was not the result of a comprehensive insight into the system of problems which science has to solve in the field of national economy. Everywhere we see the phenomenon repeated that special orientations of research, not infrequently of more or less secondary importance, make the reform of political economy dependent exclusively on their success, but deny the justification of any other orientation of research. The desire to do away with the unsatisfactory state of political economy by opening up new paths of research has led in Germany to a series of partly misleading, partly one-sided views of the nature of our science and its problems. It has led to views which separate the German economists from the movement in the literature of the subject of all other nations. Indeed, it has led to views which have caused the German efforts, on account of their one-sidedness, to appear unintelligible in individual cases to the non-German economists.

There is scarcely need to remark that in this situation a reform of political economy on the universal bases I indicated above was far removed from the mental sphere of the German reformers of this science. Among all representatives of the previously characterized orientations not one mind has been found which could have surveyed the totality of those problems which a science of the laws of national economy has to solve. Not one mind has been found which would survey the individual orientations of theoretical research as justified branches of a totality of a theoretical science of national economy, or which could even survey its relationship to the remaining nontheoretical branches of research in the field of national economy. Indeed, nowhere has even the desire for such a universal conception of the methodological problem come to light. Everywhere, on the contrary, we meet orientations of research, partly misleading and partly justified per se, but more or less secondary in respect to all of political economy. Yet each one of these is identified with research in the field of national economy in general.

But in this is to be found the real perniciousness of the present state of political economy in Germany. It is not the circumstance that the reformers of our science, who came to the fore with such confidence, did not truly do away with its defective state, which forms the real core of the evil. Nor is it that in pursuing relatively secondary problems they lost sight of the main goals of research in the field of political economy and even lost sight of the science itself. The core is to be found in the poorly cloaked contempt for and basic negation of all other orientations of research, not infrequently of those which prove to be the most significant in respect to the whole of our science.

With this, to be sure, the time has come when methodological investigations in the field of political economy necessarily take first place in scientific interest. The progress of our science at present is hindered by the sway of erroneous methodological principles. Methodology thus has the floor and will keep it until, through clarification of the goals of research and subsequent clarification of the ways to attain the goals, those obstacles are removed which arose for the progress of political economy in Germany in virtue of misleading methodological principles.

As regards the results I have reached, I think it hardly necessary to say anything about them. I have presented them in words as simple and clear as I could, considering the difficulty of the questions dealt with. I have also sorted and arranged them as far as I was able. Let them speak for themselves. But I cannot keep from making one remark here, for it concerns my attitude toward my colleagues in Germany.

The largely polemic character of this writing, of which I am aware, was not caused even in a single instance by ill will toward meritorious representatives of our science. It came about rather because of the nature of the task I set myself. It was produced of necessity by my conception of the present state of political economy in Germany. The polemics against the presently prevailing orientation of research in economics were for me neither an end in themselves nor even a merely superficial ornamentation. They were an essential part of my task; indeed, they had to be forcible and sweeping, even at the risk of hurting feelings in individual cases.

Even if this should prove somewhat prejudicial to the external success of my writing, at least at first, I will not complain of this. The modern literature on economics in Germany, really but little scrutinized by the outside world and hardly understandable to it because of its trends, was not influenced by serious opponents in the decades of its constant isolation. It frequently lacked even any really strict self-criticism in its unshakable confidence in its methods. Anyone who followed a different direction in Germany was ignored rather than refuted. Thus long-lasting practice developed a phraseology concerning the basic problems of methodology in our science which is in part senseless. It is a phraseology which became so much the more harmful to the development of political economy in Germany as it was repeated thoughtlessly, untouched by serious criticism. It could even make the claim of signifying an epoch-making upheaval in the field of our science. Under such circumstances there was above all need of an unprejudiced survey and examination, and of a serious criticism. In this direction so much that had been neglected by others had to be made up.

But the unprejudiced reader will at once realize how little it was my intention in this case to belittle my German colleagues. I have nowhere neglected to do justice to the merits of others, to the best of my knowledge. Even where I had to oppose erroneous orientations of research or one-sidedness, I have always endeavored to stress most carefully the elements of truth in the doctrines I have attacked. Nor have I disposed of anything with mere general phrases, but in each case have tried to get to the bottom of the points at issue. I was guided by the thought of making research in the field of political economy in Germany aware of its real tasks again. I thought of liberating it from the one-sided aspects harmful to the development of our science, of freeing it from its isolation in the general literary movement, and thus of preparing for the reform of political economy on German soil, a reform which this science so urgently needs in the light of its unsatisfactory state.

All great civilized nations have their specific mission in the development of sciences, and every aberration of the scholarly world of a nation, or of a considerable part of it, leaves a gap in the development of scientific knowledge. Political economy, too, cannot dispense with the single-minded co-operation of the German mind. To contribute to bringing it back to the right paths was the task of this work, which was pursued without secondary considerations.

Vienna
December, 1882

THE AUTHOR

BOOK ONE

Economics as a Theoretical Science and Its Relationship to the Historical and Practical Economic Sciences

BOOK 1

CHAPTER 1

The Various Aspects of Research in the Field of National Economy

The contrast between the historical and the theoretical sciences in general and in particular between those of economy.—Nature and problems of the historical sciences of economy.—Nature, problems and significance of a theory of economy.—Nature and problems of the practical sciences of economy; their relation to theoretical economics and to the practice of economy.

The world of phenomena can be considered from two essentially different points of view. Either there are concrete phenomena in their position in space and time and in their concrete relationships to one another, or else there are the empirical forms recurring in the variation of these, the knowledge of which forms the object of our scientific interest. The one orientation of research is aimed at cognition of the concrete, or more correctly, of the *individual* aspect of phenomena; the other is aimed at cognition of their *general* aspect. Thus, corresponding to these two main orientations of the striving for cognition, two great classes of scientific knowledge confront us, the first of which we will in short call *individual,* the latter *general.*[1]

[1] We use the expression "individual" here merely to designate the contrast to what is "general," the contrast between *concrete phenomena* and *phenomenal forms.*[a] The expressions "concrete" and "abstract" were avoided by us here intentionally, because they are ambiguous and furthermore do not characterize the above contrast exactly.

[a] "Concrete phenomena" and "phenomenal forms" proved the best that could be done with Menger's language at this point. It is quite literal, for Menger writes *concreten Erscheinungen* and *Erscheinungsformen.* Fortunately, the intent of his contrast is plain enough. L.S.

The interest which the human mind takes in the cognition of concrete phenomena (of what is individual) and the significance of this for practical life is self-evident; so is the formal nature of the results of the striving for cognition aimed at what is individual. Not quite so obvious to general understanding are the nature and significance of general knowledge; and therefore, because of the importance of this subject for the understanding of the nature of the theoretical sciences and their contrast to the historical ones, a few pertinent observations may be in place here.

In spite of the great variety of concrete phenomena, we are able, even with cursory observation, to perceive that not every single phenomenon exhibits a particular empirical form differing from that of all the others. Experience teaches us, rather, that definite phenomena are repeated, now with greater exactitude, now with lesser, and recur in the variation of things. We call these empirical forms *types*. The same holds true of the relationships among concrete phenomena. These also do not exhibit a thorough individuality in every single case. We are able, rather, to observe without much difficulty certain relationships among them recurring now with greater, now with lesser regularity (e.g., regularities in their succession, in their development, in their coexistence), relationships which we call *typical*. The phenomena of purchase, of money, of supply and demand, of price, of capital, of rate of interest are examples of typical empirical forms of economy. On the other hand the regular drop in price of a commodity as a result of the increase in supply, the rise in price of a commodity as a result of an increase in currency, the lowering of the rate of interest as a result of considerable accumulation of capital, etc., present themselves to us as typical relationships among economic phenomena. The contrast between what we call general and individual phenomena, or general and individual knowledge of phenomena, respectively, is probably completely clear after what has been said.

The investigation of types and of typical relationships of phenomena is of really immeasurable significance for human life, of no less significance than the cognition of concrete phenomena. Without the knowledge of empirical forms we would not be able to comprehend the myriads of phenomena surrounding us, nor to classify them in our minds; it is the presupposition for a more comprehensive cognition of the real world. Without cognition of the typical relationships we would be deprived not only of a deeper understanding of the real world, as we will show further on, but also, as may be easily seen, of all cognition extending beyond immediate observation, i.e., of any *prediction* and *control* of things. All human prediction and, indirectly, all arbitrary shaping of things is conditioned by that knowledge which we previously have called *general*.

The statements made here are true of all realms of the world of phenomena, and accordingly also of human economy in general and of its social form, "national economy,"[2] in particular. The phenomena of the latter we also can consider from the above two so thoroughly different points of view; and in the field of economy, also, we will thus have to differentiate on the one hand between individual (concrete) phenomena and their individual (concrete) relationships in time and space, and on the other between types (empirical forms) and their typical relationships (laws in the broadest sense of the word). Also in the field of economy we encounter individual and general knowledge, and correspondingly sciences of the individual aspect of phenomena and sciences of the general aspect. To the former belong history and the statistics of economy, to the latter theoretical economics; for the first two have the task of investigating the individual[3] economic phenomena, even if from different points of view. The latter have the task of investigating the empirical forms and laws (the general nature and general connection) of economic phenomena.[4]

[2] See Appendix I: "The Nature of National Economy."

[3] The "individual" is by no means to be confused with the "singular," or, what is the same thing, *individual phenomena* are by no means to be confused with *singular phenomena*. For the opposite of "individual" is "general," whereas the opposite of a "singular phenomenon" is the "collective phenomenon." A definite nation, a definite state, a concrete economy, an association, a community, etc., are examples of individual phenomena, but by no means of singular phenomena (but of collective phenomena instead); whereas the phenomenal forms of the commodity, of the use value, of the entrepreneur, etc., are indeed general, but not collective phenomena. The fact that the historical sciences of economy represent the *individual* phenomena of the latter by no means excludes their making us aware of these from the collective point of view. However, the contrast between the investigation and description of the *individual* and the *general* aspect of human phenomena is always what distinguishes the historical social sciences from the theoretical.

[4] Theoretical economics has the task of investigating the *general nature* and the *general connection* of economic phenomena, not of analyzing economic *concepts* and of drawing the logical conclusions resulting from this analysis. The phenomena, or certain aspects of them, and not their linguistic image, the concepts, are the object of theoretical research in the field of economy. The analysis of the concepts may in an individual case have a certain significance for the *presentation* of the theoretical knowledge of economy, but the goal of research in the field of theoretical economics can only be the determination of the general nature and the general connection of economic *phenomena*. It is a sign of the slight understanding, which individual representatives of the historical school in particular have for the aims of theoretical research, when they see only *analyses of concepts* in investigations into the *nature* of the commodity, into the *nature* of economy, the *nature* of value, of price and similar things, and when they see "the setting up of a system of concepts and judgments" in the striving for an exact theory of economic phenomena (*cf.* particularly Roscher's *Thukydides,* p. 27). A number of French economists fall into a similar error when, with an erroneous view of the concepts "theory" and "system," they understand by these terms nothing more than theorems obtained deductively from a priori axioms, or systems of these (cf. particularly J. B. Say, *Cours* [1852], I, p. 14 ff. Even J. Garnier says "C'est dans le sens de doctrine erronnée qu'on prend le mot 'système' en économie politique." *Traité d'Econ. Pol.* [1868], p. 648).

The above contrast is not infrequently characterized, even if in a somewhat different sense, by the separation of the sciences into *historical* and *theoretical*. History and the statistics of economy are historical sciences in the above sense; economics is a theoretical science.[5]

Besides the two above large groups of sciences we must bear in mind here still a third one, the nature of which is essentially different from that of the two previously named: we mean the so-called *practical sciences* or *technologies*.

The sciences of this type do not make us aware of phenomena, either from the historical point of view or from the theoretical; they do not teach us at all what *is*. Their problem is rather to determine the basic principles by which, according to the diversity of conditions, efforts of a definite kind can be most suitably pursued. They teach us what the conditions *are supposed* to be for definite human aims to be achieved. Technologies of this kind in the field of economy are *economic policy* and the *science of finance*.

We will accordingly have to distinguish in the field of economy three groups of sciences for our special purposes: first, the *historical* sciences (history[6]) and the statistics[7] of economy, which have the task of investigat-

[5] Cf. below Appendix II: "The Concept of Theoretical Economics and the Nature of Its Laws."

[6] Knies (*Pol. Oek.* [1853], p. 3 ff.) specifies the problem of economic history in the following way: "It has the task of comprehending and describing not only the historical development of theory of economics, the intentions and the practice of the general state powers for the fulfillment of their needs in material goods and for the furthering of national economic interests, but also the economic conditions and developments in the real life of various nations and times." To us the problem of scientific economic history seems to be a threefold one: 1. the investigation of the sources of economic history, 2. the external and internal criticism of these sources, 3. the description of the development of those *collective* phenomena which we call "economy" on the basis of the historical material thus obtained. The more comprehensive the study of the sources, the more careful and methodical the criticism of them, and the greater the art of description, so much the more will the historian succeed in offering us a *coherent* picture of the economic history of single nations, of certain groups of nations, or else of humanity that does justice to the real conditions. On the other hand, the procedure of those people seems unscientific to us who merely compile from collected works the economic history of nations, without going back to the sources and without exercising the slightest critical check on them. In particular, the procedure of those who offer a more or less externally arranged mass of historical material, but no coherent picture of economic developments, and designate such collections of more or less uncritical notes as history seems still more unscientific.

[7] *Statistics, as a historical science,* has the same problems to solve as history, yet not in respect to the *development,* but to the *state* of societies. Uncritical compilations, or merely superficial arrangements of statistical material lacking higher unity, do not come within the domain of scientific description. The definitions of

ing and describing the individual nature and the individual connection of economic phenomena; second, *theoretical* economics, with the task of investigating and describing their general nature and general connection (their laws); finally, third, the *practical* sciences[8] of national economy, with the task of investigating and describing the basic principles for suitable action (adapted to the variety of conditions) in the field of national economy (economic policy and the science of finance).

By *political economy*,[9] however, we will understand that totality of the

---

historical statistics as "history at rest," as "the average of historical development," as "description of society at a definite point in time," and other such concepts allow a great variety of misinterpretations of the true nature of this science. Historical statistics does *not* have the task of offering us the *external picture of society at a definite point of time*, which, in accordance with the selection of this point, could not help being extremely deviant and extremely incomplete, considering the totality of the life of the people. Rather, it has the task of offering a description of all factors of social life (*even the ones latent at a given moment*) from which the movement of society results, while *history* has to portray this movement itself. To be distinguished from statistics, as a historical science, are the statistical data obtained from mass observations, which, in contrast to historical statistics as well as to theoretical statistics, present themselves as mere scientific material. Historical sources brought to light and even critically determined historical facts are not "history" per se, and in the same way mere statistical material cannot be designated as "statistics." Also the *method* for obtaining statistics, as really should be obvious, must be differentiated from the scientific description of statistical results. "Statistics as a science" can never be merely a method. What is commonly called *"the theory of statistics"* is usually by its nature the *methodology* (so-called theory of cognition!) of this science. More correctly only the results of a truly *theoretical* consideration of statistical material, the *laws* of the coexistence and the succession of social phenomena, should be designated as *theoretical*-statistical knowledge and the totality of these should be designated as theoretical statistics. The *"laws of great numbers"* form the most important constituent but by no means the exclusive content of theoretical statistics.

[8] Cf. Appendix III: "The Relationship of the Practical Sciences of National Economy to Economic Practice and to Theoretical Economics."

[9] Montchrêtien Sieur de Vateville, who in 1615 brought out his *Traicté de l'économie politique* in Rouen with Jean Osmont, is mentioned as the first to use the expression "political economy" (*économie politique*). This expression, which has attained such wide circulation, is found however only on the title page of the work, not in the royal patent, where this is designated as *Traicté économique du profit*, nor anywhere in the text. It seems, therefore, to have been the result of a momentary inspiration of the author; perhaps it was borrowed from a piece of contemporary writing after the type of the text was set. The work, which is divided into three books, on trade, commerce, and shipping, is chiefly practical economics (cf. J. Garnier, *Journal des économistes* [Aug.-Sept., 1852]. Duval, *Mémoire sur Antoine de Montchrétien* [Paris, 1868]). The expression "political economy" is probably indicated already in the pseudo-Aristotelian economics, yet only in the sense of the economy of a city. In medieval Latin the word *politia*, more frequently still *politica*, is used in the sense of art of government (in the

theoretical-practical sciences of national economy (theoretical economics, economic policy, and the science of finance) which at present are commonly grouped together under the above designation.[10]

---

oldest glosses these expressions are translated with: "statordenunge, regiment eyner stat, kunst von der regierung der stat, ein kunst von statten zu regieren").[b] *Oeconomia* usually had in medieval Latin the meaning of *praedium, villa rustica; Oeconomus* the meaning of *steward, defensor, advocatus,* etc. The combination of the two expressions I have found nowhere else among early writers, not even in the church fathers (cf. Du Cange [1845], V, 333 ff. and IV, 696, Laur. Diefenbach, *Glossarium Latino-german.* [1857], p. 445). The writings which appeared before Montchrétien, always in connection with Aristotelian terminology, deal with politics, or with economics, but never with political economy.

[10] Cf. Appendix IV: "The Terminology and the Classification of the Economic Sciences."

[b] "City order, government of a city, art of governing the city, art of governing cities." F.J.N.

BOOK 1

CHAPTER 2

The Errors Which Result from the Failure to Recognize the Formal Nature of Theoretical Economics

Confusion of the historical sciences of economy and economic theory.—Confusion of the historical and the theoretical understanding of economic phenomena.—The error of applying the points of view of historical jurisprudence to theoretical economics.—Inadequate separation of the latter from practical economic sciences.—Explanation of this error through the history of political economy.—Evils which have resulted from this for the strategy, methodology, and the advancement of political economy in general.

The nature and significance of the so-called historical point of view in political economy will be set forth thoroughly in Book Two, and the errors will be indicated which result for our science from the failure to recognize this point of view—from what might be called the unhistorical point of view in political economy. But before we go on to the solution of this problem, we should first like to make mention of those errors which have resulted from the failure to recognize the formal nature of political economy and its place in the sphere of the sciences in general. Not only have these errors appeared particularly among German political economists, but also, as will be shown, they are rooted to no slight extent precisely in the endeavor—justified per se, yet up to now vague and misguided—to make the historical point of view valid in our science. However, we shall first speak here of the confusion of historical and theoretical research in the field of economy, and then of the confusion of the theoretical and the practical economic sciences.

It was stressed above that phenomena can be investigated from a double point of view, from the *individual* (the historical in the broadest sense of this word), and from the *general* (the theoretical). The task of the first orientation of research is the cognition of concrete phenomena in their individual nature and their individual connection. The task of the latter is the cognition of empirical forms (types) and of typical relationships (the laws of phenomena). It is *concrete* acts, destinies, institutions of definite nations and states, it is concrete cultural developments and conditions whose investigation constitutes the task of history and statistics, whereas the theoretical social sciences have the task of elaborating the *empirical forms* of social phenomena and the *laws* of their succession, of their coexistence, etc.

The contrast between the historical and the theoretical sciences becomes still more clearly evident if we make ourselves aware of it in a definite realm of phenomena. If for this purpose we select the phenomena of economy, then the determination of the empirical forms and of the laws, the types and typical relations of economic phenomena, is presented to us as the task of theoretical research. We work at the development of theoretical economics by seeking to determine the empirical forms recurring in the alternation of economic phenomena, for example, the general nature of exchange, of price, of ground rent, of supply, of demand, and the typical relations between these phenomena, e.g., the effect on prices of the increasing or decreasing of supply and demand, the effect of population increase on ground rent, etc. The historical sciences of economy, on the contrary, teach us the nature and development of individually definite economic phenomena, thus, e.g., the state or the development of the economy of a definite nation or of a definite group of nations, the state or the development of a definite economic institution, the development of prices, of ground rent in a definite economic district, etc.

The theoretical and historical sciences of economy, accordingly, do exhibit a fundamental difference, and only the complete failure to recognize the true nature of these sciences can produce this confusion of these with each other, or occasion the opinion that they can replace each other mutually. Rather, it is clear that, just as theoretical economics never can take the place of the history or the statistics of economy in our striving for cognition, not even the most comprehensive studies in the field of the two last-mentioned sciences, on the other hand, could take the place of theoretical economics without leaving a gap in the system of economic sciences.[11]

[11] Concerning the confusion that prevails even on this extremely elementary problem of the methodology of economics, cf. in addition W. Roscher, *System*

If nonetheless a number of writers on economic matters imagine they are concerned with economics, whereas in truth they are occupied with historical studies in the field of economy, it is truly worth the effort to inquire about the explanation of such an extraordinarily conspicuous error. The following investigations are to give the answer to this question, which is to a great extent practical when the historical school of German economics is considered.

The goal of scholarly research is not only the *cognition,* but also the *understanding* of phenomena. We have *gained cognition* of a phenomenon when we have attained a mental image of it. We understand it when we have recognized the reason for its existence and for its characteristic quality (the reason for its *being* and for its *being as it is*).

But we are able to attain understanding of social phenomena in two ways.

We understand a concrete phenomenon in a specifically *historical* way (through its history) by investigating its individual process of development, i.e., by becoming aware of the concrete relationships under which it has developed and, indeed, has become what it is, in its special quality.

It is well known to what a great extent the understanding of a series of significant social phenomena has been advanced by investigation of their history, i.e., in a specifically historical way, and in how praiseworthy a manner German scholarship has participated in this work. I need only to call attention to law and language. The law of a specific land, the language of a specific people are concrete phenomena. They become intelligible to us to a much greater extent when we become aware of their process of development, that is when we investigate how this specific law code, this specific language gradually developed, what influences were at work here, etc., than if we wanted to attain understanding of them exclusively on the basis of study of the present, no matter how thorough and basic. "The subject matter of law," says Savigny, "is given through the collective past of the nations . . . it has emerged from the fundamental nature of the na-

---

der Volkswirthschaft, I, § 26, where the *simple presentation* first of the economic nature and needs of a nation, second of the laws and institutions which are aimed at the satisfaction of these needs, and finally of the greater or lesser success which they have had, is designated as the task of *theory,* and the results of *this* orientation of research are designated "so to speak as the anatomy and physiology of economy!" The most recent writings by Knies, Schmoller, Held, and very recently also Scheel (preface to Ingram's *Die nothwendige Reform der Volkswirthschaftslehre* [Jena, 1879], p. vi) testify that even among the adherents of the historical school a reaction is making itself felt against the above misunderstanding, which appears still more in the practice than in the theory of research. The error is similar to that which in the field of jurisprudence identifies legal history with historical jurisprudence.

tion and its history!"[12] History—Savigny continues—is not merely a collection of examples, but the sole (!) way to the true cognition of our actual conditions. And in another place: "The historical view of jurisprudence . . . lays the maximum weight on recognizing the living connection which joins the present to the past and without the knowledge of which we only perceive the external appearance of the state of the law of the present and do not comprehend its fundamental nature."[13]

Probably there is little need to remark that the above orientation of research, thoroughly justified per se, may also be analogously applied in the field of economic phenomena. The understanding of certain institutions, endeavors, and results of economy, of the state of economic legislation in a definite land, etc., can also be advanced by investigation of their process of development, i.e., in a specifically historical way, just as in the field of law. The specifically historical understanding of concrete phenomena is also completely adequate for the field of economy.

The historical understanding of concrete social phenomena, however, is by no means the only thing that we can attain by way of scientific research.[14] Rather, the *theoretical* understanding of social phenomena is of completely equivalent value and of equal significance. We understand a concrete phenomenon in a *theoretical* way (on the basis of the correspond-

[12] *Zeitschrift für geschichtliche Rechtswissenschaft* (1815), I, p. 436.

[13] *System des heutigen Römischen Rechtes* (Berlin, 1840), I, p. xv.

[14] Those who find a parallel between the historical orientation of research in the field of *theoretical economics* and that in the field of *jurisprudence* and consider themselves justified in simply transferring the methodological viewpoints of the historical school of jurists to our science overlook a very important circumstance in doing this. The historical school of jurists, along with the investigation of law in its concrete configurations and in its historical development, acknowledges no theoretical science of law in the true sense of the word. For the historical school of jurists, accordingly, jurisprudence is in general a *historical* science and its goal is the *historical understanding* of law, along with which only *dogmatics* also asserts its rights. In the field of economy, on the contrary, even the most advanced representatives of the historical orientation acknowledge a science of the general nature and laws of economic phenomena, a *theory* of the latter. The *historical orientation* of research in theoretical economics can accordingly not consist in the negation of the *theoretical* character of the latter, in the exclusive acknowledgment of the history of economy, as means for the understanding of economic phenomena. Rather, the peculiarity of such phenomena can be pursued rationally only in the retention of the historical point of view in the *theory of economy*. What the historical school of jurists wants, and what the adherents of the historical method in economics must of necessity strive for, as long as the character of the latter as a *theoretical science* is retained, are thus different, like *history* and *theory*, or, rather, like history and a *theory clarified by historical studies*. Both schools, despite their common motto, are in fundamental methodological contrast. And the mechanical transference of the postulates and viewpoints of research from historical jurisprudence to our science is therefore a process with which no methodologically trained scholar will agree after brief reflection.

ing theoretical sciences) by recognizing it to be a special case of a certain regularity (conformity to law) in the succession, or in the coexistence of phenomena. In other words, we become aware of the basis of the existence and the peculiarity of the nature of a concrete phenomenon by learning to recognize in it merely the exemplification of a conformity-to-law of phenomena in general. Accordingly, we understand, e.g., in concrete cases, the increase of ground rent, the decrease of the interest on capital and other such things in a *theoretical* way, since the pertinent phenomena present themselves to us (on the basis of our theoretical knowledge) merely as particular exemplifications of the laws of ground rent, of the interest on capital, etc. Both the history and the theory of social phenomena in general provide us thus with a certain understanding of social and economic phenomena. However, this is in each case something individual, something essentially different, just as different as theory and history themselves.

That our historical economists do not always keep separate with sufficient strictness these two ways of understanding economic phenomena which are so different in their nature and bases, and that as a result of this circumstance the opinion could develop that, as regards the understanding of the phenomena of economy, the theory of economy could replace its history and conversely its history replace its theory—this seems to me to be the first reason for that confusion of the history and theory of economy, of which the above school of economists gives us such a rare example. In the effort to attain *historical* understanding of economic phenomena, the school purports to recognize the application of an historical orientation proper to *theoretical* economics.

To this is added another circumstance which has led, to an even greater extent, to the above vagueness about the formal nature of theoretical economics and its position in the sphere of economic sciences.

The understanding of *concrete* facts, institutions, relationships, etc., in brief, the understanding of concrete phenomena, of whatever type it may be, is to be strictly distinguished from the *scientific basis of this understanding,* i.e., from the theory and the history of the phenomena in question; and the *theoretical understanding* of concrete economic phenomena is especially to be distinguished from the *theory of economy.* The scientific activity directed toward establishing and presenting the theory of economy must, of course, not be confused with that which has for its goal the understanding of the concrete economic phenomena on *the basis of the theory.* For no matter how carefully and how comprehensively an individual strives for theoretical understanding of the *concrete* phenomena of economy—for instance, on the basis of the prevailing theories!—this still does not make him a theorist in economy. *Only* the one is so to be considered who makes the *development and description of the theory itself* his task. The understanding of the *concrete* phenomena of economy *by means of the theory,* the application of theoretical economics as *means* for this understanding, the utilization of the theory of economics for the history of economy—all these are, on the contrary, problems for the *historian,* for whom the social sciences, considered in this way, are *auxiliary sciences.*

If we summarize what has been said, then the question is easily answered concerning the true nature of those errors into which the historical school of German economists has fallen, as far as the view that theoretical economics is a *historical* science is concerned. It does not distinguish the specifically *historical* understanding of economy from the *theoretical* and confuses the two. That is, it confuses the striving for the understanding of *concrete* economic phenomena by means of history or *by means of the theory* of economy with the research in these sciences itself, and most particularly with the research in the field of theoretical economics. It thinks it is contributing to the theory of economy and describing it by undertaking to attain the understanding of concrete facts and developments of economy, and to deepen *this* understanding, by calling upon history and the theory of economy.

Just as great an error concerning the nature of theoretical economics and its position in the sphere of social sciences is perpetrated by those who confuse it with *economic policy,* who confuse the science of the general nature and connection of economic phenomena with the science of the maxims for the practical direction and advancement of economy. The error is no less a one than if chemistry were to be confused with chemical technology, physiology and anatomy with therapy and surgery, etc. It has already been so well elucidated in the theory of knowledge that we properly hesitate to discuss it any further. If furthermore this error appears not only at the beginnings of our science, but strangely enough even today sporadically in economic literature,[15] and if in spite of all concessions in principle it still influences the methodology and strategy of our science to a high degree, the basis of this can properly be sought only in the peculiar historical development of knowledge in general and especially of that in the field of economy.

Theoretical knowledge has everywhere developed only gradually from practical judgments and with the growing need for a deeper scientific substantiation of practice. Theoretical knowledge in the field of economy has

[15] Cf. recently especially Bonamy Price, *Practical Polit. Economy* (London, 1878), p. 1 ff.

also taken this course of development. It, too, had originally only the character of an occasional motivating of practical maxims, and by nature there still adhere to it traces of this origin and of its previous subordination to economic policy. However, especially in all questions of the *strategy* and *methodology* of our science, it becomes clear how important, in the present-day state of economic discernment, the strict separation of theoretical and practical knowledge in the field of our science is, and to what perplexing consequences the confusion of the above two sciences leads.

The copresentation or cotreatment of theoretical and practical knowledge has of necessity the consequence that practical knowledge must be classified in the system of theoretical knowledge, or conversely that the latter must be classified in the system of practical knowledge. This is a process which, of course, completely invalidates any stricter scheme of presentation which does justice to the nature of the field of knowledge in question, as regards at least one of the two sciences; and the same process constantly fails to render the character of the other science.

To this is added the circumstances that the treatment in combination of the above two sets of scientific knowledge almost makes a certain completeness impossible. At least, in the form in which this treatment in combination has prevailed recently in our science, it probably offers, for the most part, the theory of economy in a more or less adequate way, but it offers economic policy only in occasional, extremely fragmentary expositions. These treatments of political economy by no means make special writings about economic policy dispensable. Accordingly, at least where the need for comprehensive presentations of economic policy has already become evident, we cannot disregard the doubtfulness of the advantage which the above combination of theoretical and practical knowledge is really due to provide in the presentations of political economy.

The above fusion of the theoretical and practical points of view has influenced the theoretical investigations in the field of our science in a most unfavorable way. For if theoretical and practical political economy are not kept strictly apart, what value can be shown by investigations into *the* method of economics, that is, into the method of two sciences (a theoretical science and a practical one) which are so completely different in nature? Indeed, what value can be shown by investigations into *the* method of political economy in the sense of a theoretical-practical science confusing theoretical economics, economic policy, and the science of finance?

It cannot be denied that German economics, more strictly than any other literature in this field, has understood how to avoid the error under discussion here, and also with this, in part at least, its consequences for the strategy and methodology of our science. The active need of the German cameralists for comprehensive presentations of economic administration has obviously contributed essentially to this success.

On the other hand, to be sure, that error which we mentioned previously—the confusion of the historical and the theoretical points of view in scientific research in economy—has, precisely in the German literature, led to the most confusing consequences. Arising from the desire, absolutely justified per se, for expanding and deepening the historical understanding of *concrete economic phenomena,* the above error has nevertheless influenced both the strategy and the methodology of our science most unfavorably. It has influenced the strategy, in that interrupting the presentation of the theory by numerous historical digressions was considered practical, and indeed was viewed as the application of the "historical method" in our sciences; it has influenced the methodology, in that through false understanding points of view and postulates of historical research were carried over into the methodology of theoretical economics.

But also in the proper field of theoretical research the above error has hindered the progress of our sciences in the most destructive way. Not merely a negligible number, but really the majority of the adherents of the erudite school under discussion here cannot be absolved of the charge of concerning themselves with the history of economy and with the deepening of the understanding of it, while they expressly or at least tacitly start out with the presupposition that they are presenting and developing the *theory* of economy from the historical point of view. The desire of the above scholars, justified per se, to do away with the unhistorical tendency in *theoretical* economics has led in this way, as a result of the methodological error under discussion here, to an abandonment of the theoretical character of economic science. It has led to putting historical research, the *writing of history,* in place of theoretical research in general and in particular of theoretical research with retention of the historical point of view.

Probably there is little need to remark that in Germany research in the field of theoretical economics has been unproductive chiefly as a consequence of this misunderstanding. The *historical* understanding of single fields of economy has been opened up and deepened in the last decades by the scholarly diligence of German economists. The *theory* of economy, on the contrary, and indeed not only that theory which fails to recognize the historical point of view in economy, but unfortunately *the theory of economy in general,* has plainly fallen behind.

We have no desire in any way to belittle the merit that the historical school of German economists has earned for having emphasized in principle the historical point of view in political economy in general and in theoretical economics in particular, although the form in which this notion previously took shape, as we will subsequently see, lacks clarity just as much as consistency. Certainly no unprejudiced person, no matter how much he stresses the significance of the historical point of view in our science, can deny that even the complete failure to recognize this point of view, as far as the range of the error is concerned, cannot even remotely be parallel to that error which confuses theoretical economics with the history of economy. By having so failed to recognize the formal nature of theoretical economics and its position in the sphere of sciences, a large number of the German economists have fallen into a more grievous error than economists of any unhistorical orientation at all. This is, to be sure, the most fundamental error of which a school can be the victim, for they have bypassed the very science which they thought to develop.

If theoretical economics now were a highly developed science, or at least one perfected in its basic features, criticism could at any rate silently pass by the above misunderstanding which benefits true historical studies in the field of economy. But how can it do this in respect to an erudite school which became a victim of such a misunderstanding in a science whose fundamental principles have not yet been attained, in a science in which up to now almost everything still stands in question?

How pertinently an incidental remark about certain scientific systems made by the great founder of our science applies to the above scholars, who are usually able historians, but weak theoreticians: "Systems, which have universally owed their origin to the lucubrations of those, who were acquainted with the one art, but ignorant of the other, who therefore explained to themselves the phenomena, in that (art), which was strange to them, by those (phenomena) in that (art) which was familiar to them."[16]

[16] A. Smith, *History of Astronomy*, Dugald Steward, ed. (Basel, 1799), p. 28 ff.

BOOK 1

CHAPTER 3

The Special Nature of Theoretical Knowledge in the Field of Economy Does Not Invalidate the Character of Economics as a Theoretical Science

The theoretical sciences are not equally strict; this circumstance nevertheless has no influence on their general formal character.—Whatever the degree of strictness may be which the truths of theoretical economics display, the character of the latter as a theoretical science remains intact.—Thereby, it cannot become either a historical or a practical science.—The value of the theoretical sciences for the cognition and understanding of phenomena is by no means invalidated by the fact that their truths are less strict.

The types and typical relationships (the laws) of the world of phenomena are not equally strict in all cases. A glance at the theoretical sciences teaches us rather that the regularities in the coexistence and in the succession of phenomena are in part without exception; indeed they are such that the possibility of an exception seems quite out of the question. However, some are such that they do indeed exhibit exceptions, or that in their case exceptions seem possible. The first are called *laws of nature,* the latter *empirical laws.*

Now among the methodologists no view is more widespread than the one that in certain realms of the world of phenomena, and predominantly in that of nature, strict types and typical relationships can be observed; in others on the contrary, and especially in that of social phenomena, only those of lesser strictness can. In other words, "laws of nature" can be observed only in the first realm; only "empirical laws," on the contrary, can be observed in the latter. This opinion, frequently found in the general theory of knowledge, will prove erroneous in the sequel. At this point we want briefly in passing to characterize the error only to this extent: that which on close examination turns out to be the result of different *orientations* of theoretical research in the individual realms of the world of phenomena is construed as the result of the differing natures of the *phenomena*. But we intend to speak of this only in what follows. What we would like, however, to emphasize right here most emphatically is the circumstance that, whatever the degree of strictness of the laws characteristic of the realm of social phenomena may be and whatever the results are to which investigations into the special nature and the different types of these laws lead us, the character of economics as a *theoretical* science is by no means affected. The types and the typical relationships of economy may be of greater strictness or lesser, or in general of any nature—the nature of theoretical economics can under all circumstances consist in nothing else than in the exposition of just these types and typical relationships. In other words, it can consist only in the exposition of the general nature and the general connection of the laws of economic phenomena, but by no means, for instance, in the exposition of the nature and connection of individual phenomena of economy, i.e., in historical presentations, or else in practical rules for the economic activity of people. The *theory* of economy must in no case be confused with the *historical* sciences of economy, or with the *practical* ones. Only the person who is completely in the dark about the formal nature and the problems of theoretical economics could perceive in it a *historical* science because the general (theoretical) knowledge which it embraces ostensibly, or really, shows less strictness than in the natural sciences; or else perhaps for the further reason that the development of economic phenomena, as we will see, is not without influence on the way and manner in which economics is able to solve its theoretical problems. Only a person who cannot keep apart the natures of theoretical and practical sciences could perceive in economics a *practical science*—perhaps for the reason that it, like other theories, forms the basis of practical sciences.

Just as erroneous is the frequently met opinion that the value of economics as a theoretical science is invalidated, as a result of the above-stressed circumstances. Even if it were admitted a priori and without closer investigation that the theoretical knowledge in the realm of economic phenomena was not of a strictness admitting no exception, and in particular that the fact of the development of the phenomena under discussion here excluded laws of nature pertaining to these, even then, we say, the above conclusion could by no means be drawn. The number of natural sciences which absolutely comprise strict laws of nature is also small, and the value of those which show only empirical laws is nevertheless beyond question. It does not, for example, occur to a natural scientist to deny the character of theoretical sciences to a series of sciences which present the laws of organic life because they comprise empirical laws. It would be just as foolish if we were to disdain in the field of economy the powerful aid which even less rigorous theories offer for understanding, for predicting and controlling phenomena, and to limit ourselves to research in the history and the statistics of economy, or indeed to work in practical economic science, because a strict theory of economic phenomena were not attainable. Such a procedure would leave a gap in the system of the sciences of economy, a gap of just the same kind as if the historical or the practical sciences of economy remained uninvestigated.

Whether the laws of the coexistence and of the succession of phenomena are of greater or lesser strictness is, of course, not devoid of significance, either for understanding or for predicting and controlling the phenomena. The greater the strictness of the laws, the greater also the degree of certainty with which, on the basis of these laws, conclusions can be drawn beyond direct experience about the occurrence of future phenomena, or about the coexistence of simultaneous phenomena not directly observed. Without doubt the fact that laws of the succession and the coexistence of phenomena are not rigorous ones accordingly diminishes the certainty of the conclusions based on them and with this also that of predicting and controlling the phenomena. All these differences, however, are, in respect to the prediction and control of phenomena, differences in degree, not in principle. Theoretical sciences, too, which only exhibit empirical laws have accordingly a great practical significance for human life, even if a now greater, now lesser probability takes the place of complete certainty of the knowledge mediated by them. *Historical* knowledge and the historical understanding of phenomena per se, on the contrary, do not offer us this prediction (etc.) at all and they can therefore never replace theoretical knowledge. Historical knowledge, on the contrary, can never be anything but the material on the basis of which we can determine the laws of phenomena (e.g., the laws of development of economy). Even the practical politician must first gain more general knowledge (rules) from history before he can draw his conclusions in respect to shaping future events.

The circumstances that in the realm of economic phenomena results of theoretical research of an absolute strictness are viewed by individual schools as unattainable can indeed impart a separate character to theoretical research in the field of economic phenomena and establish certain characteristics of that field. But it can never bring it about that in the economic realm of the world of phenomena the historical or the practical orientation of research can take the place of the theoretical and substitute for it. The same is true of the circumstances that theoretical research in the economic realm does, indeed, encounter difficulties which are foreign to natural-science research in its individual branches. It is true, finally, of the circumstance that for theoretical economics there are not always present problems of exactly the same kind as for the theoretical natural sciences. *Theoretical* economics can never be viewed as a *historical* science nor, as many wish, as a *practical* one.

We must try to keep ourselves from making a double mistake in research in the field of political economy. It would be a serious error to misunderstand the characteristics of the realm of phenomena which we call economy, and thus also misunderstand the peculiarity of the problem which is offered to us by *theoretical* research in the economic realm. It would, however, be a still greater error if, in the endeavor to do justice to the indicated characteristics of research, we were to sacrifice theoretical work in the realm of economic phenomena, whether explicitly or tacitly, and if we were to lose sight of the theory of economy itself in order to comprehend this theory under a special aspect, for instance, the historical.

BOOK 1

CHAPTER 4

The Two Basic Orientations of Theoretical Research in General and of That in the Field of Economy in Particular

The opinion that there is only one orientation of theoretical research.—The *realistic-empirical* orientation of theoretical research and its advantages.—That it is not suited to producing strict laws, so-called "laws of nature" of phenomena.—Nature and kinds of theoretical knowledge which it can produce.—The realistic-empirical orientation of theoretical research in the field of economy.—The *exact* orientation of theoretical research in general.—Its object and theoretical basis.—The exact orientation of theoretical research in the social sciences in general and in economics in particular.—An exact theory by its nature always offers us only the understanding of a special side of the phenomena.—Exact economics can only provide us with the theoretical understanding of the *economic* side of social phenomena.—Only the totality of the exact social sciences could reveal to us the exact understanding of social phenomena, or of a definite part of them, in their full empirical reality.

In Book Two the nature of the "historical point of view" in political economy is to be described; or, more correctly, that influence is to be described which is exercised on the theoretical and practical sciences of economy and on the nature of their truths by the fact that economic phenomena exhibit development. However, before we go on to the solution of this problem, we must mention another error that has contributed to no smaller extent than those characterized in the two preceding chapters to the confusion of the methodological doctrines of the historical school of German economists and discussion of which can therefore not be avoided at this point.

But we should most particularly like to direct the attention of our readers to the following investigations, not merely because they expose a basic methodological error of the historical school, without the knowledge of which the attitude of the latter to the questions discussed here cannot be completely understood. They simultaneously throw a bright light on the theoretical problems of our science in more than one respect.

Above we have distinguished between the two main orientations of research in general and in the realm of economic phenomena in particular: the *individual* (the historical) and the *general* (the theoretical). The former strives for the cognition of the individual nature and the individual connection of phenomena, the latter for that of their general nature and general connection. Now it would be a gross one-sidedness to believe that the general orientation of research in the various realms of the world of phenomena, and even in one special realm of it, e.g., in that of economy, is of necessity one without differences. Just as the individual orientation of research breaks down into various special orientations (the historical one in the narrower sense, the statistical one, etc.), which all to be sure bear the character of the individual orientation of research, but simultaneously exhibit certain special features when compared to one another, so theoretical research also breaks down into several branches. Each one of these, to be sure, bears the character of the general orientation of research, i.e., it has as its object the determination of the types and the typical relationships of the phenomena; nevertheless it does not necessarily solve this problem from the same point of view. The subject of the following investigations is the determination of the orientations of theoretical research which are most important for our science. Along with this goes an attack on the opinion held almost universally by the methodologists that there is only one orientation of theoretical research, or else that only one orientation of the latter (e.g., the empirical, or the exact, or else even the historical-philosophical, the theoretical-statistical, etc.) is adequate for certain realms of the world of phenomena in general and those of economy in particular.

The purpose of the theoretical sciences is understanding of the real world, knowledge of it extending beyond immediate experience, and control of it. We understand phenomena by means of theories as we become aware of them in each concrete case merely as exemplifications of a general regularity. We attain a knowledge of phenomena extending beyond immediate experience by drawing conclusions, in the concrete case, from certain observed facts about other facts not immediately perceived. We do this on the basis of the laws of coexistence and of the succession of phenomena. We control the real world in that, on the basis of our theoretical knowledge, we set the conditions of a phenomenon which are within our control, and are able in such a way to produce the phenomenon itself.

The desire for knowledge of so great a scientific and practical interest, the desire for cognition of the types and typical relationships of phenomena, is as old as civilization. Only the degree of development of this desire for knowledge has increased in the course of cultural development in general and in the development of the sciences in particular.

The most obvious idea for solving the above (the theoretical) problem is to investigate the types and typical relationships of phenomena as these present themselves to us in their "full empirical reality," *that is, in the totality and the whole complexity of their nature;* in other words, to arrange the totality of the real phenomena in definite empirical forms and in an empirical way to determine the regularities in their coexistence and succession.

This idea has also led in all realms of the world of phenomena to the corresponding orientation of theoretical research, the *realistic-empirical* one. It has done this not only for the reason that, as said, it presents itself to us as the most obvious one, but for the reason that the purposes which theoretical research serves seem at the same time to be attained most simply and completely by means of this orientation of research.

The theoretical sciences are, as we saw, supposed to teach us the types (the empirical forms) and the typical relationships (the laws) of phenomena. By this they are to provide us with theoretical understanding, a cognition going beyond immediate experience, and, wherever we have the conditions of a phenomenon within our control, control over it. How could we now solve the above problems more simply, more suitably, and yet at the same time in a more complete way than by arranging in strict types the phenomena of the real world as they are presented in their empirical reality and by obtaining their strictly typical relationships—"laws of nature"?

Close examination, however, teaches us that the above idea is not strictly feasible. Phenomena in all their empirical reality are, according to experience, repeated in certain empirical forms. But this is never with perfect strictness, for scarcely ever do two concrete phenomena, let alone a larger group of them, exhibit a thorough agreement. There are no strict types in "empirical reality," i.e., when the phenomena are under consideration in the totality and the whole complexity of their nature. This might be the case if each individual concrete phenomenon were set up as a particular type. By this the purpose and usefulness of theoretical research would be completely invalidated. The desire to determine strict categories of empirical forms comprising "all empirical realities" (according to their full content) is therefore an unattainable goal of theoretical research.

So also with respect to the second problem of theoretical research: the determination of typical relationships, *laws* of phenomena. If the world of phenomena is considered in a strictly realistic way, then laws of the latter signify merely the actual regularities, determined by way of observation, in the succession and in the coexistence of real phenomena which belong to certain empirical forms. A "law" obtained from the above point of view can in truth only state that in reality, regularly or without exception, phenomena belonging to the empirical form C have followed the concrete phenomena belonging to the empirical forms A and B, or that they were observed coexistent with them. The conclusion that the phenomenon C follows the phenomena A and B *in general* (that is, in all cases, even those not observed!), or that the phenomena under discussion here are *in general* coexistent, transcends experience, the point of view of strict empiricism. From the standpoint of the above manner of consideration it is *not strictly* warranted. Aristotle recognized this correctly when he denied the strictly scientific character of induction. But even the inductive method perfected essentially by Bacon was only able to increase the guarantees of the absoluteness of the laws gained in the above way (empirical induction); it was never able to offer absolute guarantee of it. Strict (exact) laws of phenomena can never be the result of the realistic school of thought in theoretical research even if this were the most perfect conceivable and its fundamental observation the most comprehensive and most critical.

The scientific knowledge to which the above orientation of theoretical research, the empirical-realistic, can lead, merely in consideration of the methodological presuppositions of the latter, can only be of two kinds:

(a) *real types,* basic forms of real phenomena, within the typical image of which, however, a more or less broad scope is given for particularities (also for the development of the phenomena!), and

(b) *empirical laws,* theoretical knowledge, which make us aware of the actual regularities (though they are by no means guaranteed to be without exception) in the succession and coexistence of real phenomena.

If we derive from what has been said its practical application for theoretical research in the realm of economic phenomena, we arrive at the result that, as far as the latter are brought into consideration in their "full empirical reality," only their "real types" and "empirical laws" are attainable. Properly there can be no question of strict (exact) theoretical knowledge in general or of strict laws (of so-called "laws of nature") in particular for them, under this presupposition.

But what needs no less to be emphasized is the circumstance *that with this presupposition the same thing also holds true of the results of theoretical research in all the remaining realms of the world of phenomena.*[17] For even natural phenomena in their "empirical reality" offer us neither strict types nor even strictly typical relationships. Real gold, real oxygen and hydrogen, real water—not to mention at all the complicated phenomena of the inorganic or even of the organic world—are in their full empirical reality neither of strictly typical nature, nor, given the above manner of looking at them, can exact laws even be observed concerning them.

Not only in the realm of the ethical world, and of economy, but also in that of natural phenomena, the realistic orientation of theoretical research can lead only to *"real types"* and *"empirical* laws." And in the above point of view, at any rate, no *essential* difference between the ethical and the natural sciences exists, but at most only one *of degree. The realistic orientation of theoretical research excludes in principle, rather, in all realms of the world of phenomena the possibility of arriving at strict (exact) theoretical knowledge.*

If there were only the one, just now characterized orientation of theoretical research, or if it were the only justified one, as the economists of the "historical orientation" in fact seem to believe, then the possibility of or the justification for any research aimed at exact theories of phenomena would a priori be out of the question. Not only in the realm of ethical phenomena in general and of economy in particular, but also in all other realms of the world of phenomena any success would a priori be denied to the above-mentioned effort.

It scarcely needs to be stated that the above presupposition is invalid in the realm of natural phenomena. The task of the following investigations will be to show that the situation is the same in the realm of human phenomena in general and of economy in particular. It will also be to show that the opinion of our historical economists, that the realistic-empirical orientation of theoretical research is the only justified one in

[17] See Appendix V: "In the Realm of Human Phenomena Exact Laws (So-Called Laws of Nature) Can Be Established Under the Same Formal Presuppositions as in the Realm of Natural Phenomena."

the field of economy, accordingly involves one-sidedness and its inevitable consequences.

The realistic-empirical orientation of theoretical research, as we saw, offers us in all realms of the world of phenomena results which are formally imperfect, however important and valuable they may be for human knowledge and practical life. They are theories which give us only a deficient understanding of the phenomena, only an uncertain prediction of them, and by no means an assured control of them. From the very beginning, too, the human mind has followed another orientation of theoretical research beside the one discussed above. It is different from the latter both in its aims and in its approaches to cognition.

The aim of this orientation, which in the future we will call the *exact* one, an aim which research pursues in the same way in all realms of the world of phenomena, is the determination of strict laws of phenomena, of regularities in the succession of phenomena which do not present themselves to us as absolute, but which in respect to the approaches to cognition by which we attain to them simply bear within themselves the guarantee of absoluteness. It is the determination of laws of phenomena which commonly are called "laws of nature," but more correctly should be designated by the expression *"exact laws."*[18]

[18] The expressions *"empirical laws"* and *"laws of nature"* used in theoretical investigations by no means characterize exactly the contrast between the results of the realistic orientation in theoretical research and of the exact. Even in the realm of natural phenomena (e.g., in that of the organic world, of weather phenomena, etc.) the realistic orientation of research leads merely to "empirical laws." There are, accordingly, laws of nature (in the true sense of the word) which are only "empirical laws" and hence not "laws of nature" in the above technical sense of the word, whereas conversely we can in other realms of the world of phenomena (not merely in that of the phenomena of nature) arrive at strict laws, "laws of nature," which again are not laws of nature (laws of the phenomena of nature). The contrast under discussion here is expressed much more exactly by the phrases *"empirical"* and *"exact"* laws of phenomena. The laws of theoretical economics are really never *laws of nature* in the true meaning of the word. On the contrary, they can be only empirical or exact *laws of the ethical world.*

Another terminology stands in close connection with the above terminology. It is likewise incorrect and has already contributed much to confusion in the theoretical problems of our science. The contrast between the theoretical *natural sciences* and the theoretical *social sciences* is merely a contrast of the phenomena which they investigate from a theoretical point of view. It is by no means a contrast of methods, as both the realistic and the exact orientation of theoretical research are admissible in both realms (natural and social) of the world of phenomena. A contrast exists only between the *realistic* and the *exact* orientation of theoretical research, and between the sciences comprising the results of both orientations, the empirical and the exact theoretical sciences. There are natural sciences which are not exact ones (e.g., physiology, meteorology, etc.), and conversely there are exact sciences which are not natural sciences (e.g., pure economics). Accordingly it is not an accurate expression when this latter is called a

The nature of the research activity generally directed toward the goal just described and of economic research in particular will become clear directly from the following statements.

There is one rule of cognition for the investigation of theoretical truths which as far as possible is verified beyond doubt not only by experience, but simply by our laws of thinking. This is the statement that *whatever was observed in even only one case must always put in an appearance again under exactly the same actual conditions;* or, what is in essence the same thing, that strictly typical phenomena of a definite kind must always, and, indeed in consideration of our laws of thinking, simply *of necessity,* be followed by strictly typical phenomena of just as definite and different a type. Phenomena A and B *must* under the same conditions always be followed by the strictly typical phenomenon C in so far as A and B are thought of as strictly typical and the succession of phenomena under discussion here has been observed even in only a single case. This rule holds true not only of the *nature* of phenomena, but also of their *measure,* and experience not only offers us no exception to it, but such a thing simply seems inconceivable to the critical mind.

A further rule of cognition likewise highly significant for the exact orientation of theoretical research is only a correlate of the above statement. This is the statement that a circumstance which was recognized as irrelevant only in one case in respect to the succession of phenomena will always and of necessity prove to be irrelevant under precisely the same actual conditions in respect to the same result.

If, therefore, exact laws are at all attainable, it is clear that these cannot be obtained from the point of view of empirical realism, but only in this way, with theoretical research satisfying the presuppositions of the above rule of cognition.

But the way by which theoretical research arrived at the above goal, a way essentially different from Bacon's empirical-realistic induction, is the following: it seeks to ascertain the *simplest elements* of everything real, elements which must be thought of as strictly typical just because they are the simplest. It strives for the establishment of these elements by way of an only partially empirical-realistic analysis, i.e., without considering whether these in reality are present as *independent* phenomena; indeed, even without considering whether they can at all be presented independently in their full purity. In this manner theoretical research arrives at empirical forms which *qualitatively* are strictly typical. It arrives at results

"*natural* science." It is in truth an *exact ethical* science. It is just as wrong, finally, to speak of the *natural science* method in the social sciences in general and in theoretical economics in particular. The method of the latter can be either the empirical or the exact one, but in truth never that of "natural science."

of theoretical research which, to be sure, must not be tested by full empirical reality (for the empirical forms here under discussion, e.g., absolutely pure oxygen, pure alcohol, pure gold, a person pursuing only economic aims, etc., exist in part only in our ideas). However, these results correspond to the specific task of the exact orientation of theoretical research and are the necessary basis and presupposition for obtaining *exact laws.*

In a similar way exact research solves the second problem of the theoretical sciences: the determination of the typical relationships, the *laws* of phenomena. The specific goal of this orientation of theoretical research is the determination of regularities in the relationships of phenomena which are guaranteed to be absolute and as such to be complete. We have already demonstrated that laws of this kind are not attainable in respect to the full empirical reality of phenomena, and, indeed, because of the not strictly typical nature of real phenomena. Exact science, accordingly, does not examine the regularities in the succession, etc., of *real* phenomena either. It examines, rather, how more complicated phenomena develop from the simplest, in part even unempirical elements of the real world in their (likewise unempirical) isolation from all other influences, with constant consideration of exact (likewise ideal!) measure. It does this without taking into account whether those simplest elements, or complications thereof, are actually to be observed in reality uninfluenced by human art; indeed, without considering whether these elements could be found at all in their complete purity. In this case it is also aware that a completely exact measure is not possible in reality. Science starts out, however, with these assumptions, since it would never be able otherwise to reach the goal of exact research, the determination of strict laws. On the other hand, with the assumption of strictly typical elements, of their exact measure, and of their complete isolation from all other causative factors, it does to be sure, and indeed on the basis of the rules of cognition characterized by us above, arrive at laws of phenomena which are not only absolute, but according to our laws of thinking simply cannot be thought of in any other way but as absolute. That is, it arrives at exact laws, the so-called "laws of nature" of phenomena.

The circumstance that certain differences of phenomena (deviations from their strictly typical character) appear as irrelevant in respect to definite results (e.g., the different color, the different taste of substances in respect to their weight, the same and numerous other differences in respect to their numerical relationships, etc.) permits an incomparable expansion of exact research over numerous realms of the world of phenomena.

Thus we arrive at a series of sciences which teach us strict types and typical relationships (exact laws) of phenomena, and indeed not only in respect to their nature, but also to their measure. We attain to sciences, no single one of which teaches us to understand full empirical reality, but only particular sides, and therefore must not be judged rationally from the point of view of one-sided empirical realism. But the totality of these sciences conveys to us an understanding of the real world which is just as distinctive as it is profound.[19]

Also in the realm of the ethical world the above orientation of theoretical research has from the beginning found outstanding representatives who have vigorously pursued the kind of striving for cognition under discussion here, even if without complete clarity about the related theoretical problems. Indeed they have already given to it the form corresponding to the particular nature of ethical phenomena.

The nature of this exact orientation of *theoretical* research in the realm of ethical phenomena, however, consists in the fact that we reduce human phenomena to their most original and simplest constitutive factors. We join to the latter the measure corresponding to their nature, and finally try to investigate the laws by which *more complicated* human phenomena are formed from those simplest elements, thought of in their isolation.

Whether the individual constitutive factors of human phenomena, thought of in their isolation, are real; whether these can in reality be measured exactly; whether those complications, in the case of which (according to the nature of exact research) an abstraction must be made from the effect of a variety of factors of real human life, actually put in an appearance—all this is no less irrelevant for the exact orientation of theoretical research in the realm of social phenomena than in the realm of nature. Only complete lack of understanding of the exact orientation in general can apply to the results of the latter the standard of the postulates of the empirical-realistic orientation of theoretical research.

As we pursue this orientation of research we attain to a series of social theories, each single one of which opens up for us, to be sure, only the understanding of a special side of the phenomena of human activity (abstracted from the full empirical reality). The totality of this, however, if the theories corresponding to the above orientation of research are ever to be recognized for what they are, will teach us to understand human phenomena in a way similar to that in which those theoretical sciences,

[19] The method of exact research, that is, the part which experiment plays in it, which the speculative element transcending experiment and all experience plays, especially in the formulation of "exact laws," is not the object of our presentation in this book. It will find a separate presentation in another place in connection with a critique of Bacon's induction.

which are the result of an analogous consideration of natural phenomena, have opened to us the understanding of the latter. Not just any one theory of human phenomena, only the totality of such theories, when they are once pursued, will reveal to us in combination with the results of the realistic orientation of theoretical research the deepest theoretical understanding attainable by the human mind of social phenomena in their full empirical reality. And however remote the realization of the above thought may be, considering the lagging state of the theoretical social sciences—there is no other way to reach the great goal.

As far as the exact orientation of theoretical research in the realm of economic phenomena is specifically concerned, its general nature is given by the postulates of exact research. Its particular nature is given by the particularity of the realm of the phenomena on which it has the task of working. By *economy* we understand the precautionary activity of humans directed toward covering their material needs; by *national economy,* the social form of this activity.[20] The problem of the above orientation of research can accordingly be nothing else than the investigation of the most original, the most elementary factors of human economy, the determination of the measure of the phenomena concerned, and the investigation of the laws by which more complicated forms of the phenomena of human economy develop from those simplest elements.[21]

The most original factors of human economy are the needs, the goods offered directly to humans by nature (both the consumption goods and the means of production concerned), and the desire for the most complete satisfaction of needs possible (for the most complete covering of material needs possible). All these factors are ultimately given by the particular situation, independent of human choice. The starting point and the goal of all economy (need and available quantity of goods on the one hand and the possible completeness of satisfaction of the material needs on the other) are ultimately given to the economic human, strictly determined in respect to their nature and their measure.[22] The function of the exact orientation of theoretical research is to apprise us of the laws by which not real life in its totality but the more complicated phenomena of human economy are developed on the basis of the thus given situation from these most elementary factors in human economy, in their isolation from other factors exerting influence on the real human phenomena. It is to teach us this not only in respect to the nature, but also to the measure of the above

[20] See Appendix I.

[21] Compare my *Grundsätze der Volkswirthschaftslehre* (1871), p. vii ff.

[22] See Appendix VI: "The Starting Point and the Goal of All Human Economy Are Strictly Determined."

phenomena, and thus to open up for us an understanding of these which has a significance analogous to that which the exact natural sciences offer us in respect to natural phenomena.

When we allude to the nature and the significance of the exact orientation of theoretical research in the realm of human phenomena in general and in particular in that of economy, and thus confront the one-sided realism of the social sciences, we are, to be sure, far from denying usefulness and significance to the realistic orientation, and far from underestimating it and thus of falling into the opposite one-sidedness. This charge, however, is made against all those who, one-sidedly pursuing the exact orientation of theoretical research in the field of economy, consider the determination of its empirical laws as worthless, or for any methodological reasons whatever consider the attempt to attain such laws as inadmissible. For it may be admitted ever so unreservedly that people are governed in economic things neither exclusively by a single definite propensity, in our case by their egoism, nor are uninfluenced by error, ignorance, and external compulsion. It may accordingly be admitted that the results of the realistic orientation of theoretical research in the field of economy cannot exhibit complete rigor. But from this it by no means follows that no *regularities* at all in the nature and connection of phenomena can be observed from the realistic point of view in the realm of the world of phenomena under discussion here. It does not follow that their determination is not of great significance for the understanding of economy and the prediction and control of its phenomena. On the contrary, wherever we look, economic life confronts us with regularities both in the coexistence and in the succession of phenomena. This is a fact which must probably be attributed to the circumstance that people in their economic efforts, even if not exclusively and without exception, nevertheless are predominantly and regularly governed by their individual interests and on the whole and regularly recognize the latter correctly, even if not in all cases and absolutely. The real phenomena of economy actually present to us types and typical relationships, real regularities in the recurrence of definite forms of phenomena, *real* regularities in coexistence and succession, which, to be sure, are not of absolute strictness, but to determine which is under all circumstances the task of theoretical economics and particularly of its realistic orientation.

Both the exact and the realistic orientation of theoretical research are therefore justified. Both are means for understanding, predicting, and controlling economic phenomena, and to these aims each of them contributes in its own way. But whoever denies the justification and usefulness of the one or the other is comparable to a natural scientist who one-sidedly values physiology highly, perhaps under the pretext that chemistry and physics are based on abstractions, and would deny the justification of the latter or their justification as means for the understanding of organic structures. Or else, conversely, he resembles a physicist or chemist who would deny to physiology the character of a science because its laws are for the most part only "empirical." If analogous doctrines in the field of theoretical social sciences are not only possible, but are announced by influential erudite schools as fundamental, indeed, as epoch-making truths, we find in this, perhaps, the best evidence for the imperfect state of these sciences. It is also an admonition to the experts in them seriously to take counsel with themselves about the theoretical bases of their scientific efforts.

There is scarcely any need to remark that the nature and significance of the exact orientation of research is completely misunderstood in the modern literature on national economy. In German economics, at least in the historical school, the art of abstract thinking, no matter how greatly distinguished by depth and originality and no matter how broadly supported empirically—in brief, everything that in other theoretical sciences establishes the greatest fame of scholars is still considered, along with the products of compilatory diligence, as something secondary, almost as a stigma. The power of truth, however, will finally also be tested for those who, sensing their inability to solve the highest problems of the social sciences, would like to raise their own inadequacy as a standard for the value of scientific work in general.

BOOK 1

CHAPTER 5

The Relationship of the Exact Orientation of Research in the Field of the Social Sciences to the Realistic-Empirical Orientation

The common element of the two above orientations and their difference.—Why their results are not usually treated separately in scientific presentation.—That the two orientations of research do not refer to different realms of economic phenomena, but each of them tries in principle to make us understand all of economy from the points of view characteristic of it.—Why the exact orientation is predominantly accustomed to strive for the understanding of the more elementary phenomena of economy, the empirical-realistic for the understanding of the more complicated ones.—An opinion on this from Auguste Comte and J. St. Mill.—Relationship in which the guarantees of the truth of the results of the two orientations stand to each other.—Error, that the results of the exact orientation of theoretical research find their criterion in the results of the realistic-empirical orientation.—Examples by which a clearer light is cast on the relationship between the nature and the guarantees of the results of the two orientations of theoretical research in the field of economy.

We should not like to conclude our investigations into the nature of the two above basic orientations of theoretical research in the realm of ethical phenomena without making mention in a few words of the relationship in which they and their results stand to one another. But this is done not only for the sake of the interest which the questions pertinent here have per se for the methodology of our science, but also to prevent from the start a few obvious misunderstandings about the theories presented in the previous section.

The results of the exact orientation of theoretical research and those of the realistic have in common that they teach us the general nature and the general connection of phenomena. For the rest, however, as we have seen, they also exhibit not unessential differences, as far as their formal nature is concerned. In scientific *presentation,* however, exact and realistic knowledge are seldom treated separately.

The reason for this is essentially a practical one. The theoretical sciences are supposed to provide us with understanding of phenomena, a knowledge of them extending beyond immediate experience, and a certain ability to foresee them. These are purely problems, the solution of which, even if in a different sense, is advanced not only by the results of the exact orientation of theoretical research, but also by those of the realistic orientation. Given this state of affairs it meets practical needs if we group together in presentation all the theoretical knowledge, realistic as well as exact, which has reference to a realm of the world of phenomena (e.g., to economy) and within this group all which refers to specific matters (e.g., value, price of goods, money, etc.). And thus, in fact, the theoretical sciences usually offer us the picture of a presentation combining items of knowledge of partially different formal nature. Physics and chemistry, e.g., exact sciences according to their bases, by no means exclude individual items of knowledge obtained only empirically. On the other hand, physiology, according to its basis a result of realistic research, does not take only realistic knowledge into its sphere of presentation, but also numerous items of exact knowledge. The situation is similar in theoretical economics. This, too, comprises the exact as well as the realistic results of theoretical research. And if, as is self-evident, no obstacle in principle opposes a separate presentation of the two above groups of theoretical knowledge; if, rather, one such presentation can be imagined for the exact results of research (an *exact* economics), another for pertinent realistic knowledge in general and for the laws of the historical development of economic phenomena, the laws of great numbers, etc., in particular—yet the above-stressed practical interest speaks strongly for a comprehensive presentation of all theoretical truths referring to economic matters. It does this so strongly that such a presentation has actually and everywhere found admission to a greater or lesser extent in the universal presentations of theoretical economics. For example, in price theory not only are the results of exact research treated in a comprehensive presentation, but usually also pertinent empirical laws in general and related laws of development, of great numbers, etc., in particular.

While knowledge from the exact and from the realistic orientation of theoretical research in the field of economy is thus brought together in presentation, writers in the field of national economy still, as stated, follow only practical considerations, clearly without thereby doing away with the distinctive formal character of relevant knowledge.

All this touches only the external relationship between the exact and the realistic results of theoretical social research. Meanwhile the question might arise of the inner relationship of exact and realistic knowledge in the realm of social phenomena in general and of economy in particular. And here we should like to oppose a few widespread errors about the nature of this relationship.

In theoretical economics, as in the theoretical sciences in general, exact and realistic knowledge are the result of orientations of theoretical research differing in certain respects, and accordingly exhibit a variety of formal differences. The field of research is, however, common to both orientations and comprises in each case all of economy. Both the exact and the realistic orientation of theoretical research have the aim of making us understand theoretically *all* phenomena of economy, each in *its* way.

These two orientations of research, accordingly, do not at all complement each other, for instance, by revealing to us the understanding of different fields of economy. Rather, the function of each of them consists in making us understand the total realm of economic phenomena in *its* characteristic way. Only where one or the other orientation leads to no results, whether because of deficient objective presuppositions or for reasons involved in the technique of research, does one or the other orientation of research dominate in definite fields of economy, and this only as long as this relationship persists.

The more complicated a realm of phenomena is, the more difficult and comprehensive is the task of reducing the phenomena involved to their simplest elements and of investigating the process by which the former are built up from the latter according to laws. So much the more difficult is a full and satisfactory outcome of exact research. Thus it becomes understandable that, just as in the natural sciences, only empirical laws usually appear to us in the field of social research in respect to the complicated phenomena; whereas in respect to the less complicated phenomena of nature and of human life the exact understanding achieves predominant significance. Thence also the well-known fact that the realistic orientation of research is likely to predominate where it is a question of theoretical knowledge which refers to more complicated phenomena of an empirical realm. In respect to less complicated phenomena the exact orientation predominates. Yet in principle both orientations of research are adequate not only for all realms of the world of phenomena, but also for all stages of the complexity of phenomena. When such an excellent thinker as Auguste Comte sets up the requirement that the social sciences should find their laws empirically and thereupon confirm them from the general laws of human nature, obviously lack of clarity in feeling for the above described fact is ultimately at the basis of this view. The same is true when J. Stuart Mill attributes a really decisive significance for social research to this method, which he calls the inverse deductive.

Still another question may claim our interest at this point. It is the question about the relationship to one another in which the guarantees for the truth of the exact and the realistic results of theoretical research in the field of economy stand. It is important for the reason that the underestimation of "exact economics" appearing particularly among German economists is based predominantly on the failure to recognize the true nature of this relationship.

Among economists the opinion often prevails that the empirical laws, "because they are based on experience," offer better guarantees of truth than those results of exact research which are obtained, as is assumed, only deductively from a priori axioms. Accordingly the latter would have to be modified and corrected by the former in case of a contradiction between the two kinds of scientific knowledge. Exact research appears thus as methodologically more subordinate, and realism, on the contrary, as the better guaranteed road to cognition. This is a view which, as scarcely needs to be noted, touches in its most sensitive spot the position of exact research in the field of political economy. Indeed, it actually implies a negation of its independent value.

The error at the basis of this view is caused by the failure to recognize the nature of the exact orientation of theoretical research, of its relationship to the realistic, and by applying the points of view of the latter to the former.

Nothing is so certain as that the results of the exact orientation of theoretical research appear insufficient and unempirical in the field of economy just as in all the other realms of the world of phenomena, when measured by the standard of realism. This is, however, self-evident, since the results of exact research, and indeed in all realms of the world of phenomena, are true only with certain presuppositions, with presuppositions which in reality do not always apply. Testing the exact theory of economy by the full empirical method is simply a methodological absurdity, a failure to recognize the bases and presuppositions of exact research.

At the same time it is a failure to recognize the particular aims which the exact sciences serve. To want to test the pure theory of economy by experience in its full reality is a process analogous to that of the mathematician who wants to correct the principles of geometry by measuring real objects, without reflecting that the latter are indeed not identical with the magnitudes which pure geometry presumes or that every measurement of necessity implies elements of inexactitude. Realism in theoretical research is not something higher than exact orientation, but something different.

The results of realistic orientation stand in an essentially different relationship to the empirical method than those of exact research. The former are based, of course, on the observation of phenomena in their "empirical reality" and complexity, and of course the criterion of their truth is accordingly the empirical method. An empirical law lacks the guarantee of absolute validity a priori, i.e., simply according to its methodological presuppositions. It states certain regularities in the succession and coexistence of phenomena which are by no means necessarily absolute. But bearing this firmly in mind, we note that it must agree with full empirical reality, from the consideration of which it was obtained. To want to transfer this principle to the results of exact research is, however, an absurdity, a failure to recognize the important difference between exact and realistic research. To combat this is the chief task of the preceding investigations.

In stating this we are far from denying that it would be extremely desirable if we could gain *exact* knowledge which simultaneously agrees with full empirical reality, in the here definitive sense. Or, what is in essence the same thing, it would be desirable if we could gain empirical knowledge which would simultaneously exhibit the advantages of exact knowledge. Human cognition, the prediction and control of phenomena, would be essentially aided and simplified by this. What we are trying to make clear here is, however, that this is not attainable given the actual relationships which the world of real phenomena regularly offers.

Since it is a question here of an error deeply rooted among the German economists and at the same time of a subject about which vagueness frequently exists even in the theoretical investigations of the best foreign writers, the relationship between the results of exact and of realistic research in the field of our science may be elucidated by an example. This, indeed, will be one which will at the same time explain the causes of the confusion which prevails in the respect considered.

Exact research in the realm of the phenomena of price teaches us, for example, that the increase in need for a certain item of goods appearing in a definite trade area can under certain circumstances lead to a *price increase which can be determined exactly according to measure* (whether the increase in demand is the result of population growth or of the greater intensity with which the need for the item concerned appears among the individual economic subjects).[23] Those presuppositions which automatically result from any orderly presentation of theoretical economics are: (1) that all the economic subjects considered here strive to protect their economic interest fully; (2) that in the price struggle they are not in error about the economic goal to be pursued nor about the pertinent measures for reaching it; (3) that the economic situation, as far as it is of influence on price formation, is not unknown to them; (4) that no external force impairing their economic freedom (the pursuit of their economic interests) is exerted on them.

There is scarcely need to remark that the above presuppositions in real economy all hold only in rare cases and that therefore as a rule *real* prices deviate more or less from *economic* ones (those corresponding to the economic situation). In the practice of economy people in fact endeavor only rarely to protect their economic interests *completely*. Many sorts of considerations, above all, indifference to economic interests of lesser significance, good will toward others, etc., cause them in their economic activity not to protect their economic interests at all in some cases, in some cases incompletely. They are, furthermore, vague and in error concerning the economic means to attain their economic goals; indeed, they are often vague and in error concerning these goals themselves. Also the economic situation, on the basis of which they develop their economic activity, is often insufficiently or incompletely known to them. Finally their economic freedom is not infrequently impaired by various kinds of relationships. A definite economic situation brings to light precisely *economic* prices of goods only in the rarest cases. *Real* prices are, rather, more or less different from the *economic*.

But if this is correct it is also clear at the same time that in the above typical case the real increase in need for an item of goods will not necessarily have as a result a *real* increase of prices corresponding exactly to the thus changed economic situation; indeed, there are circumstances in which it will not result in an increase at all. Accordingly, the law that the increased need for an item results in an increase of prices, and indeed that a definite measure of the increase of need also results in an increase in prices determined according to its measure, is not true—is unempirical, when tested by reality in its full complexity. But what else does this

[23] Cf. my *Grundsätze der Volkswirthschaftslehre*, I, p. 172 ff.

prove than that the results of exact research do not happen to find their criterion in experience in the above sense? The above law is true in spite of all this, absolutely true, and of the greatest significance for the theoretical understanding of price phenomena, as soon as it is merely considered from the point of view which is adequate for exact research. If one considers it from the point of view of realistic research, then, to be sure, one gets into contradictions. The error in this case, however, lies not in the law but in the wrong way of considering it.

If we now attempt to obtain an analogous law of price phenomena considered from the realistic point of view, there is probably no one experienced in economic matters who needs the special remark that this law is apparently very similar to that which is the result of exact research. It is an observation known to all that the increase of demand for an item regularly (even if not always) results in an increase in its price. This "empirical" law, however, in spite of its superficial similarity, exhibits a fundamental difference from the one previously presented, a difference that is all the more instructive as the superficial similarity of the two laws under discussion here causes it to be overlooked only too easily in cursory observation. The exact law states that *with definite presuppositions* an increase in need, definite by measure, must be followed by an increase in prices just as definite by measure. The empirical law states that an increase in need *as a rule* is actually followed by one in *real* prices, and, to be sure, an increase which as a rule stands in a certain relationship to the increase in need, even if this relationship by no means can be determined in an exact way. The first law holds true for all times and all nations which exhibit a traffic in goods. The latter allows exceptions even with one definite nation, and for each market is easily a different one to be determined only by observation, as far as the *measure* of the effects of demand on prices is concerned.

We have intentionally chosen an example in which an exact and an empirical law of economy show a superficial similarity just to present by this the fundamental difference between the two categories of theoretical knowledge under discussion here. It would, however, be easy to show that in numerous other cases the exact laws and the analogous empirical laws also show differences just in their superficial form. And it is accordingly clear that these laws must not be confused with each other, much less be tested from the same points of view.

Those who apply to the results of the exact orientation of theoretical research in the field of economy the standard of empirical realism and its theoretical results overlook one really decisive circumstance. This is that exact economics by nature has to make us aware of *the laws holding for an analytically or abstractly conceived economic world,*[c] whereas empirical-realistic economics has to make us aware of the regularities in the succession and coexistence of the *real* phenomena of human economy (which, indeed, in their "full empirical reality" also contain numerous elements *not emergent from an abstract economic world!*).

To want to look for the criterion of the guarantees of the exact laws of economy in their congruence with its empirical laws signifies a failure to recognize the most elementary principles of scientific methodology. Such a procedure would be comparable to that of a natural scientist who wants to test and rectify the laws of physics, chemistry, and mechanics by the empirical laws of natural phenomena; or even that of one who wants to test and rectify the results of the exact research of a Newton, Lavoisier, or Helmholtz by rules for farmers, surely extremely useful in their own way, as they are found in writings intended for country folk—just because they are usually based on experience of very long standing!

[c] Menger's actual phrasing is *Gesetze der Wirthschaftlichkeit,* which might be translated as "laws of economicity" if there were such a word as "economicity." Several lines below, where the translation reads, *"not emergent from an abstract economic world,"* Menger's crucial term is *Unwirthschaftlichkeit* ("noneconomicity"). I have noted three other instances of the use of *Wirthschaftlichkeit* in the special sense of reference to a "pure" economic realm governed by exclusively economic laws without contamination by any "noneconomic" phenomena. One of these occurs at p. 250, where reference is made to "the principle of economic reality." Another occurs at p. 212, where Menger is translated as writing "abstract economic reality." And the third occurs at p. 218, where Menger is again translated as writing "abstract economic reality." With so convenient a usage of *Wirthschaftlichkeit* even Menger can be concise. L.S.

BOOK 1

CHAPTER 6

The Theory that Economic Phenomena Are to Be Treated Only in Connection with the Total Social and Political Development of Nations

That the above way of looking at social phenomena is adequate for research in history.—Also for the specifically historical orientation of jurisprudence.—That mechanically applying the above point of view to the social sciences in general, and to theoretical economics in particular, involves, on the other hand, a fundamental error.—The above point of view considered in relation to the *exact* orientation of theoretical research.—That this clashes with the idea of exact theories in general and those of an exact theory of economic phenomena in particular.—The above point of view considered in relation to the *empirical-theoretical* orientation of theoretical research.—That it is by no means adequate for the latter. —That even the most realistic orientation of theoretical research imaginable cannot dispense with certain abstractions from full empirical reality.—That the above view in its ultimate logical consequence leads to the negation of any theory of economy and to recognizing the writing of history as the solely justified orientation of research in the field of economy.

There is a doctrine closely connected with the errors set out in the previous sections, the confusion of the historical and the theoretical understanding of social phenomena on the one hand, and the one-sided conception of the theoretical problem of the social sciences as an exclusively realistic one on the other. This doctrine more than any other has become all-prevailing in modern German economics and is repeated not only in the writings of almost all prominent contemporary economists of the historical school, but by their own admission really determines the character and orientation of their research.

I am speaking here of the opinion of those who want to have "the phenomena of economy understood only in inseparable connection with the social and political development of nations";[24] of those who characterize "as unhistorical and unreal when compared with life the act of making the economic element independent, and of separating it from the total complex of the life of the state and nation," and speak of this therefore as "the cause of erroneous results, as soon as the full truth of actual life is to be reproduced by science from that point of view."[25]

The above[d] view,[26] as is well known, is not a new one in the field of *historical research*. The concrete phenomena of the life of nations are the result of innumerable factors acting together, and there probably is scarcely one phenomenon of this life which would not feel the influence of all the factors which are determinative in shaping human phenomena. The historian would at least not escape the reproach of the most extreme one-sidedness from all expert historians if he tried to explain and make us understand a complicated phenomenon of the life of nations or indeed a set of such phenomena merely by one single propensity of human effort

[24] C. Dietzel, *Die Volkswirthschaft und ihr Verhältniss zu Gesellschaft und Staat* (Frankfurt a.M., 1864), p. 52.

[25] C. Knies, *Die politische Oekonomie vom Standpunkte der geschichtlichen Methode* (Braunschweig, 1853), pp. 29 and 109 ff.

[26] It must be designated as a not wholly successful formulation of the above basic thought when Schmoller (*Ueber einige Grundfragen des Rechts und der Volkswirthschaft* [Jena, 1875], p. 42 ff.) requires that the science of political economy also investigate the *"psychological and ethical* causes . . . systematically in their significance for economy" along with the *"technical-natural"* causes. For a strict contrast does not exist between the above two groups of causes. Human needs and the resulting desire to satisfy them, in any case by far the most important factors of the human sciences, are e.g., certainly just as much natural causes of economic phenomena as they are psychological ones. And yet Schmoller, as is clear from the context of his presentation, includes them among the natural ones, or indeed, even among the "technical-natural" ones, and thus contrasts them to the psychological and ethical causes of economy. A contrast does in truth exist between the specifically economic propensity (directed toward satisfying the need for goods) and others—the noneconomic drives of humans—from which and in the midst of which real social life arises, a social life whose reality should not be presented solely as the result of the economic propensity. This observation, extremely simple per se, is not made more profound by Schmoller's categories, but is made obscure.

[d] By "the above view" Menger evidently means the "holistic" outlook in economics which he has described in the previous paragraph. L.S.

or even exclusively by one single factor in the shaping of history. This applies to a historian who, for example, should try to interpret the facts of the foreign policy of states merely through the character and the propensities of the leading diplomats, to interpret the artistic development of an age merely through the individuality of its leading artists, battle victories merely through the talents of the generals. This is true in all the above cases if the historian does not at the same time interpret the relevant phenomena by way of political, cultural, and economic conditions of the nations as far as they have affected great historical facts.

What has been said clearly applies also to the historical facts of law and economy. As Savigny went about making German jurists more clearly aware of the significance of historical law studies for understanding law than had previously been the case, he was not in doubt for a moment. He knew that law, "whose organic connection with the essence and character of the nation"[27] was clear to him, had no existence by itself, but that its essence, like that of language, was the life of man himself, viewed from a particular side.[28] He had no thought of interpreting law historically in its concrete formations by some definite propensity or in general by some one-sided point of view and at the same time of failing to recognize the influence of all the other cultural factors and all the other historical facts affecting it. He had no more thought of doing this than a historian of economy has the idea of wanting one-sidedly to explain its historical development exclusively by some definite propensity, e.g., the economic self-interest of the nations or of the members of a nation. Law and economy in their concrete form are parts of the total life of a nation and can be understood historically only in connection with the entire history of the nation. There can be no rational doubt that the facts of economy must be traced back by the historian to the totality of the physical and cultural factors which have aided in shaping them. There can be no doubt that the *historical* understanding of economy and its phenomena can be attained "only in their connection with the social and political development of the nations." And the separation of the economic element from the total complex of the life of the state and the nation, its separation in the above characterized sense, would not be historical nor adequate to real life. We repeat, about all these things there can be no rational doubt and—if we disregard a few philosophers of history who undertake to construct the historical facts from one-sided propensities—they have never been actually doubted by historians, either, as far as a question of the historical understanding of economic phenomena is involved.

[27] Fr. C. v. Savigny, *Vom Beruf unserer Zeit zur Gesetzgebung und Rechtswissenschaft* (Heidelberg, 1814), p. 11.

[28] *Ibid.*, p. 30.

Only the complete failure to recognize the nature of the *theoretical* sciences and the true nature of the understanding of phenomena rendered by them, of the theoretical understanding of phenomena in general, and of that understanding in particular which has the task of providing us with theory in the realm of economic phenomena—only this failure could meanwhile mislead a number of writers on economics into applying simply, i.e., in a thoroughly mechanical way, to the theory and the *theoretical* understanding of economic phenomena the above points of view relating to history and the *historical* understanding.

But here we will speak of the above research postulate first in respect to the *exact* orientation of theoretical research in the field of economy, then in respect to the *realistic* orientation.

In the sphere of exact theories there is not even one which could per se provide us with *universal* theoretical understanding of the world of phenomena or any definite realm of the latter—indeed, even of a single complicated phenomenon of the real world, thought of in its totality. Rather, only the exact sciences in their *totality* are able to offer us such things, since each of them opens up only the understanding of a specific side of the real world.

Anyone who wants to understand the phenomena of nature as experience offers them to us, anyone who wants to understand even a single phenomenon of nature in an exact way, i.e., as an exemplification of the strict regularity in all natural things, must not seek this understanding, for instance, merely in the laws of chemistry, of mechanics, or exclusively in those of physics, etc. but can attain them only through the totality, or at least a majority of the exact sciences. For only in this way will he reach an exact understanding of those phases and sides of real phenomena which from the point of view of a *single* exact science would perhaps present themselves to him as *irregularities,* as exceptions to the strict regularity of the world of phenomena. No one exact science happens to include the universal theoretical understanding of even the slightest part of the real world. As stated, it always teaches us only *a special side of this regularity*.

Will chemistry perhaps, or physics, or mechanics, etc., be designated as one-sided sciences for this reason? Will it for this reason occur to a natural scientist to want to expand each one of the above sciences to a theory of the phenomena of nature in general? Or will a person to any extent informed about theoretical questions scorn the disciplines under discussion here as "abstract" because each of them, taken by itself, is not sufficient for the explanation of even one single more complicated phenomenon of nature in its full empirical reality?

It is a fundamental principle of all methodology that the individual exact sciences open up for us only the theoretical understanding of *individual sides* of the real world. Anyone who, instead of trying to attain universal understanding of concrete phenomena by the totality of these sciences, wants to reach this goal by desiring to expand the individual exact sciences into universal theories in definite realms of real phenomena, misunderstands the most elementary principles of the theory of science. He does so to such an extent that his qualification to join the discussion of the difficult problem dealt with here would really have to be questioned.[29]

Now what else do the representatives of the previously characterized doctrine want but to expand theoretical economics, which as an exact science is—can be!—only a theory of the *economic* side of the life of a nation, into the phantom of a universal theory of social phenomena?

If humanity should ever arrive at a *universal* exact understanding of social phenomena in general and economy in particular (thought of in its full empirical reality), then this could assuredly happen only by way of a *majority* of exact social sciences, the totality of which would have to open up for us the universal exact understanding of social phenomena. Then, to be sure, it would be possible for us to learn to understand in those real phenomena which we preferably call the phenomena of economy the noneconomic influences and effects. We could learn to understand them thus not by means of pure economics, but by means of other social sciences, in the domain of which these influences fall; to understand them in an exact way, i.e., not as exceptions to the regularity of economic phenomena, but as exemplifications of social laws, even if, as is self-evident, not as those of economy. The economists may extend their best wishes to the development of these sciences and aid it as much as they are able. Until then, however, we will endeavor, in line with the particular scientific task that has been given us, to free exact economics from *its* errors and to fill in *its* gaps. We do this to provide an ever clearer exact understanding of what is *our* immediate occupation and, given the really la-

[29] The matter is so clear that the above error, which incidentally is very old, could not help striking the attention of an author like J. B. Say, who otherwise is not exactly authoritative in methodological matters. He writes: "Les phénomènes de la politique eux-mêmes n'arrivent point sans causes, et dans ce vaste champ d'observations un concours de circonstances pareilles ammène aussi des résultats analogues. L'économie politique montre l'influence de plusieurs de ces causes; mais comme il en existe beaucoup d'autres . . . toutes les sciences n'en feraient qu'une, si l'on ne pouvait cultiver une branche de nos connaissances sans cultiver toutes celles qui s'y rattachent; mais alors quel esprit pourrait embrasser une telle immensité! On doit donc, je crois, circonscrire les connaissances qui sont en particulier le domaine de l'économie politique" (J. B. Say, *Cours d'E. P.* [1852], I, p. 5 ff).

mentable state of economic theory, is our most urgent occupation, the *economic* side of social phenomena.

But those who perceive one-sidedness in this and want to sublimate pure economics into a theory of social phenomena in their totality also confuse here the points of view of historical and theoretical understanding. They overlook the fact that *history,* to be sure, has the task of making us understand *all* sides of *certain* phenomena, but that exact *theories* have the task of making us understand only *certain* sides of *all* phenomena in their way. A science can never be called *one-sided* if it completely fulfills *its* task.

The view that economic phenomena are to be treated in inseparable connection with the total social and political development of nations is accordingly a methodological absurdity, at least as a postulate for the exact orientation of theoretical research in the field of economy.

But also in the *realistic* orientation of theoretical research in the field of human economy a treatment of the latter in inseparable connection with the total social and political development of nations is properly out of the question. The "real types" and "empirical laws" of economy, too, are by no means the result of a consideration of social phenomena comprising all sides of the life of a nation. They are likewise, however realistically theoretical research may be thought of, in more than one respect the result of an abstraction from individual sides of these phenomena.

Even in the most realistic conception of theoretical problems imaginable, laws of phenomena never state anything else than that phenomena of a certain empirical form regularly follow those of other empirical forms or are coexistent with them. In this, therefore already in the idea of "laws" and, indeed, even of empirical laws, there is present, in more ways than one, an evident abstraction from full empirical reality. This is clear from the circumstance that in "laws," of whatever type they be, the succession or coexistence of *concrete phenomena* does not come into question (as in history!), but the succession or coexistence of *empirical forms* does. Accordingly, just for this reason an abstraction from certain features of the phenomena in their full empirical reality is unavoidable. Furthermore, abstraction is also involved in the circumstance that "laws," by stating the succession or coexistence of *certain* empirical forms without, as is self-evident, incorporating all other conceivable empirical forms, necessarily isolate the former and abstract them from all the remaining phenomena. With the idea of "laws of phenomena" there is accordingly given simply a certain abstraction from the full empirical reality of concrete phenomena. This abstraction is not a chance happening; not, for instance, a lack of a definite orientation of theoretical research, which is certainly to be avoided. It is so inevitable in determining the "laws of phenomena" of any kind at all that the attempt to avoid it *would really nullify the possibility of determining the laws of phenomena.*[30]

Even the most realistic orientation of *theoretical* research imaginable must accordingly operate with abstractions. The aspiration for types and typical relationships of real phenomena which refer in each case to the "*full* empirical reality" of the latter is accordingly an aspiration that simply contradicts the nature of theoretical research as it presents itself on the basis of reality.

If, however, the above abstraction resulting of necessity from the nature of theoretical research is disregarded, it is difficult to recognize what reform the realistic orientation of theoretical research still needs, in the sense of considering full empirical reality. If, corresponding to the above orientation of theoretical research, the laws of economy are obtained in a purely empirical way, by observing the real succession and coexistence of phenomena, then there is present in this procedure just per se a complete consideration of empirical reality—disregarding the circumstances stressed above. The *real* prices of goods, the *real* ground rents, the *real* income on capital, etc., are in any case not only the result of specifically economic propensities, but also of ethical ones. By determining the regularities of the succession and coexistence of *these* phenomena empirically, we therewith take into account, as far as this is at all conceivable, the influence of law, custom, and so on, typical economic relationships. Nor is there any foretelling how much further this influence is to be taken into account, especially as it is self-evident that *empirical* laws of phenomena are valid only for those spatial and temporal relationships, from the consideration of which they were obtained.

The aspiration to take into account the noneconomic factors of economy in the realistic orientation of theoretical research is accordingly superfluous since it is necessarily implied by the very character of this orientation. Here no special method is needed, still less an erudite school. On the contrary, minds of a very peculiar constitution would be needed to investigate "*empirical* laws" of economic phenomena, in which the noneconomic factors of human economy would be eliminated in the way our historical economists imagine this.

[30] The above postulate contradicting so completely the nature of theoretical research was actually set up by a few extreme representatives of the historical school of German economics. With complete misunderstanding of the nature of theoretical research, in determining the (realistic!) laws of economy, they always pretend to bring into consideration the entire life of the nation (why only this, and not the whole universe, since an abstraction is present in this, too?). With this, however, they arrived ultimately and logically at *a complete aberration from theoretical research and entered into the field of writing history.*

The above postulate involves a strange misunderstanding in respect both to the exact orientation of *theoretical* research and to its empirical orientation.

Truly the demand "that economic phenomena are to be treated in connection with the entire social and political development of nations" is rooted in the dim aspiration to carry the specific points of view of historical research over into theoretical economics, in an effort that is in contradiction with the character of the latter. Here also our historical economists evidence their slight methodological sophistication by asking more of an orientation of research than it can provide. They also show this lack of sophistication by straying, for fear of seeming *one-sided,* from their really proper field of knowledge, political economy, into the realm of historical research. This is a form of many-sidedness which German science, at any rate, could well be spared.

BOOK 1

CHAPTER 7

The Dogma of Self-Interest in Theoretical Economics and Its Position in Relation to the Theoretical Problems of the Latter

What is understood by the above "dogma" and the significance that is ascribed to it for the theory of economy.—The opinion that strict laws of economic phenomena are possible only under the erroneous assumption that people in their economic dealings are *in reality* guided merely by their well understood interest.—Line of argument by which the above opinion is refuted.—Inadequacy of this line of argument, as *error, ignorance, external complsion,* etc., in addition to *public spirit,* would exclude exact laws of economy, in case the line of argument in question were valid.—That the latter is based on a failure to recognize the nature of the exact orientation of theoretical research in general and of that in the field of economy in particular.—That the exact orientation of theoretical research by no means starts with the presupposition that economic humans would be *actually* guided only by their economic interests.—What the case really is in regard to the so-called dogma of self-interest in theoretical economics.

"*Private egoism,* self-interest, plays such an important role in the theory of economics, it has been brought into such an immediate and deeply radical connection with the method of obtaining laws of economy, it has exerted such a determinative effect on the whole position of our science" that we can pass over its relationship to the theoretical problems of our science here so much the less as, in our opinion, "the historical method of political economy stands in a very special relationship to the dogma of unalterable self-interest."[31]

By the "dogma of self-interest" some economists understand the basic principle that the pursuit of private interest on the part of single economic individuals, uninfluenced by politico-economic government measures, must have as a consequence the highest degree of common welfare which a society can attain, considering its spatial and temporal conditions. However, we do not intend to deal here with this opinion, which is erroneous at least in its general form, for it has no immediate connection with those methodological questions which will occupy us in this section.

What claims our interest at this point is, rather, the thesis, known under the above designation, that humans truly are guided in their *economic* activity exclusively by consideration of their individual interests. This is a thesis which, as the representatives of the historical school of German economists assume, is placed like a basic axiom at the head of their systems of political economy by the adherents of the "unhistorical" schools of our science, at least. Its significance for the theoretical problems dealt with by us here may, meanwhile, be clear simply from the circumstance that on the part of the historical school the possibility of strict laws of economic phenomena and thus also of an economic science is thought of as dependent on its correctness. Or, with reference to the erroneousness of the above "dogma," the possibility of a science of the "laws" of economy is simply denied and a special method, the historical method of dealing with our science, is demanded.

The line of argument of our historical economists in this case is, however, the following:

Man's will is guided by innumerable motives in part really in contradiction with each other. Thereby, however, a strict regularity of human actions in general and of economy in particular is a priori out of the question. Only when we think of man as always being guided by the same motive, e.g., self-interest, in his economic actions, does the factor of arbitrariness appear to be out of the question, only then does each action appear to be strictly determined. Only with the above presupposition are laws of economy conceivable, accordingly, and with them also an economics in the sense of an exact science.

But now people in their actions are guided, to judge by experience, neither in general nor even in particular in their economic actions exclu-

[31] K. Knies, *Die Politische Oekonomie vom Standpunkte der geschichtlichen Methode* (1853), p. 147.

sively by a definite motive. For along with self-interest, which at most can be recognized as the mainspring of human economy, also public spirit, love of one's fellow men, custom, feeling for justice, and other similar factors determine man's economic actions. And the presupposition with which the (nonhistorical) economists of the Smith school start is accordingly false. But with the above presupposition there also collapses the basis for strict laws of economy independent of temporal and spatial conditions, and with that the basis for a science thereof, that is, a theoretical economics in the previously conceived sense of the word. The entire orientation of research thus characterized is therefore unempirical, one that violates truth. And only research purified of these erroneous presuppositions could attain results in the field of our science which correspond to the real phenomena of economy.

This is approximately the line of argument of Germany's historical economists in fighting the "dogma of human self-interest."[32]

Here we should like above all to point to a gap in the above line of argument which catches the eye of anyone to any extent familiar with psychological investigations. The circumstance that people are not guided exclusively by self-interest prohibits, in the above sense, the strict regularity of human action in general, and of economic action in particular—and thereby eliminates the possibility of a rigorous economic theory. But there is another factor, equally important, that does the same thing. I mean *error,* a factor which surely can be separated still less from human action than custom, public spirit, feeling for justice, and love of one's fellow man can be separated from economy. Even if economic humans always and everywhere let themselves be guided exclusively by their self-interest, the strict regularity of economic phenomena would nonetheless have to be considered impossible because of the fact given by experience that in innumerable cases they are in error about their economic interest, or in ignorance of the economic state of affairs. Our historians are too considerate of their scholarly opponents. The presupposition of a strict regularity of economic phenomena, and with this of a theoretical economics in the multiple meaning of the word, is not only the dogma of ever-constant self-interest, but also the dogma of the "infallibility" and "omniscience" of humans in economic matters.

We are far from asserting that with the above dogmas the entirety of presuppositions of a rigorous theory of economic phenomena, in the sense in which our historians think of it, is already exhausted. Rather, it is clear to anyone not completely inexperienced in methodological investiga-

[32] Cf. Schmoller, *Ueber einige Grundfragen* (Jena, 1875), p. 42.

tions that they would have to be complemented by a series of other similar dogmas (in the realm of economic phenomena especially *the dogma of complete freedom from external compulsion,* among others). These are dogmas which, we have no doubt, could offer the representatives of the historical school just as rewarding as effortless a field of ingenious criticism. But precisely what has been said should suffice to point out what is most evident, what astonishing nonsense the greatest minds of all nations have been coming up with for thousands of years as they have sought for rigorous theories of social phenomena. In what a pitiable state of error humanity would still be today if the historical school of German economists had not opened its eyes.

To be sure, in contrast to such an epoch-making upheaval in the field of social sciences, the circumstance must appear somewhat strange that those errors with which scholars in the economic field are reproached are to be observed in a completely analogous way in all the remaining realms of theoretical research, but especially in the realm of research in nature. It is strange that accordingly a whole series of theoretical sciences becomes invalid and worthless upon closer examination, without even a suspicion of this having been aroused previously in the minds of our natural scientists.

For the most important and most basic of the theoretical natural sciences also suffer from the same weakness for which our historical economists reproach previous theories of social science. Chemistry and physics, too—no less, however, a series of other exact sciences like mechanics, mathematics, etc.—appear, when measured by the critical standard of our historians, contrary to reality, unempirical, and therefore in need of the same reform as theoretical economics.

Chemistry does not teach us "real concepts" of definite groups of concrete phenomena. Its elements and compounds are, rather, unempirical in their complete purity, they are not to be observed in nature uninfluenced by human art; indeed, to some extent, they cannot be prepared synthetically. Pure gold, pure hydrogen and oxygen, and their pure compounds are not given empirically, either per se, or in that ideally strict measure which the laws of chemistry presuppose. Chemistry operates with factors which are unempirical qualitatively and in certain respects quantitatively also. It furthermore does not deal with substances in the totality of their phenomenal form. It apprises us of their nature and laws, not in respect to all sides of their being, but only to a specific one. Chemistry, to use the language of our historical economists, starts with the dogma that the basic chemical substances and their compounds are empirically present in their complete purity, that ideally they are exactly measurable, that gold and oxygen in their *real* phenomenal form are exactly identical in all places and at all times. Moreover, it is concerned with only one single side of the real world, and its laws are accordingly, in contrast to the totality of the world of phenomena, based upon arbitrary assumptions and unempirical.

As we probably do not need to amplify any further, the same is true of physics, and in particular of mechanics and mathematics.

Pure mechanics starts in the case of its most important laws with the arbitrary and nonempirical assumption that bodies move in a vacuum, that their weights and their paths are measured exactly, that their centers of gravity are determined exactly, that the forces by which bodies are moved are known exactly and are constant, that no disturbing factors develop their activity; and thus—to use the language of our historians—it starts with a thousand other arbitrary, unempirical dogmas. And just like mathematics, whose unempirical presuppositions probably need not be pointed out particularly (think of the mathematical point, the mathematical line, the mathematical surface, etc.!), they, too, do not deal with the world of real pheenomena in its totality, but only with a single side of it. Also in this respect they are therefore, in contrast to "full empirical reality," arbitrary and unempirical; they are lamentable confusions of the human mind!

And up to now no one has suspected all these false dogmas, until the historical school of German economists finally opened our eyes, in part with full awareness, in part with the instinct of genius. It did this without becoming aware of the full extent of the really epoch-making upheaval being effected in the realm of exact research. Truly, our historical economists can be rather proud of this achievement of theirs.

But back to the matter in all seriousness! The *exact* orientation of theoretical research in the realm of social phenomena—and only in respect to this can there properly be any question of the dogma of self-interest—has, as we have already set forth fully, the task "of reducing human phenomena to the expressions of the most original and the most general forces and impulses of human nature." It has the task "of hereupon examining to what formations the free play of each individual basic propensity of human nature leads, uninfluenced by other factors (especially by error, by ignorance of the situation, and by external compulsion)." When we pursue this orientation of research, we attain to a set of social theories, each of which, to be sure, reveals to us only the understanding of a particular side of the phenomena of human activity. Accordingly, each abstracts from full empirical reality. But all, taken together, teach us to understand the ethical world in a fashion similar to that made possible by those theoretical sciences which result from comparable observation of nature.[33]

Among human efforts those which are aimed at the anticipation and provision of material (*economic*) needs are by far the most common and most important. In the same way, among human impulses that which impels each individual to strive for *his* well being is by far the most common and most powerful. A theory which would teach us to what crystallizations of human activity and what forms of human phenomena action oriented to the provision of material needs leads, on the assumption of the free play of that powerful economic impulse, uninfluenced by other impulses and other considerations (particularly error or ignorance); a theory, especially, which would teach us what *quantitative effects* would be produced by a definite *quantity* of the influence in question: such a theory simply must provide us with a certain understanding. It cannot provide understanding of human phenomena in their totality or of a concrete portion thereof, *but* it can provide understanding *of one of the most important sides of human life. "The exact theory of political economy"* is a theory of this kind, a theory which teaches us to follow and understand in an exact way the manifestations of human self-interest in the efforts of economic humans aimed at the provision of their material needs. It is thus a theory which does not have the task of teaching us to understand generally and in their totality social phenomena or even human phenomena, indeed not even those social phenomena which are commonly called "economic." It has only the task of affording us *the understanding of a special side of human life, to be sure, the most important, the economic.* On the other hand the understanding of the remaining sides of it could only be attained by other theories which would make us aware of the formations of human life from the point of view of the remaining propensities (e.g., from the point of view of public spirit, of the strict sway of the ideal of justice, etc.).

The great theoreticians in the realm of ethical phenomena have from the beginning started out with these methodological points of view. With this point of view Plato and Aristotle also approached the task of constructing theories of social phenomena. With this point of view, finally, the great founder of our science also wrote his work on the wealth of nations, but along with it a theory of moral sentiments, in which he made public spirit as well as self-interest a pivotal point in his work, which was so epoch-making for political economy.

If now we return to the so-called "dogma" of human self-interest, which, in the view of the historical school of German economists, is sup-

[33] See p. 61.

posed to form such a disturbing contrast to "full empirical reality," there is scarcely need of any further discussion for us to recognize this view as a misunderstanding of justified methodological outlooks which guided the great founders of the ethical sciences in their scholarly activity. No more than pure mechanics denies the existence of air-filled spaces, of friction, etc.; no more than pure mathematics denies the existence of real bodies, surfaces, and lines which deviate from the mathematical; no more than pure chemistry denies the influence of physical factors in the formation of real phenomena, or pure physics the influence of chemical factors, although each of these sciences considers only one side of the real world and abstracts from all the rest—no more than these does the economist assert that humans are *actually* guided only by self-interest or else are infallible and omniscient. He does not, because he makes the formations of social life the object of his research from the point of view of the free play of human self-interest uninfluenced by secondary considerations, by error, or ignorance. The dogma of human self-interest in the conception of our historical political economists is a misunderstanding.

Aristotle and Hugo Grotius were certainly not in doubt that other factors contributed to the formation of states beside the impulse for socializing or for community. Hobbes was certainly not in ignorance of the fact that the conflict of interests of separate individuals was not the sole mover of social formations, just as Spinoza knew that the impulse of self-preservation was not their sole mover. And Helvetius, Mandeville, and A. Smith knew just as well as any adherent of the historical school of German economics that self-interest does not exclusively influence the phenomena of human life. If the last of these had only written his own theory of public spirit! What distinguishes him and his school from our historians is the fact that he neither confused the history of economy with its theory nor even followed one-sidedly that orientation of research which I designated above with the expression empirical-realistic. Nor, finally, did he become a victim of the misunderstanding of seeing in theoretical investigations conducted from the point of view of the free play of human self-interest uninfluenced by other powers the acknowledgement of the "dogma" of human self-interest as the only *actual* mainspring of human actions. And I do not doubt that German economics also, as soon as its representatives become fully aware of the misunderstanding I am dealing with, will again assume the orientation of research discussed here, which is thoroughly justified and indispensable for the understanding of economic phenomena, even if it has long neglected it sadly, and it will also in turn contribute its share to the development of this orientation. The highly unsatisfactory state of exact research in the realm of economic phenomena is a powerful challenge to the German economists, too, to leave the wrong path which isolates them. It is a challenge to them to apply their strength again to the great problem of developing an exact theory of economics along with the effort to establish realistic knowledge in the field of economy and especially along with the effort to interpret economic phenomena historically.

BOOK 1

CHAPTER 8

The Charge of "Atomism" in Theoretical Economics

Nature and significance of so-called "atomism" in the theory of economy.—Origin of the above dogma in the line of argument of the historical school of jurists.—Difference in the deductions drawn from the above dogma at which the historical school of German jurists and that of German economists have arrived.—The standpoint of the historical school of jurists.—The standpoint of the historical school of German economists.—That the charge of "atomism" has its roots in the failure to recognize the true nature of the exact orientation of theoretical research and in the application of methodological points of view of specifically historical research to theoretical economics.—The contrast of *national economy* and *individual economy* in the methodological expositions of the historical school of German economists and the significance of the pertinent error for the theoretical problems of our science.

We should like to mention another opinion particularly widespread among German economists which ultimately, like the one previously discussed, has its roots in the mechanical application of certain points of view of historical research to theoretical economics and in a one-sided outlook on the problems of the latter. It can therefore be disposed of at this point. We mean the charge of *atomism* which is made in modern German literature against economics in the most frivolous way, indeed against everybody who is concerned with the true problems of theoretical economics. It is supposedly based on the fact that economic phenomena theoretically are reduced ultimately to individual economic efforts or to their simplest constituent elements, and are thus explained.

The dogma under discussion here also owes its origin above all to the historical school of jurists, from whose methods it was borrowed mechanically like many another part of the methodology of our historical school of economists. "There is," says Savigny, "no completely separate and isolated human existence. Rather, whatever can be viewed as separate is, when considered from another side, a member of a larger unit. Thus each separate human is of necessity to be considered at the same time as a member of a family, of a nation, as the continuation and development of all previous time." Savigny then speaks of the higher nature of a nation as a unit which is constantly growing, constantly developing, of which "higher nation," indeed, the present age too is but one member, etc.[34]

No one who compares the pertinent utterances of the historical economists of Germany with the above will fail to recognize their relationship, even if the results to which the two schools, starting with the same basic notion have come, are essentially different.

The historical school of jurists utilizes the above notion to arrive at the thesis that law is something above the arbitrariness of the individual, is even something independent of the arbitrariness of the temporary generation of the national body. They state that it is an "organic" structure which cannot and must not be arbitrarily shaped by individuals or by single generations, that it is a structure which, on the contrary, is opposed as something higher to the arbitrariness of the individual, of the entire age, of human wisdom. From this thesis the above school now further derived consequences which are in part extremely practical. It concluded that the desire for a reform of social and political conditions aroused in all Europe by the French Revolution really meant a failure to recognize the nature of law, state, and society and their "organic origin." It concluded that the "subconscious wisdom" which is manifested in the political institutions that came about organically stands high above meddlesome human wisdom. It concluded that the pioneers of reform ideas accordingly would do well less to trust their own insight and energy than to leave the reshaping of society to the "historical process of development." And it espoused other such conservative basic principles highly useful to the ruling interests.

The notion of an analogous conservative orientation in the field of economy was fairly obvious. And a historical school of economists comparable to the historical school of jurists, which would have defended existing economic schools and interests against the exaggerations of re-

[34] Fr. C. v. Savigny, *Zeitschrift für geschichtliche Rechtswissenschaft* (Berlin, 1815), I, p. 3 ff.

form thought in the field of economy, but especially against socialism, would have fulfilled a certain mission even in Germany and prevented many a later setback.

But nothing was further from the thoughts of the historical school of economists in Germany than the idea of an analogous conservative orientation in the field of economy. For this the historical orientation of German economists was something much too superficial and lacking in depth. On the contrary, its proponents, in a practical respect, lined up even a short time ago almost completely with the liberal policy-makers of progress in the field of economics, until no small part of them most recently offered the rare spectacle of a *historical* school of economists with socialistic tendencies. This was a scientific curiosity, the further development of which was checked more by external events than by scientific insight. In brief, the organic conception of economy remained for our historians in economics something thoroughly external, a theoretical view. It did not even remotely occur to them to draw from this view *practical* consequences, for instance, in the sense of the historical school of jurists. Not even the practical logical consequences really justified for economy have been drawn from this view by our historical economists.

The conclusions which our historical economists derived from the above basic view of the nature of economy (as an organic uniform unit) referred, on the other hand, exclusively to questions of scientific technique and thus quite clearly characterize the range of vision of this school.

If national economy was considered as a special unit differing from the singular phenomena of human economy, one could easily draw the consequence that national features should be the exclusive object of scientific treatment in theoretical *national* economy, and that the *singular phenomena* of human economy should be excluded therefrom. Not the general nature of the phenomena of human economy, not their general relationships, were henceforth to be the object of research in the field of theoretical economics. Research on the phenomena of *national* economy seemed to be the sole task of theoretical economics from this point of view. Meanwhile research on the general nature and the general relationships of the singular phenomena of human economy was banned from the field of our science. As amounting to the confusion of a mode of consideration of *private economy* and consideration of *national economy,* even as aspiration to reduce the phenomena of *national* economy to the singular phenomena of human economy, it was characterized as "atomism."

The error of this doctrine, more immediately occasioned by the confusion of historical and theoretical points of view[35] and more ultimately

[35] How very much this doctrine corresponded to the specifically historical ap-

caused by the failure to recognize the real character of "national economy" in its relations to the singular economic phenomena out of which it is constituted—the error of this doctrine is obvious.

The *nation* as such is not a large subject that has needs, that works, practices economy, and consumes; and what is called "national economy" is therefore not the economy of a nation in the true sense of the word. "National economy" is not a phenomenon analogous to the singular economies in the nation to which also the economy of finance belongs. It is not a large singular economy; just as little is it one opposed to or existing along with the singular economies in the nation. It is in its most general form of phenomena a peculiar complication of singular economies which has been characterized by us more in detail in another place.[36]

Thus the phenomena of "national economy" are by no means direct expressions of the life of a nation as such or direct results of an "economic nation." They are, rather, the *results* of all the innumerable individual economic efforts in the nation, and they therefore are not to be brought within the scope of our theoretical understanding from the point of view of the above fiction. Rather the phenomena of "national economy," just as they present themselves to us in reality as results of individual economic efforts, must also be theoretically interpreted in this light.

"Scire est per causas scire." Whoever wants to understand theoretically the phenomena of "national economy," those complicated human phenomena which we are accustomed to designate with this expression, must for this reason attempt to go back to their *true* elements, to the *singular economies in the nation,* and to investigate the laws by which the former are built up from the latter. But whoever takes the opposite road fails to recognize the nature of "national economy." He moves on the foundation of a fiction, but at the same time he fails to recognize the most important problem of the exact orientation of theoretical research, the problem of reducing complicated phenomena to their *elements.*

One-sided *collectivism* in the consideration of the phenomena of econ-

---

proach, adhered to with preference by the German economists of the historical school even in theoretical economics, scarcely needs any further comment after what was said in the preceding section. History comprises human phenomena always from the *collective* point of view, since it can do justice to its specific task in a universal way only thus, but not by reducing social phenomena to the singular phenomena of human life. Accordingly, the thought of applying the usual historical point of view to theoretical research also was obvious to the predominantly historically trained German economists of the historical orientation. And the above doctrine thus presents itself to us as a special form of that more universal methodological error of the historical school of German economists. It presents itself as one of those mechanical applications of specifically historical points of view to theoretical research which we have frequently mentioned and the combating of which is one of the main tasks of this writing.

[36] See Appendix I.

omy is simply inadequate for the exact orientation of theoretical research, and the charge of *atomism* in the above indicated sense of the word is thus a misunderstanding in respect to *exact economics*. The latter comes in for the charge of atomism along with all other exact sciences, and, indeed, *as* an exact science.

But even in respect to the *realistic* orientation of research in the field of economy the charge is not justified. Every theory, of whatever kind it may be and whatever degree of strictness of knowledge it may strive for, has primarily the task of teaching us to understand the concrete phenomena of the real world as exemplifications of a certain regularity in the succession of phenomena, i.e., genetically. Every theory, accordingly, strives first and foremost to make us understand the complicated phenomena of the research field peculiar to it as the result of the coworking of the factors responsible for its origin. *This genetic element is inseparable from the idea of theoretical sciences.*

The realistic orientation of research in the field of economy, therefore, may still strive for a determination of the empirical laws of the complicated phenomena of human economy. However, it can by no means dismiss the task of reducing the latter to their factors, to the singular phenomena of human economy, to the extent and in a form which is compatible with the idea of realistic research. Thus, to reproach a theoretician because he keeps firmly in mind the genetic factor in theory is really absurd.

Finally, as far as the charge is concerned that "national economy" is confused with "individual economy" by this genetic orientation in the theory of our science, it would have a firm basis in one case. That is, if it were not to acknowledge those complications of the singular phenomena of human economy which we call the phenomena of "national economy" and would have us fail to consider the singular phenomena of human economy as elements of "national economy." As long, however, as it tries to solve this problem, there can be no rational question of a confusion of individual with national economy.

All this, moreover, is so self-evident that certain writers are not completely able to avoid in the systematic presentation of the theory of economics the reduction of the more complicated phenomena of national economy to the singular phenomena of human economy. These include even the writers who in their methodological discussions express the anti-atomistic view, which fails to recognize the nature of the theoretical sciences. Herewith there arises also that contradiction between the theory and practice of research which is really characteristic for the historical school of German economists.

BOOK TWO

The Historical Point of View in Economic Research

Introduction

The formal nature of political economy and its subdivisions.—It is not a historical science.—Its "historical method" cannot consist in giving up the formal nature characteristic of it or its subdivisions, but only in retaining the historical point of view when it offers orientations of research adequate for political economy.—Nature of the "historical method" in theoretical economics on the one hand, and in the practical sciences of economy on the other.—It is by no means the same in both cases.—Just as little in the exact and realistic orientations of theoretical research in the field of economy.—Exaggerated significance which is attributed to the historical point of view in political economy on the part of the historical school of German economists.—Its relative importance for the present.

In the preceding book we have set forth the essential difference between the historical, the theoretical, and the practical sciences of economy. We have particularly pointed out the errors of those who see a "historical" science in political economy. Political economy (in its meaning which comprises theoretical economics, economic policy, and the science of finance) is a theoretical-practical science. The treatment of it, therefore, as a historical discipline is just as wide of the mark as if one wanted to subordinate the history or the statistics of economy to the methodological points of view of the theoretical or practical sciences.

If there is to be any question at all of a historical orientation in political economy this cannot mean the change of political economy into a "historical" science. It can, rather, designate only such a *theoretical* or *practical* orientation in research as keeps firm hold on the development of social phenomena—and without meanwhile relinquishing the character of political economy as a theoretical-practical science.

However, before we go on to the solution of the problems pertinent here, it is necessary to reject a tacit presupposition of those who have concerned themselves with these problems. It is an error in principle, the elucidation of which is necessary for a complete conception of the nature of the historical point of view in our science. We mean the error that the historical point of view is identical in theoretical economics and in the practical sciences of economy; furthermore that what is true of the historical orientation of research in the former therefore can be applied simply to the treatment of the latter from the historical point of view.

The sciences in question here are, to be sure, concerned with the same realm of human life; they are all sciences of economy. But, as we saw in the preceding book, their goals are so thoroughly different that we cannot properly speak of an identity of the cognitive methods for reaching them. The method of economic policy must not be confused with that of theoretical economics any more than the method of the latter is to be confused with that of history or statistics.

But if this is certain, then it is at the same time clear that the development of economic phenomena, as we will present it later, by no means has of necessity the same influence on the practical sciences of economy as on theoretical economics. Accordingly, the postulates of the historical point of view in the latter simply must not be applied to the former, and vice versa. Rather, it scarcely needs to be stressed that the influence of the above fact on theoretical economics on the one hand, and on the practical sciences of economy on the other, can only be established by way of a separate investigation which considers the problems of the above sciences from the historical point of view.

In *theoretical economics* the historical point of view is made valid when the development of economic phenomena is noted in its influence on the determination of empirical forms and the laws of economic phenomena. In *economic policy* the same point of view is acknowledged when the various stages of the development of economy are presented in their influence on the institutions and measures of public authority calculated to further this economy. The theoretician in economics validly adopts the historical point of view when he keeps his eye on the development of economic phenomena in his research on the *general nature and the laws of economy*. The individual concerned with economic policy does this similarly in his research on *measures for advancing economy*. The difference between the above two problems is so obvious that confusing them really should seem quite inconceivable. If it is nonetheless so frequently missed, the cause lies partly in the erroneous conception of political economy as a formally homogeneous science and in the resultant effort to determine *the* method of this science and not, on the contrary, in the *methods* of the formally quite different parts of which it consists. To no slight extent, however, it lies in a misunderstanding to which we will briefly refer here.

The common element in the above two methodological problems is to be found in the circumstance that both practical and theoretical economics are concerned with the question of whether economic laws which correspond to a definite developmental stage of economy are also adequate for developmental phases of it differing from this stage. What is not infrequently overlooked here is the decisive circumstance that in the one case it is a matter of *normative laws* (of rules for human action established by the state or through custom). In the other, however, it is a matter of *laws of phenomena* (of regularities in the coexistence and the succession of the phenomena of economy). That is, it is a matter of two completely different things and concepts which are just by chance designated by the same expression (law!).

Accordingly, one can still be of the opinion that various normative laws and institutions of economy correspond to various stages of the development of state and society in general, and of economy in particular, without having to be of the opinion, or even having a suspicion, that state and social phenomena in general, and the phenomena of economy in particular, develop in the course of time, and that this circumstance touches on the laws of the succession and coexistence of these phenomena. It is, in fact, a matter here of two different scientific questions which both have their full justification. Of these, however, only the latter refers to theoretical *economics* and the problem of keeping the "historical point of view" in it, while the former is a matter of keeping the historical point of view in *economic policy*.

A long series of writers on economics conceive of political economy at one moment as a formally homogeneous science, and as a consequence of this circumstance strive for *the* method of this science. At another moment they apply the methodological points of view and postulates of theoretical economics to the practical sciences of economy, and conversely those of the latter to the former. In particular, they conceive of keeping the historical point of view in the two kinds of sciences as an identical methodological problem. All this has become no less injurious to theoretical investigations in our science than the confusion of the history and the theory of economy, whose consequences for political economy we have presented in the preceding book.

Accordingly our problem cannot first and foremost consist in determining *in general* the nature of the historical point of view in that totality of theoretical and practical sciences which we call political economy. Rather, we will have to deal separately with the above thoroughly different methodological problems: the determination of the historical point of view in theoretical economics on the one hand, and in the practical sciences of economy on the other.

But in the treatment of the pertinent theoretical problems we will have to keep in mind a second no less important point of view. Theoretical research in the field of economy is not strictly homogeneous, either. It, too, as we have seen above, breaks down into two special orientations which show essential differences both in respect to their aims and to their ways of cognition, despite the fact that both try to solve the theoretical problem of research in the field of economy. We speak here of the *realistic* and the *exact* orientation of theoretical research, and with this it is clear that the determination of the historical point of view in each one of the above two orientations also must lead to different theoretical problems. We will have to distinguish on the one hand the historical point of view in the exact orientation of theoretical research, and on the other in the realistic one.

To be sure, the question could arise whether the problem of keeping the "historical point of view" in political economy is of such significance for our society as to assure a sufficient interest of the scholarly world for such complicated and difficult methodological investigations as those indicated above. But this question must especially suggest itself to us in a work which might destroy many illusions of the historical school of economics and at least reduce its significance to a more modest level. Nevertheless, even if it should develop from the following investigations that the historical point of view is far from showing that significance for our theoretical-practical science which a series of scholarly economists will ascribe to it, one thing must still not be overlooked. This is that in this work, which aims at the reform of the present state of political economy in Germany, it is obvious that things must not be judged exclusively according to their innate worth, but at the same time according to the significance which they have gained in the judgment of contemporaries. And what idea could have gained greater importance in this sense than that of a historical orientation of our science?

Thus the fault does not lie with us if we treat issues by no means without significance, yet of relatively small significance, in a fashion similar to that in which we treat the most important ones. The fault lies with those who have set scientific problems of secondary significance as the pivotal point of research in the field of economy and who have made the sharing of their limitations the sole criterion of the value or lack of value of scientific accomplishments. In pointing out the one-sided features, the exaggerations, and the errors of the historical school of German economists, we believe, considering the present state of political economy in Germany, that we are indeed dealing with the most important concern of our science.

BOOK 2

CHAPTER 1

The Historical Point of View in Theoretical Economics

§1. The development of economic phenomena

Nature of the development.—The development of the individual phenomena.—The two kinds of development of economic phenomena must be distinguished.—The development of empirical forms has a greater significance for social research than (the development of the species!) for the natural sciences.

It is a feature of numerous phenomena that they enter reality in a certain undeveloped form, gradually develop, follow a descending line after they have reached a certain peak, and finally give up their peculiar character, and in this sense perish. To the phenomena, in the nature of which the above process is really inherent, belong first and foremost natural organisms. But also in the case of numerous phenomena of social life in general and of economy in particular we can make a similar observation. Every single worker as such, every concrete economic enterprise, every measure aimed at elevating economy, every social connection of economic humans is a phenomenon of this type, a phenomenon which, by itself or in its effects, gradually develops and thus is subject to constant change.

Beside the above changes of concrete phenomena in time, experience makes us acquainted with developments of still another type. These, as we will at once see, are of no less importance for the theoretical sciences in general and political economy in particular than those just described. I mean those developments which come to light not in individual *concrete phenomena,* but in *empirical forms.* For we can observe in numerous groups of phenomena which recur typically that their empirical *forms* let us perceive a gradual movement. They do this in such a way, to be sure, that the concrete phenomena of a particular type occurring later in the succession, as opposed to the earlier phenomena of the same type, show a difference, a development, which we will call the *general* development, the development of empirical forms (in the natural sciences: the development of the species!) to distinguish it from that previously mentioned, the *individual* development.

Every single economic enterprise, every single economic institution, etc., exhibits for example an individual development which can easily be verified by observing it from its beginning to its point of decay. At the same time we can also perceive that the above phenomena are not always the same in their recurrence, but—just think, for example, of money—in the course of centuries have assumed different empirical forms.

The development of empirical forms, particularly those in the realm of organic life, and the significance of this fact for the natural sciences, have been stressed most emphatically by modern research in nature. But these are of far greater significance in the realm of social phenomena and particularly of economy. Natural organisms exhibit unmistakably the phenomenon of *individual* development. The development of empirical forms, however, proceeds only quite gradually, scarcely perceptibly. But in the ethical world a movement which clearly strikes the attention is perceptible in the latter respect, too. Those changes in the empirical forms of the organic world which as a result of well-established hypotheses are said to have been completed in the course of thousands of years, usually in prehistoric times, actually are completed in the realm of social phenomena in general and in particular in that of economy in a most intense manner, and, indeed, in historical times, right before our eyes, as it were. The phenomena of private property, of barter, of money, of credit are phenomena of human economy which have been manifesting themselves repeatedly in the course of human development, to some extent for millennia. They are typical phenomena. How different, nevertheless, is their present empirical form from that of previous epochs. In the beginnings of civilization want and plenty were equalized by way of more or less voluntary presents on the part of the one with plenty to those suffering want. In the course of the development of civilization crude forms of natural barter take place, and in higher civilization the equalization I refer to comes about predominantly through purchase and sale, that is, by means of money. And within the above phases of development numerous gradations of more or less developed forms of traffic in goods are to be observed. If all this is so, then we certainly have before our eyes a striking example of the development characterized above. When we perceive how with some of the most important civilized nations money first appeared in the form of domestic animals, later of base and noble metals in uncoined state, then as coins, only to pass over finally into still more involved forms (combinations of money and money tokens!), it would be difficult to fail to see here the striking development of the empirical form of money. In both cases it is the same economic phenomenon which assumes such different forms in the course of the development of civilization. In the first case it is the equalization of want and plenty; in the second, the means of barter. But what a difference of empirical forms which we, after all, have characterized here only in their most striking phases! And we meet such developments of empirical forms in the realms of social phenomena not only by way of exception; on the contrary, they form the rule.

The phenomena of human economy are thus not of strictly typical nature in time; rather, they exhibit at the same time (disregarding qualitative differences in their simultaneous appearance!) the spectacle of a double development, an individual one and one of empirical form. Concrete phenomena of economy do not resemble other simultaneous phenomena of the same kind. The "'same" concrete phenomenon of economy is not infrequently a different one in the single phases of its individual existence. But economic phenomena of the "same" kind are different even in the totality of their appearance as a result of the development of the empirical forms.

§2. The influence which the development of economic phenomena exerts on the nature and problems of the realistic-empirical orientation of theoretical research

That the development of economic phenomena cannot be without influence on theoretical economics in general and on the realistic-empirical orientation of theoretical research in the field of economy in particular.—Double problem of this orientation of research.—The influence which the above fact exerts on the desire to determine the real types and the empirical laws of economic phenomena.—How the problem of keeping the historical point of view in the realistic-empirical orientation of theoretical research is to be solved.—Limits of the significance of the historical point of view for the above orientation of research.

One thing must be clear immediately to anyone who has any understanding at all of the nature and the problems of theoretical research in general and of its realistic orientation in particular. It must be clear to him that the just noted fact of the development of economic phenomena cannot remain without influence on a theory of that development;[37] nor can it fail to influence the outcome of the realistic perspective in theoretical research in this field.

The realistic orientation of theoretical research has the double problem of investigating the types and the typical relationships (the general nature and the general connection) of *real* phenomena. It is supposed to make us aware of the empirical forms (the types) and the repeated relationships (the empirical laws) of real phenomena. How, in the solution of this problem, could it remain uninfluenced by the fact that those phenomena are variable whose general nature and whose general connection it has to determine?

A theoretical science, whose field of research would comprise phenomena that exhibit no changes in any phase of their existence, would fulfill its tasks by simply presenting to us their general nature and general relationships, i.e., at some point in time, since anyone who might have recognized the nature and laws of such phenomena at a definite moment would have recognized them in general. And a theory which would present the phenomena to us in respect to a definite point of time would solve its general pertinent problem.

But the position and correspondingly the problem of the realistic orientation of theoretical research are rather different. A theoretical science would solve the first part of the problem designated above only very imperfectly if it presented to us the general nature of the real phenomena of economy only in respect to a definite point of time, or, what is the same thing, only in respect to a definite stage of its existence. For anyone who knows the nature of these phenomena only in a certain phase of their existence has really not become acquainted with their nature at all.

The general nature of the economic phenomenon which we call a "commercial crisis" is not, for example, exhausted by our making ourselves aware of its nature at a definite stage, but only of its entire course. If we want to get the real concept of "worker" we must consider him not merely at the height of his development, but also in his period of development and in the period of the decline of his abilities. The real concept of

[37] Knies correctly stresses (*Pol. Oek.*, p. 35) that keeping the historical point of view in economic policy frequently enough goes hand in hand with a thoroughly unhistorical treatment of *theoretical* economics. He writes (*op. cit.*), "With most writers admissions in favor of basic principles concerning the historical development of political economy and claims against the absolute validity of economic theories refer only to the basic principles of *economic policy* and not to economics, i.e., they do not, therefore, refer to the general theoretical part of political economy."

an "enterprise" comprises the period of its establishment, of its development, and of its decline. Indeed, even the general nature of an apparently so slightly variable economic phenomenon as the coin shows a development from the moment when it leaves the mint up to the moment when it is worn out with use or taken out of circulation since it has been rendered obsolete by the advances of technology. Its general nature is not a static one.

Up to now we have looked only at cases of the *individual development* of economic phenomena and emphasized the effect of the fact under discussion on the determination of the general nature of the phenomena concerned. We can, however, make an analogous observation with respect to that development of economic phenomena which we have designated as one of *empirical forms*. The forms in which human needs, the possession of wealth, private property, barter, money, credit, taxes, and a thousand other institutions of human economy make a real appearance, as we have seen above, have by no means remained unchanged in all epochs of history in respect to their totality, if we disregard the possible *individual* developments of these phenomena. Their general nature would thus be comprehended only imperfectly if we were to overlook this significant fact and confuse the nature of the phenomena discussed here in the present or in any period of their development with their general nature in an absolute sense, and if we were to confuse the conception of them with respect to the present with the conception of them in the most general sense. On the contrary, it is clear that the most general conception is not a static one, but the conceptual image of these phenomena in the totality of their development.

We have met the determination of the real, typical relationships, of the empirical laws of economic phenomena, as the second problem of the realistic orientation of theoretical research in the field of economy. Now if these phenomena exhibit developments in the two previously mentioned respects, it is immediately clear that the empirical laws established in respect to a certain stage of their development do not necessarily remain valid for all the remaining stages of their development. The typical relationships which would be observed between phenomena which show no change would be independent of temporal conditions. The matter is different where it is a question of phenomena which are placed in the stream of time. Here it is clear that the empirical laws which were determined for definite stages of the existence of the pertinent phenomena do not necessarily retain validity for all phases of their development. To cite obvious examples, the physiological laws of developed organisms do not necessarily apply to the same organisms in the embryonic or in the descending stage of development. The empirical laws of the coexistence and the succession of the phenomena of the state of classical antiquity do not necessarily apply to those of the feudal state or a modern state, etc. The empirical laws of wages which apply to the worker at the peak of his development do not necessarily apply to the beginner or to the worker whose strength has already declined. The laws of the circulation of money, as we have observed them in a highly developed economy, do not necessarily apply to the periods of the beginnings of civilization. The laws by which the phenomena of credit are regulated in our day will not necessarily apply to the credit phenomena of the future.

If we summarize the statements made here, we arrive at the following result: the real phenomena of human economy exhibit a development which is presented on the one hand as one of individual phenomena, on the other as one of empirical forms. This circumstance has an undeniable influence on the results of the realistic orientation of theoretical research in the realm of the empirical world discussed here. This influence makes itself felt both in the determination of the general nature (of the real concepts) of economic phenomena and in that of their general connection (of the empirical laws): the real concepts, the types of economic phenomena are only then truly adequate if we make ourselves aware of the nature of the pertinent phenomena not merely at a definite moment, but in the totality of their individual development or of the development of their empirical forms; and the empirical laws of the phenomena discussed here, insofar as they only correspond to a definite stage of their development, do not necessarily retain their validity for other stages of the development of the above phenomena.

The development of economic phenomena characterized in greater detail above thus has a significance not to be overlooked for the realistic orientation of theoretical research in the field of economy.

What remains for us now to do at this point is briefly to characterize the way by which the above "historical thought" can most usefully be realized in the realistic orientation of research in the field of economy.

The development of economic phenomena and the necessity of taking this fact into account in the realistic theory of economic phenomena are beyond all doubt. No one to any extent familiar with theoretical investigations will, however, claim that we are to strive for the solution of the above problem, for instance, by creating just as many economic theories as there are developmental stages of economic phenomena or as there are different spatial relationships of nations at the same developmental stage. Such an effort would not be feasible simply for reasons of presentation and of scientific technique in general. The road which the theoreticians in the field of economy have to take to solve the above problem can, on the contrary, properly be one which is admissible only in light of the customary technique of scientific presentation and in light of the present need, which, indeed, is also asserting its rights in the science. This is especially the case when the road was already taken with satisfactory results in other fields of research which have a similar problem to solve. It can only consist in our taking as the basis of our presentation a specific state of the economy, especially significant with respect to time and place,[38] and merely pointing out the modifications which result for the realistic theory from differently constituted developmental stages of economic phenomena and from different spatial conditions. In the same way, for instance, a German or French anatomist or physiologist takes the well-developed bodies of the Indo-Europeans as a basis for his presentation, but also takes into consideration the developmental phases of the human body significant for anatomy and physiology, and also racial variations, for instance, those of the Negroes, the Malayans, etc. A realistic theory of economy in this sense is not a phantom, but a goal of research which can be attained with the usual means of science. At the same time, however, it is one which does proper justice to the factor of development in economy and to difference of spatial conditions without thereby sacrificing the theoretical character of economics. This would in truth be a *realistic theory of economy* with *consideration of the point of view of development* or of the *historical* point of view, if one wants to keep a more usual, if not quite apt, expression.

The more unreservedly we acknowledge this and the greater the right with which we can claim to have presented the influence of the above fact on the theory of economy more exhaustively and comprehensively than any of our predecessors, the more we nevertheless feel obligated to stress certain things. We must emphasize that in the acknowledgment of the frequently mentioned fact of the development of economic phenomena, in the recognition of the above-stated logical consequences of it for the solution of the specifically theoretical problems of our science, and in the endeavor to realize the above methodological thoughts is to be found the

[38] The state of the economy which in the concrete case must be selected as the basis for presenting theoretical economics is, of course, not necessarily the same for all times and nations. The selection is not a question of research, but one of suitable presentation, and thus conditioned by temporal and spatial conditions. Dahlmann very correctly has already remarked (*Politik* [Leipzig, 1847], I, p. 9): "Because humanity in each age produces new conditions, no state form can be presented fundamentally except in terms of means available and conditions prevailing in some era, unless it is bound to the relationships of some immediate present. Therefore all treatment of state matters in life and in theory presses on toward history and through it to a present, and, because no new form of life can be neglected, on to *our* present, *our* part of the world, *our* nation."

sum of everything which one is justified in designating as the "historical point of view" in the realistic orientation of *theoretical* research in the field of economy, in contrast to the unhistorical orientation of research. (If one wishes to be more correct, one may speak of "the consideration of the fact of development of economic phenomena" rather than of the "historical point of view.") Every postulate going beyond this, especially the effort of the historical school of German economists to transform political economy into a historical science or into a philosophy of economic history and the like comes, it must be emphasized, from a failure to recognize the most elementary bases of the theory of science, from a confusion of theory and history or of theory of economy and single special orientations of the theoretical aspiration for knowledge in the economic field.

§3. That the charge of too thorough a generalization of the theoretical knowledge of economy is by no means completely removed by the so-called historical method

Not every change of phenomena signifies a development thereof.—Those changes of phenomena in time which are not presented to us as developments are also of methodological importance for theoretical research, and only by taking them into consideration could the charge of "perpetualism" in the theory of economy be fully met.—The like is true of those differences of homogeneous social phenomena which are not of international or interlocal nature, but appear in the same place and at the same time.—These, too, are of methodological importance for the theory of economy.—Taking them into consideration would be necessary, too, if the charge of excessive generalization of theoretical knowledge in the field of economy were to be fully met.—The charge of "perpetualism" and of "cosmopolitism" in the meaning given by our historical economists thus includes only a part of the doubts about an all-too-excessive generalization of theoretical knowledge of economy.—The complete removal of these doubts is nevertheless not attainable for theoretical reasons.—A theory obtained from the point of view of empirical realism necessarily suffers from those weaknesses which the historical school thinks it removes by its method.

There is not a phenomenon of the real world which does not offer us the spectacle of constant change. All real things are located in the stream of time, the phenomena of social life just as well as those of organic nature, and the phenomena of the inorganic world no less than these. The historical point of view in the realistic orientation of theoretical research—the basic principle that the development of phenomena is not to be neglected—must, accordingly, either be adequate for all realms of the empirical world, or else something different from the mere fact of this change in time must be understood by "development of phenomena."

Now the so-called "development" of things constitutes in fact only a small portion of their changes in time, for we usually understand by "development" only those changes which result from the characteristic nature of the things, and in the case of which, accordingly, a particular individuality remains preserved in spite of change in time. We therefore do not speak of "developments" of those things which exhibit no characteristic individuality. Nor do we do so in those cases where a thing, of whatever type it be, undergoes a change merely through external or chance circumstances.

From what has just been said the following consequences result for the methodology of our science. It is above all an error when it is assumed that all difficulties of whatever nature resulting for theoretical research from the change of social phenomena in time would be removed by considering the *development* of social phenomena in the social sciences in general and in political economy in particular. It is an error to assume that a theory which considers this development thereby avoids the mistake of "perpetualism." On the contrary, it is clear that the charge of perpetualism could be completely avoided in theory only by taking into consideration in theoretical research those changes of phenomena which do not fall under the concept of "development."

A similar statement is true of the charge of "cosmopolitism." Simultaneous phenomena belonging to the same empirical form exhibit not only international or interlocal differences, but also differences in the same place and at the same time. This is a circumstance which, as scarcely needs to be noted, likewise cannot remain without influences on the more or less universal validity of theoretical knowledge. If anyone declares general economic laws inadmissible because economic phenomena exhibit *interlocal* differences, if he considers a modification of them necessary according to spatial conditions, he cannot at any rate help coming to similar conclusions in respect to the *local* differences of homogeneous economic phenomena. Also with the mere effort to avoid the charge of "cosmopolitism" in economic theory the mistake of excessive generalization of the theory is by no means removed.

The conception of so-called "perpetualism" and "cosmopolitism" which the historical school of German economists has had is thus inadequate. For the scholar who ever so carefully avoided the two errors so characterized would nonetheless not escape the fundamental weakness of an excessive generalization of theoretical knowledge, i.e., a generalization not adequate for real conditions. And only the consideration of all variations of the empirical forms of economic life stressed by us here would bestow upon the realistic theory of economy that rigor which the above school thinks it attains merely by the removal of "cosmopolitism" and "perpetualism" in the theory of economy.

Now we have already represented that the realization of the above scientific postulates is unattainable in full strictness, as far as the postulates refer to the difficulties resulting from the spatial variations of social phenomena and those resulting from their development in time. In the realistic orientation of theoretical research the desire for knowledge will always have to be satisfied with a merely approximate consideration of the facts touched on here and with that form of them, the basic lines of which we have previously determined. And however far the human mind is competent to advance in the perfection of a realistic theory of social phenomena, it will always be frustrated by the problems characterized here. The carrying out of the above postulates in research in their full strictness will always prove to be a phantom just for theoretical reasons. An approximate consideration of them will always be the only attainable goal of the realistic orientation of theoretical research in the realm of social phenomena. The form of the realization of the notions expressed here will, however, be analogous to the one we characterized further above.

The historical school of German economists has succumbed to a double error in consideration of the theoretical problems now treated. It has, on the one hand, conceived of them too narrowly. It has overlooked the fact that still other divergences of social phenomena not considered by it are entitled to the same significance for the methodology of our science as those to which it has turned its attention exclusively. Its representatives have, on the other hand, yielded to the erroneous idea that the difficulties for economic theory arising from the development of social phenomena and from their interlocal divergences can be completely removed by the historical method.

The "historical method" promises less than it should with respect to the goals it has set up, but even what it promises is unattainable in its full strictness. Every realistic theory of economy necessarily suffers, rather, to a certain extent from those weaknesses which the historical school thinks it is removing completely by its "method."

§4. The influence which the development of economic phenomena exerts on the nature and the problems of the exact orientation of theoretical research

Lesser significance of the above fact for the exact orientation of theoretical research.—Explanation of this circumstance through the nature and problems of this orientation of research.—What can constitute the historical point of view in this orientation.—That the exact orientation of theoretical research neither denies nor refuses to consider the development of economic phenomena.

Up to now we have dealt only with the influence which the development of economic phenomena exerts on the *realistic* orientation of theoretical research and on the nature of its results. There remains for us now to examine the influence of the fact of development on *exact* research. But here we can be so much the briefer as the influence on exact research is, indeed, of lesser significance.

At another point we have already stressed that the difficulties resulting from the atypical character of phenomena for the realistic orientation of theoretical research do not exist for its *exact* orientation, as a result of the peculiar conception of theoretical problems that prevail in the latter. Exact research reduces real phenomena to their simplest elements, thought of as strictly typical, and attempts to determine their strictly typical relationships, their "laws of nature." The empirical forms with which it operates are nonetheless thought of as strictly typical not only in respect to spatial conditions, but also to *temporal* ones. The development of *real* phenomena, accordingly, exerts no influence on the way in which exact research undertakes to solve the theoretical problem. Only the greater or lesser strictness of the realistic results of theoretical research is influenced by the change of phenomena and their interlocal divergences; that of the exact results is not. Accordingly, only the realistic orientation of theoretical research in the field of economy, and not the exact, has the task of testing the influence which the fact discussed here exerts on the nature of its results. It must look for ways and means to meet the above difficulty. The extensive investigations of our historical economists on the questions of "cosmopolitism" and of "perpetualism" in economic theory, in the form in which they have appeared up to now, truly concern only the realistic results of theoretical research in the field of economy, not the exact ones.

This is surely not to say that the exact orientation of theoretical research does not at all consider, or even denies, the development of economic phenomena. Exact theories are supposed to reveal to us the simplest and strictly typically conceived constitutive factors (susceptible of exact inquiry) of phenomena and the laws according to which complicated phenomena are built up out of the simplest factors. However, they fulfill this task completely only by providing us with this understanding in respect to each phase in the development of phenomena. Or, in other words, they do so by teaching us how phenomena are presented at *each step of their development* as the result of a regular genetic process. The exact sciences therefore ignore the development of phenomena just as little as they do the postulate of every theory to follow in all its phases the alternation of the phenomena which it is to make us understand. Every new empirical form which life produces, every new phase of development of phenomena offers a new problem for the exact orientation of theoretical research. Thus it considers in fact the change of phenomena—only in an essentially different way than is the case in the realistic orientation of theoretical research. The development influences the nature of the results of realistic research, its greater or lesser strictness. The same fact leaves untouched the formal character of the results of exact research. However, it modifies and expands the sphere of the *objects,* the understanding of which is to be revealed to us by the exact sciences. It modifies the aims of research.

As far as the *exact* orientation of theoretical research in the field of economy is especially concerned, the remark is scarcely needed for anyone to any extent familiar with its results and its history that *its* representatives, too, always endeavored to follow the development of economy. They endeavored to take into the sphere of their consideration every new empirical form in its field, indeed, every new phase in the development of economic phenomena. Exact research in the field of our science has never negated the development of social phenomena; it has never neglected it even in principle. However, it has, as is obvious, considered it in a way appropriate to its nature and problems.

BOOK 2

CHAPTER 2

The Pseudo-Historical Orientations of Research in Theoretical Economics

The historical orientation in *theoretical* economics does not consist in historical accessories which are added superficially to the results of the theoretical orientation of research in the field of economy.—Just as little in literary-historical studies in general and in dogmatic-historical accessories in particular. —Nor is it to be sought in the fact that only history is acknowledged as the empirical basis for theoretical research in the field of economy.—Error of specific overestimation of historical development in theoretical economics.—The desire to determine "parallelisms in economic history" is only a special orientation of theoretical research in the field of economy.—Theoretical economics is not a science of the "laws of development of economy."—Just as little a "philosophy of history."—Contradiction between the definitions of theoretical economics and the presentations of it in the historical school of German economists.

We have already seen that those who make the most noise emphasizing the significance of the historical point of view for the theory of economy are not infrequently the ones who fail most fundamentally to recognize its true nature, in pointing to the methodological errors of those who think they are retaining the historical point of view in theoretical economics. Actually, they are not concerned with the historical point of view in theoretical economics at all, but consider the phenomena of economy from a specifically historical standpoint, or from the standpoint of practical economies. Now, while we have presented the nature of the historical point of view, or rather, the significance of the fact which we call the development of economic phenomena, it still remains for us to mention certain methodological mistakes. They are made by those who, to be sure, retain the concept of theoretical economics, but recognize the nature of the "historical" point of view in it in postulates of research which deviate essentially from those presented above, which, indeed, are usually superficial and irrelevant for theoretical economics.

There are those who think they retain the historical point of view in theoretical economics when they embroider with all kinds of historical accessories the old theories gained from the so-called "'unhistorical" point of view. If one compares the representations of theoretical economics of this kind with those of an earlier, so-called "unhistorical" epoch, it is not hard to recognize that the *theoretical* knowledge which the two sorts of representations afford are essentially the same. The difference consists often enough only in the fact that the systematic presentation of the well-known theories of the old "unhistorical" schools is interrupted by historical digressions or is embroidered quite superficially with historical additions. Thus a composite results which is neither theory nor historical writing, and least of all *a theoretical economics from the point of view of historical consideration.*

But those people fall into a similar error about the nature of the historical point of view in economic theory who find it in literary-historical studies in the field of our science, or else in some special orientation of the science.

"In contrast to the absolutism of theory," says Knies,[39] "the historical conception of political economy is based on the following principle. The theory of political economy is also a result of historical development just as economic conditions of life are. It grows, in living connection with the total organism of a human and ethno-historical period, with and out of the conditions of time, of space, of nationality. It exists together with them and continues preparing for progressive development. It has its line of argument in the historical life of the nations, and must attribute to its results the character of historical solutions. Too, it can present general laws in the general part of economics in no other way than as historical *explication* and *progressive manifestation* of the truth. It can at every stage present itself only as the generalization of the truths recognized up

[39] Knies, *Politische Oekonomie nach geschichtlicher Methode* (1853), p. 19 and (1882), p. 24.

to this definite point of development, and cannot be declared absolutely self-contained according to sum or formulation. Furthermore, the absolutism of the theory, where it has obtained validity at one stage of historical development presents itself only as a child of this time and designates a definite stage in the historical development of political economy."

The error which is the basis of the above conception of the nature of the historical orientation of research in the field of *theoretical* economics is clear. The individual phases of development of our science can be understood *historically,* to be sure, only in connection with the spatial and temporal conditions from which they have emerged. Or in other words: a *literary history* of our science with a correct comprehension of its (historical!) task must not overlook the connection between the individual phases of its development and spatial and temporal conditions. This is, however, a postulate of every literary history, even one of the exact natural sciences, of chemistry and physics, indeed, of any *writing of history* in general. However, it has no immediate relationship at all to those postulates of research which we have called the historical point of view in *theoretical* economics (i.e., retaining the fact of the development of economic phenomena in the investigation of the general nature and the general connection of the laws of economy).

Those who think that they retain the historical point of view in theoretical economics are the victims of thoroughly analogous error when they add histories of dogmatic economic theories to the results of a *theoretical* research which, moreover, is not infrequently quite "'unhistorical." Presentations of histories of dogmatic theories of this type are literary history, and, to be sure, history of single theories of political economy, but not results of theoretical research from the "historical" point of view. They are thus neither per se, nor can they change an "unhistorical" theory into a "historical" one. However useful they may be for the study of theoretical economics, they signify the historical point of view in this science just as little as literary-historical studies of any other kind.

No less in error are those who try to make the historical point of view in theoretical economics valid by trying to base the theory of economy not on *experience* in general, but exclusively on the *history* of economy. That is, they recognize in the latter the solely justified *empirical* basis of theoretical research in the realm of human economy.

The falseness of the above opinion, which has really become prevalent among German economists (one-sided overestimation of historical development in theoretical economics!) is, however, obvious to anyone not completely inexperienced in methodological matters. In contrast to the theoretical sciences which have to make us aware of the general nature and the general connection of phenomena, history has the task of investigating and presenting the individual nature and the individual connection of phenomena in general and of human phenomena in particular. It cannot solve its problem by investigating and cataloging the vast quantity of *singular phenomena* of human life. Rather, it can do justice to it only by bringing together what is individual in the real world from the point of view of *collective phenomena* and making us aware of the nature and the connection of the above phenomena to those large *collective phenomena* which we call nation, state, society. The fates of single individuals, their acts per se, are not the subject matter of history, but only the fates and acts of nations. The former are proper subject matter only insofar as they are at the same time significant for the development of the whole, i.e., of the collective phenomena as such.

As is obvious, the same thing is also true of the history of human economy. Here, too, it is not the singular economic phenomena which form the subject matter of historical presentation. It is not all the innumerable efforts and successes of single individuals aimed at meeting their material needs, nor the vast myriads of single acts of production, exchange, and the economic employment of goods. What brings authentic history home to us is, rather, the concrete nature and the development of those large collective phenomena which we call economy. Only those who completely fail to recognize the nature of the historical sciences can thus yield to the illusion that, from the study of history in general and of economy in particular, insight may be gained into the general nature and the general connection of the phenomena of human economy *in general.*[40]

Those who recognize in the history of economy the only justified empirical basis for theoretical research in the realm of human economy err fundamentally. For along with the historical, surely very valuable empirical basis for theoretical research, the experience of everyday life is indispensable. Or what is the same thing, *the observation of the singular phenomena of human economy,* indeed, as must be added here, the most comprehensive possible observation of that economy, is indispensable. It is so indispensable that we cannot imagine a highly developed theory of economic phenomena without the study of the history of economy. Without the observation of the singular phenomena of human economy we cannot imagine a theory of them at all. The error of those who acknowledge the history of economy exclusively as the empirical basis for theoretical economics seems no smaller to us than that of a physicist or chemist who would like to build up the laws of physics or chemistry on the basis of

[40] Cf. especially Roscher, *Leben, Werke und Zeitalter des Thukydides* (Göttingen, 1842), p. vii.

universal representations of nature, even if they were as excellent as A. von Humboldt's. It seems no smaller than that of a physiologist who would like to build up a physiology of the human body exclusively on the basis of ethnographic descriptions.[41]

Finally they are also mistaken who recognize the nature of the historical orientation of the theoretical political and social sciences in general in the *investigation of parallelisms in the historical development* of various nations, in what was occasionally but perhaps not quite aptly called "the philosophy of history." They are mistaken if in particular they recognize the nature of the historical orientation of theoretical economics in the investigation of these parallelisms in the economic history of nations. Indeed, they are mistaken if they simply identify the results of this orientation of research with theoretical economics.

It is self-evident that the adherents of this conception of the nature of theoretical economics likewise succumb to the previously characterized error of one-sided overestimation of historical development. However, a much cruder error underlies the conception.

Only the most extreme scientific one-sidedness could assert that the

[41] Economics has to investigate not only the general nature of those phenomena of human economy which are of "economic" nature, as for example, market price, rates of exchange and stock market quotations, currency, bank notes, commercial crises, etc. It also has to investigate the nature of the singular phenomena of human economy, e.g., the nature of the needs of the individual, the nature of goods, the nature of barter, indeed, even the nature of those phenomena which, being of purely subjective nature, simply appear in the individual, e.g., use value in its subjective form. How could economics draw exclusively on *history?* To conceive of history as an exclusive empirical basis of the social sciences is a glaring error. Saint-Simon and his followers have already succumbed to a similar error. A. Comte also considers social science to be essentially a result of generalizations from history. Yet he at least feels the need to verify these by deriving them from the laws of human nature. J. St. Mill acknowledges Comte's method only for some of the problems of social science, while for others he admits the justification of the exact method (according to Mill, the concrete-deductive method). "*Political economy* especially owes its origin and development to the latter." The feature of Mill's investigations that seems one-sided and defective is his failure also to understand the necessity in all questions of methodology of separating theoretical from practical economics and the exact orientation of theoretical research from the realistic. This is a circumstance which often causes him to apply the methodological postulates of the practical and the realistic orientation to the results of exact research in the field of the social sciences. Also, Mill does not distinguish sufficiently the single branches of realistic research in the field of the theoretical social sciences (Mill, *Logic,* Book IV, Chap. IX, §3). Among the German methodologists who have expertly treated the pertinent questions Rümelin is to be mentioned among the first. But he, too, is misled by his too narrow conception of the nature of social laws and his lack of understanding for the exact orientation of theoretical research in the realm of the social sciences. He is misled into applying the standard of exact natural research to the results of specific-empirical orientations of theoretical social research (*Reden und Aufsätze,* I, p. 1 ff. and II, p. 118 ff.).

parallelisms in national and state life in general and in the development of economy in particular are absolute regularities, or, in other words, that the development of the phenomena under discussion here exhibits a strict conformity to law.[42] But even if rationally laws of nature in the development of ethical phenomena in general and of economy in particular are out of the question, there still exists no doubt in the mind of anyone at home in history that regularities are actually to be observed in the development of those phenomena, even if not with the presumed strictness. Their determination—whether they are called laws of development or mere parallelisms, mere regularities of development—is a by no means unjustified task of theoretical research in the realm of human phenomena and in that of economy in particular.

There is a lack of clarity among a number of the German scholars in the field of economics about general methodological questions and especially about the problems of the theoretical sciences. Only this could lead them into the opinion that the parallelisms under discussion here in the *historical* development of economy form the exclusive, or even only the main content of theoretical economics; or in other words, that theoretical economics is "the theory of the law of development in economy" in the above suggested sense. Theoretical economics is the science of the general nature (the empirical forms) and the general connection (the laws) of economy. In contrast to this comprehensive and significant task of our science the establishment of "laws of development" in economy in the above sense of the word must appear as one that is per se by no means unjustified, but still quite secondary. It must appear as one which must by no means be neglected in theoretical research in the realm of the phenomena of human economy. But its results constitute only the least part of the content of theoretical economics, as we are taught by just a single glance at the contents of all presentations of the latter which have to some extent come into favor. Parallelisms, as we can observe them in

[42] It is one of the most one-sided features of the historical-philosophical orientation in political economy that its representatives deny on the one hand "laws of nature" in economy, and indeed partly deny "laws of economy" in general, but on the other hand acknowledge not only *laws of development* in economy in general but occasionally even seek to vindicate for the latter the character of "laws of nature." The study of history teaches any unprejudiced person that absolute regularities are by no means to be observed in the development of historical facts in general and of economic phenomena in particular. And every more mature theory of knowledge places beyond any doubt the impossibility of a rigorously typical development of phenomena of such complicated nature as the facts of "economy." The so-called laws of development in economy accordingly can certainly claim no greater strictness than other empirical laws in this sphere of the world of phenomena (cf. in this connection especially Rümelin, *Reden und Aufsätze,* II, p. 113 ff.; J. St. Mill, *Logic,* Book VI, Chap. IX, §5 conclusion and §6).

the development of prices, of ground rent, of interest on capital with various nations, are doubtless an object of theoretical research which is as justified as it is interesting. But what a methodological error it is to confuse these with the laws which teach us how supply and demand or the quantity of means of circulation influence the price of goods, how the distance of pieces of land from the market and their differential fertility influence ground rent, how the greater or lesser thriftiness or the more or less active business spirit of the inhabitants of a land influence the rate of interest in it! These are laws which after all cannot reasonably be designated *in toto* as parallelisms of the historical development of economy!

The error discussed here is not less a one than if a school of natural scientists wanted to confuse the effort to establish laws of development of the organic world or even Darwin's theory in particular with theoretical research in the realm of the organic world (physiology, etc.), even with natural research in general. It is no less an error than if they wanted to designate as "unmethodological" and "sterile" every research effort not included in the developmental orientation, or wanted to measure the results of all other orientations of natural research by this one-sided standard.[43]

It is obvious that in scientific practice the above misunderstanding does not attain full prevalence even with the most zealous representatives of the "historical-philosophical" orientation. The above conception of the task of the theoretical social sciences is too one-sided ever to have been consistently carried out in the practice of research or in the presentations of these sciences. In methodological writings and at the apex of the presentations of theoretical sciences it may still find a place. But there can be no suggestion of realizing the idea in the theory of the social sciences. After all, even those who at the apex of their presentations of economics designate it as the "philosophy of economic history" or as the science of the "parallelisms of economic history" borrow a large part of the contents of their works from the results of exact research. They really do not present parallelisms of economic history exclusively, but, and even in the main, they also present results of exact research and those results of empirical research which are not "parallelisms of economic history." In this case the practice of research corrects its theory.

The error and one-sidedness of the here characterized conception of the

[43] It really seems odd that an erudite school which calls itself "historical" seeks its main task in determining the above "laws." What an unhistorical idea it is to compare the economic history of all nations and times—not to state, for instance, the *particularity* of individual developments, but their often extremely imperfect *parallelisms!* What an "unhistorical" notion, especially, to abstract from the particularity and the inner connection of *concrete* economic developments and institutions in order to determine external parallelisms of development!

nature of political economy is not at all exhausted by the above remarks. Anyone to any extent familiar with the efforts in the field of the philosophy of history knows that the above-indicated orientation of research means only one of the numerous forms of investigation in the philosophy of history.[44] He knows that the determination of "parallelisms of economic history" or of so-called "laws of the development of economy" is thus not even identical with the historical-philosophical orientation of research in the field of economy.

Thus the conception of theoretical economics, or even of political economy, as a science of the "parallelisms of economic history," of the "laws of development in economy," and other such things, is a one-sided monstrosity. It can only be explained by the circumstance that the historical school of German economists has developed up to now without serious contact with the other orientations of research in the field of political economy. It is a living proof of the aberrations of which a scholarly group is capable when it does not have the good fortune to find serious opponents.

[44] Other orientations of research, rather different from the above, are not infrequently designated with the ambiguous expression "philosophy of history." The proof of a constant advance of the human race in its historical development (Perrault, Turgot, Leroux); the proof that the development of the human race takes place in definite epochs (Condorcet); the proof that history is the progressive realization of the idea of freedom (Michelet), an education of the human race (Lessing), a progress toward the realization of the idea of humanity (Herder); the proof that the history of individual nations shows a rising line, a peak, and a falling line of development (Bodin, Vico); the proof that the ultimate goal of all history is the formation of a state in which freedom and necessity attain harmonious union (Schelling); indeed, even the proof that French civilization is the type of human civilization in general (Guizot)—these have all been designated already as philosophy of history. These and numerous other orientations of research in the philosophy of history could also be applied in some form or other to economy. Thus, along with that science of the "parallelisms of economic history," which our German economists of the historical orientation characterize exclusively as "philosophy of economic history," we would get numerous other "philosophies of economic history." It is, however, clear that even all the above orientations of research taken together would not be equivalent to theoretical research in the realm of economic phenomena. Even when the philosophy of economic history is understood in the broadest sense of the word, the identification of it with theoretical economics still appears as a monstrous one-sidedness.

BOOK 2

CHAPTER 3

The Historical Point of View in the Practical Sciences of Economy

Economic institutions and normative laws have to be guided by the particular conditions of the nations which they serve.—Obviousness of this basic principle for all practical sciences—The acknowledgment of the above principle is not a special method of the practical sciences.—That the so-called "historical method" in the practical social sciences has contributed essentially to the confusion of opinions about the relativity of social institutions.

We pointed out above that the historical point of view in the practical sciences of economy must not be confused with that in theoretical economics. Now, after we have presented the nature of the latter, let us deal with the nature and significance of the historical point of view in the practical economic sciences. We will, however, be able to do this so much the more briefly as the differences of opinion among German economists on the question under discussion here are relatively slight. The question has to do with the relativity of social institutions and normative laws.

Now if any notion is fully valid, without doubt it is the notion that definite political regulations, laws, institutions, customs, etc., simply do not have the same justification for all times and nations, in brief, for *heterogeneous conditions*. It is obvious that a political or social institution can have been purposeful and therefore justified in the past, even if it does not have this justification today. Conversely, an institution can be justified in the present which in the past was rightfully designated as pernicious and in the future perhaps will be rightfully again so designated. The same holds true in respect to the same point of time for two countries which exhibit different political or social conditions. In general, various institutions, regulations, laws, etc., are as a rule adequate for various political and social conditions. All this is so obvious, it has been repeated so innumerably many times by writers on "politics" (and, as we will see in Book Four, has been repeated again and again for thousands of years) that only the failure of a few scholars in their remote ivory tower to recognize the validity of the above statements is the reason for the special emphasis on them.[45]

A practical science, a technology, of whatever type it may be, is not, just because of the *general nature* of the knowledge it is supposed to give us, one which could claim the same validity for all times and nations or *without considering the difference of conditions* in general. Rather, such a science is really an absurdity for anyone who has become at all clear about the nature of technologies, since rationally there can be no basic principles for human transactions without consideration of the peculiarity of conditions.

Economic policy constitutes no exception to this general character of the practical sciences. It is the science of the basic principles by which economy can be advanced. However, it is obviously just as little as any other technology a science of *universal means,* with special reference to the advancement of economy. A scholar in economic policy who takes no consideration of the conditions under which certain aims of economic policy are to be attained, who simply advises or rejects certain regulations, considers certain institutions, customs, etc., justified under all circumstances or condemns them, is comparable to a technologist who would simply set up certain mechanical operations without considering the material to be worked on. He resembles a therapist who would set up certain methods of healing without considering the pathological state of the patient; he would resemble a field marshal who would simply set up certain strategic and tactical measures as suitable, without further ado. Economic

[45] At the same time it may remain undecided whether that absolutism of solutions in the field of economic policy which we meet in individual writers does not seem, rather, to be based in fact on their ignorance of the difference of conditions or on the circumstance that they thought they were writing only for their times and for certain economic conditions. But it is not anything in a practical science which reasonably could arouse objection if a writer in the field of economic policy has predominantly, or even exclusively, the conditions of *his* country and of *his* time before his eyes and from this point of view judges customs, laws, institutions, etc., and proposes regulations. Anyone who champions practical causes, e.g., the establishment or reform of institutions—and to this category belong most of the writers on the theory of economy—naturally feels called upon only to a slight extent to bring out the merely *relative* truth of his opinions.

policy may thus be designated with entire justification as the science which teaches us maxims by which measures for advancing economy may be taken that correspond to *particular economic conditions*. Such a definition would not be incorrect. If economic policy, however, is designated simply as the science of the basic principles for advancing economy, then that is done because the above postulate of research is characteristic of all practical science and is therefore self-evident. For just as little as the directive to consider the peculiarity of conditions is necessary in the definition of technology, therapy, or strategy, just as little is this the case in "economic policy."

Accordingly we are not able to recognize any special *method* (a special way to knowledge) of economic policy in the consideration of various conditions on the part of the scholars in economic policy. Not considering the variety of conditions is a crude error in any type of research in the realm of the *practical* sciences. Taking it into consideration is nothing which would give the character of a special method to the procedure of a scholar, unless the avoidance of any type whatever of methodological mistake had to be regarded as a special method of research.

The general statements made here about the variety of economic conditions and their influence on the basic principles of economic policy hold also for the variety which nations exhibit as a consequence of the varied *development* of their economy. There is scarcely need to remark that *these* differences in the economic conditions of nations also cannot remain without influence on their economic institutions. Different economic measures, normative laws, customs, and institutions are appropriate not only for different nations, but for the same nations at different stages of economic development. All this, however, is obvious in the light of the above general basic principle of the relativity of practical knowledge. It is so obvious that special emphasis on it must appear at least superfluous. This emphasis, however, really becomes an error when a special, "historical" method of research in the realm of economic policy is recognized in the mode of thinking characterized here. It does indeed become an error when putting this method into practice is confused with putting into practice the method of the general basic principle of the relativity of practical knowledge in the economic field.

A science of economic policy which properly considered the *various stages of development* of nations would adhere very strictly to the historical point of view in *this* sense of the word. But if at the same time it failed to take into consideration the diverse economic, geographic, and ethnographic conditions of nations at the *same stage of development*, it could not be acquitted, as scarcely needs to be remarked, of the charge of "absolutism of solutions." It would be a historical science in the sense of many of our historical economists, but nonetheless one which would do only partial justice to the basic principle of the relativity of social institutions. The idea of the "historical method" in the practical social sciences put in place of the obvious basic principle of the general relativity of practical maxims is therefore not only superfluous, but really confusing.

A science of economic policy placed at the peak of methodological demands must fulfill the obvious task which is common to all practical sciences, in respect to the furthering of economy. It must teach us the basic principles by which economy can be advanced on the part of public authority, in consideration of *all* special conditions coming into account. This method is a *historical* one in the sense of our historical economists. At the same time it is one which could with equal justification be called *geographic* or *ethnographic.*

And yet, even with all these "methods," the simple notion is still to the fore that every practical science has to do justice to the diversity of conditions, whether it refers to the formation of human conditions or of organic nature, even of inorganic nature.

The efforts of our historians in the field of economy to vindicate here, too, an exclusive significance for history has contributed nothing toward clarifying the methodological problem discussed, but it has contributed essentially to its obfuscation.

BOOK THREE

The Organic Understanding of Social Phenomena

BOOK 3

CHAPTER 1

The Analogy Between Social Phenomena and Natural Organisms: Its Limits, and the Methodological Points of View for Social Research Resulting Therefrom

§1. The theory of the analogy between social phenomena and natural organisms

The normal function of organisms is conditioned by the function of their parts (organs), and these in turn are conditioned by the combination of the parts to form a higher unit, or by the normal function of the other organs.—A similar observation about social phenomena.—Organisms exhibit a purposefulness of their parts in respect to the function of the whole unit, a purposefulness which is not the result of human calculation, however.—Analogous observation about social phenomena.—The idea of an anatomical-physiological orientation of research in the realm of the social sciences results as a methodological consequence of these analogies between social structures and natural organisms.

There exists a certain similarity between natural organisms and a series of structures of social life, both in respect to their function and to their origin.

In natural organisms we can observe a complexity almost incalculable in detail, and especially a great variety of their parts (single organs). All this variety, however, is helpful in the preservation, development, and the propagation of the organisms as *units*. Each part of them has its specific function in respect to this result. The disturbance of this function, according to its intensity or the significance of the organ concerned, results in a more or less intensive disturbance of the function of the whole organism, or of the other organs. Conversely a disturbance of the connection of the organs forming a higher unit has a similar reaction on the nature and the function of the individual organs. The normal function and development of the unit of an organism are thus conditioned by those of its parts; the latter in turn are conditioned by the connection of the parts to form a higher unit; and finally the normal function and development of each single organ are conditioned by those of the remaining organs.

We can make an observation similar in many respects in reference to a series of social phenomena in general and human economy in particular. Here, too, in numerous instances, phenomena present themselves to us, the parts of which are helpful in the preservation, the normal functioning, and the development of the unit, even conditioning these. Their normal nature and normal function in turn are conditioned and influenced by the function of the unit, and in such a way that the unit cannot be imagined in its normal appearance and function without some essential part or other. Nor, conversely, can such a part be imagined in its normal nature and function when separated from the unit. It is obvious that we have here a certain analogy between the *nature and the function* of natural organisms on the one hand and social structures on the other.

The same is true with respect to the *origin* of a series of social phenomena. Natural organisms almost without exception exhibit, when closely observed, a really admirable functionality of all parts with respect to the whole, a functionality which is not, however, the result of human *calculation,* but of a *natural* process. Similarly we can observe in numerous social institutions a strikingly apparent functionality with respect to the whole. But with closer consideration they still do not prove to be the result of an *intention aimed at this purpose,* i.e., the result of an agreement of members of society or of positive legislation. They, too, present themselves to us rather as "natural" products (in a certain sense), as *unintended results of historical development.* One needs, e.g., only to think of the phenomenon of money, an institution which to so great a measure serves the welfare of society, and yet in most nations, by far, is by no means the result of an agreement directed at its establishment as a social institution, or of positive legislation, but is the unintended product of historical development. One needs only to think of law, of language, of the origin of markets, the origin of communities and of states, etc.

Now if social phenomena and natural organisms exhibit analogies with respect to their nature, their origin, and their function, it is at once clear that this fact cannot remain without influence on the method of research in the field of the social sciences in general and economics in particular.

Anatomy is the science of the empirical forms of organisms and the structure of their parts (the organs); *physiology* is the theoretical science which apprises us of the vital phenomena of organisms and the functions of their parts (organs) with respect to the preservation and development of the organisms in their totality. Now if state, society, economy, etc., are conceived of as organisms, or as structures analogous to them, the notion of following directions of research in the realm of social phenomena similar to those followed in the realm of organic nature readily suggests itself. The above analogy leads to the idea of theoretical social sciences analogous to those which are the result of theoretical research in the realm of the physico-organic world, to the conception of an *anatomy* and *physiology* of "social organisms" of state, society, economy, etc.

In the preceding discussion we have presented the basic ideas of the theory of the analogy of social phenomena and natural organisms, an analogy which, as is well known, was already drawn by Plato and Aristotle in the political sciences. We have pointed out the two factors with respect to which this analogy is acknowledged in modern scientific literature. Not that the totality of the parallelisms between the above two groups of phenomena is exhausted with this. However, we do, indeed, believe that in the foregoing we have presented the nucleus of the above theory in the form and in the sense in which it is expounded by the most careful and most reflective writers on this subject.

§2. The limits of the justification of the analogy between natural organisms and social phenomena

The analogy of social phenomena and natural organisms refers only to a part of the former, namely, to those which are the unintended product of historical development. The rest are the result of human calculation and thus are not comparable to *organisms*, but to *mechanisms*. At any rate, the above analogy is thus not universal.—Even where it comes into question, it is not an analogy that covers the entire nature of the phenomena concerned, but only certain aspects of them. In this respect it is again only a partial analogy.—Moreover, it has not come from a clear cognition of the nature of natural organisms and of social structures, but from a vague, even rather superficial feeling.

The widespread dissemination which the previously mentioned, so-called organic, way of looking at social structures in the social science literature of all nations has enjoyed is at any rate an eloquent proof that, in the two respects stressed above, a striking, even if perhaps superficial, similarity exists between social phenomena and natural organisms.

Nonetheless, only that complete prejudice of preconceived opinion which sacrifices interest in all other aspects of the objects of scientific observation for interest in particular individual aspects could fail to recognize two things:[e]

First, that only a part of social phenomena exhibit an analogy to natural organisms.

A large number of social structures are not the result of a natural process, in whatever sense this may be thought of. They are the result of a purposeful activity of humans directed toward their establishment and development (the result of the agreement of the members of society or of positive legislation). Social phenomena of this type, too, usually exhibit a purposefulness of their parts with respect to the whole. But this is not the consequence of a natural "organic" process, but *the result of human calculation which makes a multiplicity of means serve one end.* Thus we cannot properly speak of an "organic" nature or origin of these social phenomena which, even if an analogy does come into question, are not analogous to *organisms* but to *mechanisms.*[46]

Second, that the analogy between social phenomena and natural organisms, even where it comes into question according to the previous discussion, *is not a complete one, comprising all aspects of the nature of the phenomena concerned.* Rather, it is merely one which is limited to the factors stressed in the previous section, and even in this respect it is an inexact one.

This holds true first of the analogy which is supposed to exist between the two groups of phenomena under discussion here with regard to the normal nature and the normal function of the whole being conditioned by the parts and of the parts by the whole. There is a view that the parts of

[46] Not only *organisms,* but also *mechanisms,* show a purposefulness of their parts with respect to the whole, and not only in the former, but also in the latter, the normal function of the unit is conditioned by the normal condition of the parts. The organism is distinguished from the mechanism by the fact that on the one hand it is not, like the latter, a product of human calculation but of a natural process. On the other hand its individual part (each organ) is conditioned not only in its normal *function, but* also in its normal *nature* by the connection of the parts to form a higher unit (the organism in its totality) and by the normal nature of the other parts (the organs). This is by no means the case with a mechanism.

[e] The author labels only two by number, and I have accordingly changed "three" to "two" here. F.J.N.

a whole and the whole itself are mutually *cause* and *effect* simultaneously (that a *mutual causation* takes place), a view which has frequently taken root in the organic orientation of social research.[47] It is a view so vague and inadequate for our laws of thinking that we will scarcely err if we designate it as eloquent testimony that our age in many respects still lacks a deeper understanding of the nature of natural organisms as well as of that of social phenomena. The above analogy, therefore, is by no means one which is based upon a full insight into the nature of the phenomena under discussion here, but upon the vague feeling of a certain similarity of the function of natural organisms and that of a part of social structures. It is clear that an analogy of this kind cannot be a satisfactory basis for an orientation of research striving for the deepest understanding of social phenomena.

To a much greater extent this is true of the analogy which is assumed between the *origin* of the two groups of phenomena under discussion here, an analogy which has led to the greatest variety of theories about the "*organic origin*" of social phenomena. Here the inadmissibility of the analogy is obvious.

Natural organisms are composed of elements which serve the function of the unit in a thoroughly mechanical way. They are the result of purely causal processes, of the mechanical play of natural forces. The so-called social organisms, on the contrary, simply cannot be viewed and interpreted as the product of purely mechanical force effects. They are, rather, the result of human efforts, the efforts of thinking, feeling, acting human beings. Thus, if we can speak at all of an "organic origin" of social structures, or, more correctly, of a part of these, this can merely refer to one circumstance. This is that some social phenomena are the results of a *common will* directed toward their establishment (agreement, positive legislation, etc.), while others are the unintended result of human efforts aimed at attaining essentially *individual* goals (the unintended results of these). In the first case social phenomena result from the *common will* directed toward their establishment (they are its *intended* products). In the second case social phenomena come about as the unintended result of individual human efforts (pursuing *individual interests*) without a *common will* directed toward their establishment. Only this circumstance, recognized up to now only very imperfectly (but by no means, for instance, an objectively based, strict analogy to the natural organisms!), gave occasion to designate the cause of the last mentioned social phenomena (resulting *unintentionally*) as "original," "natural," or even "organic," in contrast to the cause of those mentioned first (established intentionally, by the common will).

[47] Cf. Roscher, *System*, I, §13, especially note 5.

The so-called "organic" origin of a part of social phenomena, that process of forming social structures which we designate with this expression, thus truly exhibits *essential* differences from the process to which natural organisms owe their origin. For these differences are not of the type that can also be perceived between natural organisms. The difference in the above respect turns out, rather, to be a fundamental one, like that between mechanical force and human will, between the results of mechanical force effect and purposeful activity of the individual human.

Also that part of the social structures in reference to which the analogy with natural organisms comes in question at all exhibits this analogy, therefore, only in certain respects. Even in these respects it only exhibits an analogy which must be designated in part as vague, in part really as extremely superficial and inexact.

§3. The methodological principles resulting for social research from the incompleteness of the analogy between social phenomena and natural organisms

Along with the so-called "organic" interpretation of social phenomena the pragmatic one is indispensable.—Even where the former seems adequate to the situation it can lead us only to the understanding of certain aspects of social phenomena, but not of these in their totality.—Even in respect to the former the "organic" understanding of social phenomena can still not be the result of a mechanical application to social phenomena of the methods and results of research in the realm of natural organisms. On the contrary, the so-called "organic" interpretation of social phenomena can in truth be only a specifically sociological one.—Errors into which a number of social philosophers have fallen in respect to the organic view of social phenomena.—The analogy of the two above groups of phenomena as means of *presentation.*

If the analogy between social phenomena and natural organisms were a perfect one, as is assumed on the part of a number of social philosophers, if social structures were really organisms, then this circumstance would without doubt be of decisive significance for the methodology of the social sciences. The methods of those natural sciences which are concerned with research in the organic world, anatomy and physiology in particular, would then, of course, at the same time be those of the social sciences in general and of economics in particular.

The circumstance that the above analogy refers to only a portion of social phenomena and furthermore is in respect to these a merely partial and superficial one excludes a priori the above logical consequence. The basic theoretical principles resulting from the preceding investigations are, rather, the following:

1. The so-called organic understanding of social phenomena can first and foremost be adequate for only a portion of them, in any case, namely for those which present themselves to us not as the result of agreement, of legislation, of the common will in general. *The organic view cannot be a universal means of consideration;* the organic understanding of social phenomena cannot be the universal goal of theoretical research in the field of the latter. Rather, for the understanding of social phenomena in their entirety the *pragmatic* interpretation is, in any case, just as indispensable as the "organic."

2. Even where social phenomena do not refer back to a pragmatic origin, the analogy between them and natural organisms is not a universal one comprising the totality of their nature. It is, rather, one which refers merely to certain aspects of their nature (their function and their origin), and therefore the organic interpretation per se cannot alone provide us with an all-round understanding of them. For this, rather, still other orientations of theoretical research are necessary which have no relation at all to the so-called organic view of social phenomena.

The theoretical social sciences have to present to us the general nature and the general connection of social phenomena at large and of social phenomena in particular fields (e.g., in the economic field). They fulfill this task among other ways by making us understand partial social phenomena in their meaning and function for the whole of social structures. The problem under discussion here comprises, however, the totality of the tasks of theoretical social sciences just as little as the analogous problem in the realm of natural organisms comprises the totality of the scientific tasks in the field of natural research. Even if the justification of the so-called organic orientation of research in the above sense is acknowledged, nonetheless the determination of the laws of the coexistence and succession of social phenomena *in general* remains the task of the theoretical social sciences. The determination of the laws of their reciprocal conditioning remains just a special branch of social research.

3. But even in those respects in which the analogies discussed here seem to be present when viewed superficially, they are not strict ones. Above all they are not based on a clear insight into the nature of social phenomena on the one hand and of natural organisms on the other. They accordingly cannot be the basis of a methodology of the social sciences in

general, nor even one of any special orientations of social research. The mechanical application of the methods of anatomy and of physiology to the social sciences is therefore not permissible even within the narrow limits indicated above.

The so-called "organic" interpretation could at any rate be adequate only for a part of social phenomena, and only in consideration of certain aspects of their nature. Also, in this consideration it must not simply be borrowed from the natural sciences, but must be the result of independent investigation into the nature of social phenomena and the special aims of research in the realm of the latter. The method of the social sciences in general and of political economy in particular cannot at all be a physiological or an anatomical one. But even where it is a matter of sociological problems which have a certain superficial similarity to those of physiology and anatomy, it cannot be a method simply borrowed from physiology or anatomy, but only a *sociological*[t] one in the strictest understanding of this word. The application of the results of physiological and anatomical research by analogy to political economy[48] is, however, such nonsense that no one trained methodologically would even consider it worthy of a serious refutation.

[48] Those who simply incorporate into the social sciences the results of anatomy and physiology are victims of a similar error, even if they do not do it by way of a mechanical analogy, but seek to prove a thorough, *real* analogy between natural and so-called social organisms by all kinds of synthetic and tortuous interpretations—all this in the expectation of attaining an (organic!) understanding of social phenomena in this way. Scholars of this type do not investigate the nature of social phenomena, not *their* nature and *their* origin, in order to point out occasionally single striking analogies between the above two groups of phenomena. Rather, they start with the preconceived opinion of a thoroughly *real* analogy between natural and so-called social organisms and now look for the basis of the opinion presupposed by them with maximum effort, occasionally even with the sacrifice of all scientific impartiality. This orientation of research is as valueless as the one previously characterized, with which it exhibits not only a superficial similarity but with which, in the practice of research, it even combines regularly. Cf. recently H. C. Carey, *The Unity of Law* (Philadelphia, 1872); P. v. Lilienfeld, *Gedanken über die Socialwissenschaft der Zukunft* (1875-81), V; Schäffle, *Bau und Leben des socialen Körpers. Encyclopädischer Entwurf einer realen Anatomie, Physiologie und Psychologie der menschlichen Gesellschaft, mit besonderer Rücksicht auf die Volkswirthschaft als socialen Stoffwechsel* (Tübingen, 1875-78), IV. Also his "Ueber den Begriff der Person nach Gesichtspunkten der Gesellschaftslehre," *Tübing. Zeitschrift für die ges. Staatswissenschaften* (1875), p. 183 ff.; "Der collective Kampf ums Dasein. Zum Darwinismus vom Standpunkte der Gesellschaftslehre," *ibid.* (1876), p. 89 ff. and p. 243 ff. and (1879), p. 234 ff.; "Zur Lehre von den socialen Stützorganen und ihren Functionen," *ibid.* (1878), p. 45 ff.

[t] Here and at other points Menger actually says *socialwissenschaftliche* ("social-scientific") but this has been rendered as "sociological" to eliminate the awkwardness of the alternative in English. L.S.

The above errors are obviously no different from those of a physiologist or anatomist who wants to apply the laws and methods of economics uncritically to his science or who wants to interpret the functions of the human body by the economic theories prevailing at the moment: for instance, the circulation of the blood by one of the prevailing theories of the circulation of money or the traffic in goods; digestion by one of the prevailing theories of the consumption of goods; the nervous system by a description of telegraphy; the function of the individual organs of the human body by the function of the various social classes, etc. Our physiologists and anatomists in the field of economy deserve the same reproach to which a natural scientist of the "economic orientation" would expose himself with all serious professional contemporaries. Anyone who is acquainted with the state of the natural sciences, which even today is extremely imperfect as far as they have reference to the organic world, really cannot help noticing the humor in the effort, often practiced with an expenditure of incredible ingenuity, to explain the unknown by what is not infrequently still more unknown.[49]

Thus there seems to be no doubt that play with analogies between natural organisms and social phenomena, and especially the mechanical application of research results in one realm of phenomena to sciences which are supposed to open up a theoretical understanding of other realms of the empirical world, is a methodological procedure which scarcely deserves a serious refutation. Yet I should still not like in any way to deny the value of certain analogies between natural organisms and social phenomena for certain purposes of *presentation.* Analogy in the above sense, as method of *research,* is an unscientific aberration. As means for *presentation* it still may prove useful for certain purposes and certain stages of knowledge of social phenomena. The best minds have not infrequently attempted to explain the nature of social phenomena to their contemporaries by means of comparisons with organic structures. That was particularly true in epochs in which such procedure was still more foreign to the mind of the people than in our days. It remains to be seen whether such images have not already become obsolete, at least for purposes of scientific presentation, with the present-day development of the social sciences. But they definitely are to be rejected where what is supposed to be only a means of presentation appears as a means of research and the analogy is drawn not only where it corresponds to real conditions, but really becomes

[49] Cf. Fr. J. Neumann's remarks opposed to this orientation in Schönberg's *Handbuch der Pol. Oek.,* I, p. 114 ff. and Krohn, "Beiträge zur Kentniss und Würdigung der Sociologie," *Jena'er Jahrb. f. Nation u. Statist.,* XXXV, p. 433 ff. and XXXVII, p. 1 ff.

a principle and a universal trend of research. Also for the adherents of this orientation the author of *Inquiry into the Nature and Causes of the Wealth of Nations* has an excellent word:[g] "and with whom, on that account, the analogy, which in other writers gives occasion to a few ingenious similitudes, became the great hinge upon which everything turned."[50]

[50] A. Smith: "History of Astronomy," in his *Essays on Philos. Subjects,* published by Dugald Stewart, p. 29 of the Basel edition of 1799.

[g] The actual English is taken from the 1795 edition published in London by Codell, Davies and Creech. The German of the text does not quite faithfully render this. It reads as if Smith had written "becomes with writers of the above type the hinge," and there is no German equivalent to "and with whom, on that account." F.J.N.

BOOK 3

CHAPTER 2

The Theoretical Understanding of Those Social Phenomena Which Are Not a Product of Agreement or of Positive Legislation, but Are Unintended Results of Historical Development

§1. That the acknowledgment of social phenomena as organic structures by no means excludes the striving for the exact (the atomistic) understanding of them

The theoretical understanding of *natural* organisms, too, can be twofold: an exact one (atomistic, chemical-physical) or an empirical-realistic one (collectivistic, specifically anatomical-physiological).—The exact understanding of natural organisms is not only desired in the natural sciences, but signifies an advance over the empirical-realistic understanding.—The exact understanding of social phenomena or of a part thereof can, accordingly, not be inadmissible because the phenomena concerned are viewed as so-called "social organisms."—The circumstance that the exact understanding of natural organisms and of their functions has been successful only in part up to now does not prove that this goal is unattainable in respect to the so-called social organisms.—The theory that "organisms" are indivisible units and their functions are vital expressions of these structures in their totality does not establish an objection to the exact (the atomistic!) orientation of theoretical research either in the realm of natural or of so-called social organisms.—The exact orientation of social research does not deny the real unity of social organisms; it seeks, rather, to explain their nature and origin in an exact way.—Just as little does it deny the justification for the empirical-realistic orientation of research in the realm of the above phenomena.

In the preceding chapter we dealt with the analogy between social phenomena and natural organisms, with the limits of its justification, and finally with the logical consequences resulting from this for the methodology of the social sciences. It turned out that this analogy is only a partial one and even in those respects in which it comes in question it is only a superficial one. Also, the understanding of those phenomena which do not point to a pragmatic origin, but are the result of "organic," i.e., unintended social development, can, accordingly, not be attained merely by way of analogy to natural organisms. Nor can it be attained by applying the points of view of physiology and anatomy to social research.

What remains for us now is to investigate how those problems for social research, *the solution of which is not attainable pragmatically according to the objective state of affairs* and was undertaken previously on the basis of the above analogy ("organically"), can be answered in a way adequate to the nature of social phenomena as well as to the special goals of theoretical research in the realm of the latter.

But before we go on to the examination of the pertinent problems we should like to preface this with a few remarks of a general nature.

As we saw above, all theoretical understanding of phenomena can be the result of a double orientation of research, the *empirical-realistic* and the *exact*. This is true not only in general, but for each realm of phenomena in particular. The understanding of the social phenomena which point to an unintended or, if one prefers, to an "organic" origin, *indeed, even the understanding of natural organisms themselves,* can also be sought in the two above orientations of research. Only their combination can procure for us the deepest theoretical understanding of the phenomena considered here which is attainable in our age.

With this, of course, it is not stated that both kinds of theoretical understanding are *actually* attained in all realms of phenomena similarly. Nor is it stated that they can even definitely be designated as *attainable,* considering the present state of the theoretical sciences of the organic world. However, as a postulate of research the exact understanding of phenomena stands equally justified beside the realistic-empirical understanding in all realms of phenomena, in that of "organic social structures" no less than in that of natural organisms. It is possible that the exact analysis of natural organisms will never be *completely* successful and that realistic-empirical research, at least in certain respects, will always remain indispensable to theoretical understanding. It is possible that the physical-chemical (atomistic!) understanding of them will never attain *exclusive* dominance, simply for this reason. The empirical-realistic view of the organic world is a justified one at present. Perhaps it is one which along with the atomistic one will never lose its justification.

But only a person who is completely unfamiliar with the present state of theoretical research in the realm of natural organisms could draw the conclusion that the striving for the exact (atomistic) understanding of natural organisms is in general an unjustified one, or even an unscientific one. "Physiology," says Helmholtz, "in research into life processes, had to decide to take into account that natural forces adhere to laws without exception. It had to mean business in the pursuit of physical and chemical processes which take place within the organisms." And another outstanding scholar finds that the physical-chemical understanding of organic phenomena is really a measure for the development of the theoretical sciences of the organic world.

As has been said, the exact analysis of natural organisms has been only partly successful; it will perhaps never be *completely* successful. But it would mean being blind to the advances of the exact natural sciences if one refused to recognize the great things that have been accomplished already in the above respect or the successes of "atomism" in the realm of natural organisms, or if one wanted to designate as an unscientific aberration aspiration directed toward exact understanding of the organic world.

Even those who cling to the theory of the strict analogy of social phenomena and natural organisms cannot reject the atomistic orientation of research in the field of the social sciences. On the contrary, just those people who ceaselessly speak of this analogy ought logically to share the aspiration of the natural scientist to achieve exact (atomistic!) understanding of the organic world. They should be farthest removed from a one-sided estimation of the realistic-empirical orientation of research. Accordingly, the problem with which we plan to be occupied in this chapter may simply be designated as one of the "organic" world—the fact is thereby in no way changed that the exact understanding of the above social structures and their functions is a justified aim of theoretical research along with the empirical-realistic understanding. *The acknowledgment of a number of social phenomena as "organisms" is in no way in contradiction to the aspiration for exact (atomistic!) understanding of them.*

But what is to be said of the procedure of those who, because exact understanding has been attained *only incompletely* in the realm of natural organisms, draw the conclusion that the desire for it is unjustified, even unscientific, in the realm of social phenomena, which really can be designated only figuratively as organisms? On the contrary, is it not clear that even when exact understanding of natural organisms is simply unattainable, or even inadequate in this realm of the empirical world, the same understanding would not at all be necessarily out of the question in the realm of social phenomena? Is it not clear, rather, that the question whether such understanding would be possible can never be answered except by an original investigation taking the nature of social phenomena directly into consideration? That it can never be answered by a superficial analogy?[51]

If the opinion has nonetheless found so many representatives in modern sociological literature that only the "organic" view, more correctly the "collectivist" view, is the justified one in the realm of social phenomena, or that it is the "higher" one as opposed to the exact one, the basis for this is a misunderstanding that will be refuted here briefly on account of its importance in principle.

A widespread objection to the exact solution of theoretical problems in the realm of social phenomena is derived from the circumstance that social structures, like natural organisms, are indivisible units; in respect to their parts they are higher units; their functions, however, are vital manifestations of the organic structures in their totality. Therefore the desire for an exact interpretation of their nature and their functions, the "atomistic" point of view in the theories of the organic world, means *a failure to recognize their unitary nature.*

We have already stressed that this view is by no means shared in the

[51] The ultimate elements to which the exact theoretical interpretation of natural phenomena must be reduced are "atoms" and "forces." Neither is of empirical nature. We cannot imagine "atoms" at all, and natural forces only by a representation, and by these we really understand merely unknown causes of real motions. From this there arise ultimately quite extraordinary difficulties for the exact interpretation of natural phenomena. It is otherwise in the exact social sciences. Here the human *individuals* and their *efforts,* the final elements of our analysis, are of empirical nature, and thus the exact theoretical social sciences have a great advantage over the exact natural sciences. The "limits of knowledge of nature" and the difficulties resulting from this for the theoretical understanding of natural phenomena do not really exist for exact research in the realm of social phenomena.[h] When A. Comte concéives of "societies" as real organisms and to be sure as organisms of a more complicated nature than the natural ones and designates their theoretical interpretation as the incomparably more complicated and more difficult scientific problem, he exposes himself forthwith to a serious error. His theory would be correct only as against sociologists who might get the idea, which is really insane in the light of the present state of the theoretical natural sciences, of wanting to interpret social phenomena not in a specifically sociological way, but in the atomistic way of the natural sciences.

[h] The view expressed in the last two sentences is an extremely interesting one in the history of social science. It is worth noting that Max Weber was later specifically critical of the type of "organicism" represented by Wilhelm Roscher, on the ground that it involved the view that the task of analyzing social "organisms" is more difficult than that of analyzing natural "organisms." Weber agrees with Menger that the task of the social sciences is in principle easier on account of the accessibility to them of the inner life of the individual human units of society. See Max Weber, *Gesammelte Aufsätze zur Wissenschaftslehre,* 2nd ed. (Tübingen: J. C. B. Mohr [Paul Siebeck], 1951), p. 35, footnote 1. L.S.

realm of natural research, since the exact interpretation of organic phenomena is numbered among the highest aims of modern natural research. At this point we should not like to neglect to supply the proof that this view is untenable in the field of social research, that it is, indeed, one which has an error in principle as its basis.

The sciences in their totality have the task of offering us the understanding of all realities; the theoretical sciences have especially that of offering the theoretical understanding of the real world. This, as is obvious, is also true of those theoretical sciences whose realm is the investigation of organisms. They could, however, fulfill this task only imperfectly if they were to leave unobserved the real unity of the phenomena discussed here, if they were to make us aware of these only as a juxtaposition of parts and not as a *whole,* and if they failed to make us aware of the functions of organisms as functions of organisms in their totality.

From the circumstance that organisms present themselves to us in each case as units and their functions as vital manifestations of them in their totality, it by no means follows that the exact orientation of research is in general inadequate for the realm of phenomena discussed here. It does not follow that *only* the realistic-empirical orientation of theoretical research is adequate for this group of phenomena. The actual consequence of the above circumstance for theoretical research in the realm of organisms is that it establishes a number of problems for exact research, and the solution of these cannot be avoided by exact research. These problems are the exact interpretation of the nature and origin of organisms (thought of as units) and the exact interpretation of their functions.

The exact orientation of research in the realm of the organic world does not thus deny the unity of organisms. It tries, rather, to explain the origin and the functions of these unified structures in an exact way, to explain how these "real unities" have come about and how they function.

This problem, which is one of the most advanced problems of modern natural research, is undertaken by the exact orientation of research in the realm of social phenomena also, and especially in the realm of those which are presented to us as the unintended product of historical development. Here, too, the failure to recognize the "unity" of social organisms, to the extent that it corresponds to real conditions, cannot come into question. What the exact orientation of research strives for is on the one hand the clarification of the special nature of the "unity" of those structures which are designated as social organisms. On the other, it strives for the exact explanation of their origin and their function. It does not give way to the illusion that this unity can be comprehended merely by analogy to natural organisms. Rather, it tries to establish its unified nature by direct investigation, by consideration of "social organisms." It is not content with wanting to understand the functions of the social structures discussed here by means of the above analogy. Instead, it strives for their exact understanding without any consideration of analogies, the inadmissibility of which it clarifies instead. It tries to achieve for the social sciences by direct investigation of social structures the same thing that the exact orientation of theoretical research in the realm of natural organisms strives for, the exact understanding of the so-called "social organisms" and their functions. It opposes the understanding of social structures on the basis of mere analogies, however, for *general, methodological* reasons, the same ones for which physiology, for example, had to reject the "politico-economical" understanding of human organisms as a principle of research. It rejects the opinion that theoretical problems which as yet have not been solved in the realm of natural research or which appear insoluble to our age are likewise to be characterized as insoluble a priori in the realm of social research. Rather, it investigates those problems without considering the results of physiology and anatomy, in the mere light of social structures themselves, just like physiology, which in its striving for the empirical or the exact understanding of natural organisms is not concerned with the results of social research. However, none of this is the result of the failure to recognize the unified nature of social organisms, but comes about for general methodological reasons.[51a]

The opinion that the unified nature of those social structures which are designated as "social organisms" excludes the exact (atomistic!) interpretation of them is thus a crude misunderstanding.

But in the following we will deal first with the exact understanding of "social organisms" and their functions, then with the realistic-empirical understanding of them.

§2. The various orientations of theoretical research which are the consequence of viewing social phenomena as "organic" structures

[51a] The "organic" view—more correctly, the "collectivist" view—of economy neither forms a contrast to the problems of theoretical political economy in general, nor does it comprise the totality of the tasks of the latter. It is nothing else than a part, a particular aspect of the science which teaches us to understand the phenomena of economy in theory. The acknowledgment of it is nothing which could nullify or in any way alter the concept of economics as a theoretical science. Also, the acknowledgment of the "organic" view of economy cannot change our science into either a historical or practical one, nor can it change it to a science of the mere "organic" understanding of human economy (to a mere "anatomy and physiology").

A portion of the social structures is of pragmatic origin and must thus be interpreted pragmatically.—Another portion is the unintended result of social development (of "organic" origin!) and the pragmatic interpretation of this is inadmissible.—The major problem of the theoretical interpretation of the origin of the social structures arising unintentionally ("organically").—The above problem and the most important problems of theoretical economics exhibit a close relationship. —Two other problems of the theoretical social sciences in general and of theoretical economics in particular, which come from the "organic" view of social phenomena: (a) the effort to understand the reciprocal conditioning of social phenomena; (b) the effort to understand social phenomena as functions and vital manifestations of society (or of economy, etc.) as an organic unit.—The striving for the exact (atomistic!) solution of the above problems and for the empirical-realistic (collectivistic, anatomical-physiological!) solution.—Plan of the presentation.

There are a number of social phenomena which are products of the agreement of members of society, or of positive legislation, results of the purposeful common activity of society thought of as a separate active subject. These are social phenomena, in connection with which there can properly be no thought of an "organic" origin in any admissible sense. Here the interpretation appropriate to the real state of affairs is the *pragmatic* one—the explanation of the nature and origin of social phenomena from the intentions, opinions, and available instrumentalities of human social unions or their rulers.

We interpret these phenomena *pragmatically* by investigating the aims which in the concrete case have guided the social unions, or their rulers, in the establishment and advancement of the social phenomena under discussion here. We investigate the aids which have been at their disposal in this case, the obstacles which have worked against the creation and development of those social structures, the way and manner in which the available aids were used for establishing them. We fulfill this task so much the more perfectly the more we examine the *ultimate* real aims of the active subjects on the one hand, and the most *original* means which they had at their command on the other, and the more we come to understand the social phenomena referring back to a pragmatic origin as links in a chain of regulations for the realization of the above aims. We make use of historical-pragmatic criticism of social phenomena of the above type when in each concrete case we test the real aims of the social unions or of their rulers by the needs of the social unions in question, when we test the application of the aids to social action, on the other hand, by the limitations of success (the fullest satisfaction possible of the social needs).

All this is true of those social phenomena which refer back to a pragmatic origin. Another portion of them, however, is not the result of agreement of members of society or of legislation, as we have already explained. Language, religion, law, even the state itself, and, to mention a few economic social phenomena, the phenomena of markets, of competition, of money, and numerous other social structures are already met with in epochs of history where we cannot properly speak of a purposeful activity of the community as such directed at establishing them. Nor can we speak of such activity on the part of the rulers. We are confronted here with the appearance of social institutions which to a high degree serve the welfare of society. Indeed, they are not infrequently of vital significance for the latter and yet are not the result of communal social activity. It is here that we meet a noteworthy, perhaps the most noteworthy, problem of the social sciences:

How can it be that institutions which serve the common welfare and are extremely significant for its development come into being without a common will[1] *directed toward establishing them?*

With this the problem is by no means exhausted of the theoretical interpretation of those social phenomena which do not refer back to a pragmatic origin in the above sense. There are a number of extremely significant social phenomena which are of "organic" origin in exactly the same sense as the previously characterized social structures. However, because they do not appear in their respective concrete forms as social "institutions" such as law, money, markets, etc., they cannot be grouped in common as "organic structures" and interpreted accordingly.

Here we could point to a long series of phenomena of this kind. We intend, however, to set forth the above idea by an example that is so striking that it excludes any doubt of the meaning of what we plan to present here. We mean the example of the social prices of goods. As is well known, these are in individual cases completely or at least in part the result of positive social factors, e.g., prices under the sway of tax and wage laws, etc. But as a rule these are formed and changed free of any state influence directed toward regulating them, free of any social agreement, as unintended results of social movement. The same thing holds true of interest on capital, ground rents, speculative profits, etc.

What is the nature of all the above social phenomena—this is the ques-

[1] The words "common will" (*Gemeinwellen*) appear in boldface in the original. L.S.

tion of importance for our science—and how can we arrive at a full understanding of their nature and their movement?

The remark is hardly needed that the problem of the origin of unintentionally created social structures and that of the formation of those economic phenomena that we have just mentioned exhibit an extremely close relationship. Law, language, the state, money, markets, all these social structures in their various empirical forms and in their constant change are to no small extent the unintended result of social development. The prices of goods, interest rates, ground rents, wages, and a thousand other phenomena of social life in general and of economy in particular exhibit exactly the same peculiarity. Also, understanding of them cannot be "pragmatic" in the cases considered here. It must be analogous to the understanding of unintentionally created social institutions. The solution of the most important problems of the theoretical social sciences in general and of theoretical economics in particular is thus closely connected with the question of theoretically understanding the origin and change of "organically" created social structures.

Here we must mention two more problems of the theoretical social sciences which likewise are rooted in the organic view of social phenomena.

It was already stressed above, where we talked of the analogy between natural organisms and individual structures of social life in general and of economy in particular, that the observer of the latter is struck by an aggregate of institutions. Each one of these serves the normal function of the whole, conditions and influences it, and in turn is conditioned and influenced by it in its normal nature and its normal function. Also in a number of social phenomena we meet with the appearance of the reciprocal conditioning of the whole and its normal functions and the parts, and vice versa. As a natural result of this fact we are met with a special orientation of social research which has the task of making us aware of this reciprocal conditioning of social phenomena.

In addition to the above-characterized orientation of theoretical social research another one closely related to that just presented could be designated as "organic." It is the one that tries to make us understand economic phenomena as functions, as vital manifestations of the whole of economy (the latter thought of as an organic unit!). It thus stands in a relationship, not to be discussed in any more detail, to certain problems of theoretical research in the realm of natural organisms.

All these orientations of research resulting from the organic view of society (or of economy) and the theoretical principles adequate for them can justly attract the interest of social philosophers. The empirical-realistic (the specifically physiological) orientations of research have most recently, however, been developed so comprehensively, especially in Germany, that we can properly dispense with a detailed presentation of them and confine ourselves to the *exact* interpretation of the so-called organic social structures. Thus, in the following we will deal with the striving for the exact understanding of unintentionally created social structures, both those which are commonly acknowledged to be "organisms" and those that have not had their "organic" character sufficiently stressed as yet. But we will preface the pertinent discussions with a survey of the chief attempts which have thus far been undertaken to solve the problems resulting from the organic view of social phenomena.

§3. The previous attempts to solve the problems resulting from the organic view of social phenomena

Pragmatism as a universal mode of explaining the origin and change of social phenomena.—Contradiction between it and the teaching of history.—The interpretation of the *origin* of unintentionally created social structures by characterizing them as "organic," as "original."—Aristotle's opinion.—The striving for the organic understanding of the *alterations* of social phenomena.—The conception of them as functions and vital manifestations of real social organisms (of society, of economy, etc.) in their totality.—The striving for the understanding of the reciprocal conditioning of social phenomena.—The physiological-anatomical orientation of social research.

The most obvious idea for arriving at understanding of social institutions, of their nature, and of their movement was to explain them as the result of human calculation aimed at their establishment and formation, to attribute them to agreement between people or to acts of positive legislation. This (pragmatic) approach was not adequate to real conditions and was thoroughly unhistorical. It still offered the advantage of interpreting from a common, easily understood point of view all social institutions, both those which are presented to us actually as the result of the common will of socially organized human beings and those in which such origin is not detectable. This is an advantage which will be underestimated by no one who is familiar with scientific works and knows the history of their development.

The contradiction to the facts of history in which the above merely formally satisfactory approach (stressing the exclusively *pragmatic* origin of the cause and change of social phenomena) stands brought it about nevertheless that a number of mostly meaningless attempts were undertaken in scientific investigations into the problem treated here. Along with the pragmatic, obviously one-sided mode of interpretation, and indeed, partially in direct opposition to it, there were attempts which document quite well the inadequacy of the previous "organic" views of social phenomena.

In this category belong above all the attempts of those who think that they have solved the problem involved merely by designating as "organic" the developmental process we are discussing. The process by which social structures originate without action of the common will may well be called "organic," but it must not be believed that even the smallest part of the noteworthy problem of the social sciences that we alluded to above has been solved by this image or by any mystic allusions attached to it.

Just as meaningless is another attempt to solve the problem discussed here. I mean the theory, which has attained widespread currency, that recognizes in social institutions something *original,* that is, not something that has developed, but an *original* product of the life of the people. This theory (which, incidentally, is also applied by a few of its adherents, for whom a unified principle means more than historical truth or the logic of things, by way of a peculiar mysticism to social institutions created by positive laws) indeed avoids the error of those who reduce all institutions to acts of positive common will. Still, it obviously offers us no solution of the problem discussed here, but evades it. The origin of a phenomenon is by no means explained by the assertion that it *was present from the very beginning* or that it *developed originally*. Aside from the question of the historical establishment of this theory, it involves a paradox with respect to every complicated phenomenon. Such a phenomenon must obviously have developed at some time from its simpler elements; a social phenomenon, at least in its most original form, must clearly have developed from individual factors.[52] The view here referred to is merely an analogy between the development of social institutions and that of natural organisms which is completely worthless for the purpose of solving our problem. It states, to be sure, that institutions are unintended creations of the human mind, but not *how* they came about. These attempts at interpretation are comparable to the procedure of a natural scientist who thinks he

[52] Obviously Aristotle was unfamiliar with such nonsense, no matter how often he is alluded to as the founder of the theory that the state is something "original," that it is something given with the existence of man itself. See Appendix VII: "The Opinion Ascribed to Aristotle That the State Is an Original Phenomenon Given Simultaneously with the Existence of Man."

is solving the problem of the origin of natural organisms by alluding to their "originality," "natural growth," or their "primeval nature."

The previous attempts to interpret the *changes* of social phenomena as "organic processes" are no less inadmissible than the above theories which aim to solve "organically" the problem of the *origin* of unintentionally created social structures. There is hardly need to remark that the changes of social phenomena cannot be interpreted in a social-pragmatic way, insofar as they are not the intended result of the agreement of members of society or of positive legislation, but are the unintended product of social development. But it is just as obvious that not even the slightest insight into the nature and the laws of the movement of social phenomena can be gained either by the mere allusion to the "organic" or the "primeval" character of the processes under discussion, nor even by mere analogies between these and the transformations to be observed in natural organisms. The worthlessness of the above orientation of research is so clear that we do not care to add anything to what we have already said.

If this significant problem of the social sciences is truly to be solved, this cannot be done by way of superficial and, for the most part, inadmissable analogies.[53] It can be done, in any case, only by way of direct consideration of social phenomena, not "organically," "anatomically," or "physiologically," but only in a *specifically sociological* way. The road to this, however, is *theoretical* social research, the nature and main orientations of which (the exact and the empirical-realistic) we have characterized above.

We should further like to mention an orientation of social research at this point which is likewise in the sphere of the "organic" approach to social phenomena. We mean the striving to understand their *reciprocal conditioning*. This orientation of research has at its basis the idea of a "mutual causation" of social phenomena. The value of this idea for a deeper theoretical understanding of such phenomena, as we have already stated in another place,[54] is not entirely beyond question. Nonetheless, this approach is one so close to common understanding that it justly can claim the respect of social scientists, at least as long as the exact understanding of more complicated social phenomena has not yet been gained.

It would be an error to conceive of the above approach as the only justified one or even, as many want it, "*the* method" of the social sciences. It would be just as wrong, however, voluntarily to fail to recognize its significance and its usefulness for the theoretical understanding of social phenomena in general.[55]

[53] See p. 131 ff.

[54] See p. 132 ff.

[55] It is here, too, that the works by A. Comte, H. Spencer, Schäffle, and Lilien-

The name that is applied to this orientation of research is a matter of terminology and thus without objective importance from the standpoint of methodology. But we still believe that it could, for lack of a better expression, be designated as "organic" or "physiological-anatomical," in consideration of a certain similarity, even if not a fully clarified one, to certain orientations of theoretical research in the realm of natural organisms. Only, it must be kept firmly in mind that the expressions here in question are merely symbolic and that really a specifically *sociological* orientation of theoretical research is designated by them which would have its objective justification even if sciences of natural organisms in general and anatomy and physiology in particular did not exist at all. Let the orientation be called "organic" or '"physiological-anatomical"; it really is still a branch of the empirical-realistic orientation of theoretical social research.

§4. The exact (atomistic) understanding of the origin of those social structures which are the unintended result of social development

Introduction. Course of the presentation.—(a) The *origin of money:* The phenomenon of money.—Characteristics of it.—The theory that money originated through agreement or law.—Plato, Aristotle, the jurist Paulus.—Insufficiency of this theory.—Exact explanation of the origin of money.—(b) *The origin of a number of other social institutions:* The genesis of localities, of states.—The genesis of the division of labor, of markets.—Influence of legislation.—Exact explanation of the origin of the above social structures.—(c) *Concluding remarks:* General nature of the social-pragmatic origin of social phenomena and of their so-called "organic" origin; the contrast between these.—The methods for the exact understanding of the origin of "organically" created social structures and those for the solution of the main problems of exact economics are the same.

INTRODUCTION

In the preceding section I have presented the previous attemps to solve our problem and alluded to their insufficiency. If there is

feld, which are excellent in their way, have really contributed essentially to a deepening of the theoretical understanding of social phenomena. This is furthermore the case even if we do not consider the analogies between natural organisms and structures of social life placed in the foreground of presentation by some of these authors.

to be any question of a serious solution, it must be sought in other ways than the previous ones.

But I will first present the theory of the origin of the social structures under discussion here by way of a few examples, that of the genesis of money, of states, of markets, etc., and thus by the genesis of social institutions which serve social interests to a high degree and the first origins of which in the great majority of cases can in no way be traced back to positive laws or other expressions of intentional common will.

(a) *The origin of money.*[56]

In the markets of nearly all nations which have advanced to the barter stage in their economic culture certain goods are gradually accepted in barter by everyone in return for wares brought to market. Initially, according to varying conditions, these are heads of cattle, hides, cowrie shells, cocoa beans, tea tiles, etc.; with advancing culture they are metals in the uncoined state, then in the coined state. They are, indeed, accepted even by people who have no immediate need for these goods or have already covered this need sufficiently. In a word, in trade markets certain wares emerge from the sphere of all the others and become means of barter, "money" in the broadest sense of the word. This is a phenomenon that from the beginning social philosophers have had the greatest difficulties in understanding. That in a market an item is readily turned over by its owner for another that seems more useful to him is a phenomenon which is clear to the meanest understanding. But that in a market anyone who offers goods for sale is ready to turn these over for a definite other item, that is, according to varying conditions, for cattle, cocoa beans, certain amounts by weight of copper or silver, even when he has no direct need for these goods or has completely satisfied his possible need for them, while he nevertheless rejects certain other goods under the same presupposition—this is a paradoxical procedure. It is so contradictory to the sense of the individual oriented simply to his own interest, that we must not be astonished when it seemed really mysterious even to so excellent a thinker as Savigny and its explanation by individual human interests appeared impossible to him.[57]

The problem which science has to solve here consists in the explanation of a *social* phenomenon, of a homogeneous way of acting on the part of the members of a community for which public motives are recognizable, but for which in the concrete case individual motives are hard to discern.

[56] Cf. my *Grundsätze der Volkswirthschaftslehre,* p. 250 ff., where the above theory is already presented.

[57] Savigny, *Obligat.,* II, 406.

The idea of tracing these back to an agreement or to a legislative act was fairly obvious, especially with respect to the later coin form of money. Plato thought money was "an *agreed-upon* token for barter,"[58] and Aristotle said that money came about through *agreement,* not by nature, but by *law.*[59] The jurist Paulus[60] and with few exceptions the medieval theoreticians on coined money down to the economists of our day are of a similar opinion.[61]

It would be an error to reject the opinion as wrong in principle, for history actually offers us examples that certain wares have been declared money by law. To be sure, it must not be overlooked that in most of these cases the legal stipulation demonstrably had the purpose not so much of introducing a certain item as money, but rather the acknowledgment of an item which had already become money. Nonetheless, it is certain that the institution of money, like other social institutions, can be introduced by agreement or legislation, especially when new communities are formed from the elements of an old culture, e.g., in colonies. Moreover, there is no doubt that the further development of such institutions takes place as a rule in the latter way in times of higher economic culture. Therefore the above opinion has its partial justification.

It is otherwise with the understanding of the social institution discussed here when it can by no means be historically viewed as the result of legislative activity, that is, when we see that money developed from the economic conditions of a nation without such activity, "primevally," or, as others express it, "'organically." Here the above, pragmatic approach is at any rate inadmissible, and the task of science is to make us understand the institution of money by presenting the process by which, as economic culture advances, a definite item or a number of items leaves the sphere of the remaining goods and becomes money, without express agreement of people and without legislative acts. This is to pose the question of how certain items turn into goods which are accepted by everyone in exchange for the goods offered for sale to him, even when he has no need for them.

The explanation of this phenomenon is given by the following considerations. As long as mere barter prevails in a nation economic individuals naturally first pursue one aim in their barterings. They exchange their excess only for goods for which they have an immediate need and reject those that they do not need at all or with which they are sufficiently supplied. For somebody who is bringing his excess to market to be able to get in exchange the goods he desires he must not only find somebody who

[58] *De republica,* II, 12.
[59] *Ethic. Nicom.,* V, 8.
[60] *Dig. de contr. empt.,* Lib. 1, 18, 1.
[61] Cf. the pertinent literature in my *Volkswirthschaftslehre,* p. 255 ff.

needs his wares but also somebody who offers for sale the goods desired. This is the circumstance that presents so many obstacles to traffic when pure barter prevails and limits it to the narrowest confines.

In this state of affairs itself there lay a very effective means to do away with this untoward circumstance which is such a burden on the traffic in goods. Each individual could easily observe that there was a greater demand in the market for certain wares, namely those which fitted a very general need, than there was for others. Accordingly, among the competitors for these goods he more easily found those who offered for sale certain goods desired by him than if he went to market with less marketable wares. Thus everyone in a nomadic tribe knows from his own experience that, when he brings cattle to the market, he will more easily find among the many who try to get these goods by barter those who offer the goods he wants than if he brought another item that has only a small circle of takers. Thus every individual who brought to the market items of slight marketability in the above sense had the obvious idea of exchanging them not only for the goods he needed, but also, when these were not directly available, for others. These others were ones which he, to be sure, did not need at the moment, but which were more marketable than his. By this he did not, of course, directly attain the final goal of his planned economic operation (procuring by exchange the goods *he* needed!), but he approached it essentially. The economic interest of the economic individuals, therefore, with increased knowledge of their *individual* interests, without any agreement, without legislative compulsion, *even without any consideration of public interest,* leads them to turn over their wares for more marketable ones, even if they do not need the latter for their immediate consumer needs. Among the latter, however, as is readily evident, they again select those which are most easily and most economically suited to the function of a means of barter. Thus there appears before us under the powerful influence of custom the phenomenon to be observed everywhere with advancing economic culture that a certain number of goods are accepted in exchange by everybody. These are, with respect to time and place, the most marketable, the most easily transported, the most durable, the most easily divisible. They can, therefore, be exchanged for any other item. They are goods which our predecessors called *Geld,* from *gelten,* i.e., to perform, to "pay."[j]

The great significance that *custom* has for the genesis of money is directly clear from the consideration of the just described process by which

[j] *Geld* is the German word for "money"; it is a derivative of *gelten,* which, however, means "to compensate, to atone for." F.J.N.

Compare Menger's own philological discussion of designations for money in his *Principles of Economics,* pp. 312-314. L.S.

certain goods become money. The exchange of less marketable wares for those of greater marketability, durability, divisibility, etc., is in the interest of every *single* economic individual. But the actual closing of such an exchange operation presupposes the knowledge of this interest on the part of those economic subjects who for the sake of the above characteristics are to accept in barter for their wares an item which per se is perhaps utterly useless to them. This knowledge will never arise simultaneously with all members of a national group. Rather, at first only a number of economic subjects will recognize the advantage accruing to them. This happens because they accept in exchange other more marketable wares for their own where a direct barter of their wares for useful goods is not possible or is highly uncertain. This is an advantage *which is per se se independent of the general acknowledgment of an item as money,* since such an exchange always and under all circumstances brings the economic individual considerably closer to *his* ultimate aim, the procuring of useful goods that *he* needs. But, as is well known, there is no better means to enlighten people about their economic interests than their perceiving the economic successes of those who put the right means to work for attaining them. Therefore it is also clear that nothing may have favored the genesis of money as much as the receiving of eminently marketable goods for all other goods, which had been practiced for quite a long time on the part of the most perspicacious and ablest economic subjects for their own economic advantage. Thus practice and custom have certainly contributed not a little to making the temporarily most marketable wares the ones which are received in exchange for their wares not only by many economic individuals, but ultimately by all.

Money, an institution serving the common good in the most outstanding sense of the word, can thus, as we saw, come into being legislatively, like other social institutions. But this is no more the only way than it is the most original way that money developed. This is rather to be sought in the process described above, the nature of which would be explained only imperfectly if we wanted to call it "organic," or if we wanted to designate money as something "primeval," "original," etc. It is clear, rather, that the origin of money can truly be brought to our full understanding only by our learning to understand the *social* institution discussed here as the unintended result, as the unplanned outcome of specifically *individual* efforts of members of a society.

(b) *The origin of a number of other social institutions in general and economy in particular.*

The question of the origin of a number of other social structures can be answered in a similar way. These likewise serve the common welfare, indeed, even cause it, without being regularly the result of an intention of society directed toward advancing this welfare.

The *development of new localities* takes place today only in the rarest cases because a number of people of different abilities and different professions unite with the intention of founding a locality and thereupon realize this intention by planning. To be sure, such a means of starting new settlements is not out of the question and has even been attested by experience. As a rule, however, new localities arise "unintentionally," i.e., by the mere activation of individual interests which of themselves lead to the above result furthering the common interest, i.e., without any intention really directed toward this. The first farmers who take possession of a territory, the first craftsman who settles in their midst, have as a rule only their *individual* interest in view. Likewise, the first innkeeper, the first shopkeeper, the first teacher, etc. With the increasing needs of the members of the society still other economic subjects find it advantageous to enter new professions in the gradually growing community or to practice the old ones in a more comprehensive way. Thus there gradually comes into being an economic organization which is to a high degree of benefit to the interests of the members of the community. Indeed, their normal existence finally could not be imagined without it. Yet this organization is by no means the result of the activation of the common will directed toward its establishment. This will is more likely to appear as a rule only in more advanced stages of development of communities, and it is more likely to produce, not the establishment, but the perfection of the "organically" created social structures.

A similar statement holds true for the *origin of the state*. No unprejudiced person can doubt that under favorable conditions the basis for a community capable of development can be laid by the agreement of a number of people with a territory at their disposal. Nor can it reasonably be doubted that from the natural conditions of power in the family new states capable of development could be established by individual rulers or groups of them, even without the agreement of all subjects of the new state. The theory, according to which that social structure which we call the state will simply arise "organically," is thus one-sided, at any rate. Just as erroneous, indeed to a still greater degree unhistorical, is the theory that all states originally came into being *by an agreement directed toward establishing them* or by the conscious activity of individual rulers or groups of rulers directed toward this aim. For it can scarcely be doubted that at least in the earliest epochs of human development states developed in the following way. Family heads joined by no political bond and living side by side came to have a state community and organization even if it was undeveloped at first. They did this without special agreement, merely because they progressively recognized their *individual* interests and endeavored to pursue them (by voluntary subjection of the weaker to the protection of the stronger, by the effective aid which neighbor gave to neighbor in those cases in which the latter was to be coerced under circumstances under which the remaining inhabitants of a territory also felt threatened in their welfare, etc.). Conscious agreement and power relationships of different kinds directed toward the goal of strengthening communities as such may actually have aided this process of state formation in particular cases. The correct recognition and the activation of the *individual* interests on the part of individual family heads living side by side have certainly in other cases led to state formation even without the above influences, indeed even without any consideration of the common interest by individuals. That social structure, too, which we call the state, has been the unintended result of efforts serving individual interests, at least in its most original forms.

In the same way it might be pointed out that other social institutions, language, law,[62] morals, but especially numerous institutions of economy, have come into being without any express agreement, without legislative compulsion, even without any consideration of public interest, merely through the impulse of *individual* interests and as a result of the activation of these interests. The organization of the traffic in goods in markets which recur periodically and are held in definite localities, the organization of society by separation of professions and the division of labor, trade customs, etc., are nothing but institutions which most eminently serve the interests of the common good and whose origin seems at first glance to be based necessarily on agreement or state power. They are, however, not the result of agreement, contract, law, or special consideration of the public interest by individuals, but the result of efforts serving individual interests.

It is clear that legislative compulsion not infrequently encroaches upon this "organic" developmental process and thus accelerates or modifies the results. The unintended genesis of social phenomena may factually be the exclusively decisive genesis for the first beginnings of social formation. In the course of social development the purposeful encroachment of public powers on social conditions becomes more and more evident. Along with the "organically" created institutions there go those which are the result of purposeful social action. Institutions which came about organically find

[62] See Appendix VIII: "The 'Organic' Origin of Law and the Exact Understanding Thereof."

their continuation and reorganization by means of the purposeful activity of public powers applied to social aims. The present-day system of money and markets, present-day law, the modern state, etc., offer just as many examples of institutions which are presented to us as the result of the combined effectiveness of individually and socially teleological powers, or, in other words, of "organic" and "positive" factors.

(c) *Concluding remarks.*

We might ask now about the general nature of the process to which those social phenomena owe their origin which are not the result of socially teleological factors, but are the unintended result of social movement. This is a process, which in contrast to the genesis of social phenomena by way of positive legislation, can still be designated as "organic." The answer to the above question can scarcely be in doubt any longer.

The characteristic element in the socially teleological genesis of social phenomena is in the intention of society as such directed toward establishing these phenomena, under the circumstance that they are the intended result of the common will of society, thought of as an acting subject, or of its rulers. The social phenomena of "organic" origin, on the other hand, are characterized by the fact that they present themselves to us as the unintended result of individual efforts of members of society, i.e., of efforts in pursuit of individual interests. Accordingly, in contrast to the previously characterized social structures, they are, to be sure, the unintended social result of individually teleological factors.

But in the preceding we believe we have not only presented the true nature of that process to which a large part of social phenomena owe their origin, a nature which has up to now been characterized merely by vague analogies or by meaningless phrases. We believe we have also come to another result which is important for the methodology of the social sciences.

We already alluded above to the fact that a large number of the phenomena of economy which cannot usually be viewed as "organically" created "social structures," e.g., market prices, wages, interest rates, etc., have come into existence in exactly the same way as those social institutions which we mentioned in the preceding section.[63] For they, too, as a rule are not the result of socially teleological causes, but the unintended result of innumerable efforts of economic subjects pursuing *individual* interests. The theoretical understanding of them, the theoretical understanding of their nature and their movement can thus be attained in an

[63] See p. 146 ff.

exact manner only in the same way as the understanding of the above-mentioned social structures. That is, it can be attained by reducing them to their elements, to the *individual* factors of their causation, and by investigating the laws by which the complicated phenomena of human economy under discussion here are built up from these elements. This, however, as scarcely needs saying, is that method which we have characterized above[64] as the one adequate for the exact orientation of theoretical research in the realm of social phenomena in general. The methods for the exact understanding of the origin of the "organically" created social structures and those for the solution of the main problems of exact economics are by nature identical.

[64] See p. 60 ff.

BOOK FOUR

The Development of the Idea of a Historical Treatment of Political Economy

BOOK 4

CHAPTER 1

That the Basic Notions of the Historical School of German Economists Have Long Been Known in Political Science

1.

It is an obvious thought that history is an excellent teacher for the statesman and thus also an important basis for politics, the science of the statesman. It is so obvious that it could not be left to the nineteenth century to express it. We might almost believe that the study of history has so much the greater significance for the practical statesman the poorer the development of the science we call "politics." We might almost believe that a writer on the art of government appears to be the more completely dependent on history the less his insight into the nature of state affairs is and the less his direct experience with such affairs is. Thus it is certainly nothing to be surprised at if the writers of antiquity and the Renaissance not only did not fail to recognize the importance of the study of history for science and the practice of politics, but emphasized it in innumerable variations, upon occasion even to excess.

Plato expressly emphasizes that investigations into political matters *"are not to be based* on empty theories, *but on history and actual events."*[65] This is a view which, as is well known, actually becomes a principle of research with Aristotle.[66]

With the revival of learning in the West a number of excellent writers again began to make the "art of government" the object of scientific investigation. Then, along with the writings of the ancients which had dealt directly with politics, it was the historical works of classical antiquity which understandably were the chief sources from which they drew and

[65] *De Legibus,* III, 684 and 692.
[66] *Pol.,* IV, 1.

whose significance for the "politician" they could not possibly overlook. On the one hand—this became the prevailing opinion—the "politician" would find examples written down in historical works that he could use for guidance in similar cases. On the other hand the judgment of writers on history was also of no slight value concerning historical facts. The more a nation stood out because of its deeds and successes and the more excellent the historical writer, the more useful the study of history was thought to be in respect to the science and the practice of the art of government. Therefore the history of Greece and Rome was considered especially instructive, particularly the history of their golden ages, as presented by the outstanding historians of antiquity.

N. Macchiavelli believed that in the political confusions of his time it was necessary *"ad ea remedia confugere, quae a veteribus per leges instituta et excogitata fuerunt,"* and lamented as the main reason for the collapse of the governmental conditions of his time *"quod historiarum usu legitimo destituamur nec eos fructus ex illarum lectione percipiamus, quos illae natura sua alias producere queunt."*[67]

However, even this high estimation of history by the Florentine statesman and historian did not seem sufficient to many of his contemporaries. Does not the anonymous author of the work *"De regno adversus Nic. Macchiavellum libri III"* (*Innoc. Gentiletus*) reproach his great opponent with ἀνιστορησίαν when he stresses the great value of a basic study of history for the writer on politics, and does he not show the intention of wanting to be more historical than his opponent?[68]

To no less a degree J. Bodin is convinced of the importance of the study of history, for the politician, the statesman, and the lawgiver.

"Cum historia," he writes, *"laudatores habeat complures, qui veris eam ac propriis laudibus exornarunt, ex omnibus tamen nemo verius ac melius, quam qui vitae magistram appellavit; nam ea vox omnes omnium virtutum ac disciplinarum utilitates amplexa, significat, hominum* vitam universam ad sacras historiae leges . . . dirigi oportere . . . *ex quibus (historiis) non solum praesentia commode explicantur, sed etiam futura colliguntur certissimaque rerum expetendarum ac fugiendarum praecepta conflantur."*[69]

And in another place: *"Nec tamen Rempublicam idearum sola notione terminare decrevimus, qualem Plato, qualem etiam Thomas Maurus inani opinione sibi finxerunt: sed optimas quasque civitatum florentissimarum leges, quantum quidem fieri poterit, proxime consequemur."*[70]

[67] *Disputationum de Republica* (Lugd. Bat., 1643), Lib. I, Proëm. fol. 7 ff.
[68] (Lugd. Bat., 1647), Lib. I, Praef. p. 3 ff.
[69] *De Methodo* (Argent., 1627), Proëm. p. 1 et Praef. fol. 6.
[70] *De Republica* (1591), Lib. I, Cap. I, p. 4.

Even Bacon is no exception to this. After all, he characterizes history as the repertory of models of the past, as *"fundamentum prudentiae civilis,"* and even justifies his ability to deal with politics expressly by his historical studies.[71]

2.

The idea must early have struck the reflective political writers *of comparing all state constitutions and laws and thus arriving at a science of the constitution and legislation of states, that is, at a "politics" on a thoroughly historical basis.* If history is the teacher, and, as assumed, the best teacher of statesmen, what notion was more obvious than to establish a science of politics by comparing state institutions and their results in various nations? In fact, Plato already expressed this notion and thus set up a problem which Aristotle attempted to solve in a certain sense. And a J. Bodin marked its solution as the most important task of his life. He says of the politicians of his time:

"Legissent Platonem qui legum tradendarum ac moderandae civitatis unam esse formam putavit, si omnibus omnium aut magis illustrium rerum publicarum legibus in unum collectis viri prudentes eas inter se compararent atque optimum genus ex eis conflarent. *Ad hoc igitur institutum omnia mea studia, omnes contuli cogitationes."*[72]

Macchiavelli already expresses the same thought. He says: *"Vetus dictum est quod ut sapientissime pronunciatur, ita diligenter observari debet: Res futuras ex contemplatione praeteritarum conjici cognoscique posse.* Quaecunque enim per universum orbem fiunt, habuerunt olim aliquid simile, *quod eodem modo antiquitus et ex iisdem causis ut haec quae nunc videmus factum fuit . . . Eo magis etiam videris, ex praeteritis futurarum rerum eventus posse conjicere."*[73]

Prof. Nic. Stupanus of Basel (1599) expresses himself similarly in the dedication to his edition of Macchiavelli's *Prince:*

"Non faciunt sapientes Reipublicae gubernatores omnia, quae ab aliis facta esse in historiis perhibentur; sed propterea historiarum lectioni diligentissime incumbunt eorum optimi quique, ut insignem rerum praeteritarum cognitionem nacti, ceu rebus illis, quos legerunt, gerendis interfuissent, deinde in capiendis novis consiliis et rerum agendarum deliberatione Causas, Consilia, Progressus, Eventusque praeteritarum rerum promptos in animo habeant, praesentia exempla cum praeteritis, domes-

[71] *De augm. scient.*, Lib. II, Cap. V, *pass.* et Lib. VIII, Cap. III, §1.

[72] J. Bodini, *De Methodo ad historiarum cognitionem, 1566* (Argentorati, 1627), Praef. p. 3.

[73] *Disput. de Republica* (Lugd. Bat., 1643), Lib. III, Cap. XLIII, p. 410 ff. Conf. Lib. I, Cap. XXXIX, p. 115.

tica cum peregrinis, similia cum similibus, contraria cum contrariis ubique possint conferre et ex praeteritis futurarum rerum eventus praevidere. *Quae si ita se habere omnes intelligimus.*"[74]

3.

The same constitution and legislation is not adequate for all nations and times. Rather, each nation and each age needs particular laws and state institutions corresponding to its own character. These ideas, too, were not so recondite that writers of the nineteenth century had to be the first to establish them. That nations are not completely alike and that it is dangerous to apply uncritically the state constitutions and laws of one nation to another was known both to the ancients and to the writers of the Renaissance.

Plato stresses that the geographical location of a country is of no slight influence on the nature of its people and that legislation must not neglect to take this fact into consideration. The lawgiver, he says, must keep his eyes open for all differences of this kind and he must try to examine them, as far as is humanly possible, before he undertakes to devise laws.[75]

And in another place:

"It is hardly possible that any definite political institution can be preserved uncontested in practice as in theory. This seems, rather, to be just as impossible as to prescribe for each body *one* definite way of living in which one and the same thing would not prove harmful to it at one time and useful at another."[76]

Aristotle emphasizes no less decisively the relativity of political institutions. "Politics," he says, "has not merely to examine the per se most desirable constitution or government most desirable in itself but also the one which under certain circumstances is the most suitable, which is best adapted to these circumstances. It is the duty of the politician to examine every state and its institutions as they really are, and to investigate the peculiarity of its institutions. He must be acquainted with the real state of affairs before he can go ahead to improve them."[77]

[74] (Montsibelgardi, 1599), p. 1 ff.

[75] *De Legibus,* V, 747.

[76] *Ibid.,* I, 636. Plato goes so far in considering the individuality of social and political conditions that he even declares it an absurdity to want to limit a far-sighted statesman by laws. For these, since they are general, never are fully fitted to the peculiarity of individual people and situations, and especially, since they are fixed, they could never keep pace with *changing conditions.* Only where the true art of government is lacking, it is, to be sure, better to stick to laws (which are tested by experience!) than to follow the selfish and irrational pleasure of the rulers.

[77] *Pol.,* IV, 1.

N. Macchiavelli also is not unfamiliar with the spatial and temporal relativity of political institutions. He writes:

"Sicuti diversae causae esse solent, quibus urbium fundamenta ponuntur, ita quoque diversae ipsis rationes legum et institutorum existere consueverunt."[78]

And in another place: *"Qui cupit vel rempublicam vel sectam suam diuturnam esse, eam saepe corrigere debet et veluti ad prima sua principia revocare . . . praecipue sunt respublicae atque sectae, quibus salutares sunt illae mutationes, per quas corriguntur, emendantur et ad primam suam originem principiumque revocantur."*[79]

J. Bodinus expresses himself quite in detail on the relativity of political institutions. In his *Republic* he writes a separate chapter: *"De conformando civitatum statu pro regionum ac populorum varietate, quibusque disciplinis populorum mores dissimilesque naturae percipiantur."*[80]

He further expresses himself as follows: *"In toto genere animantium non modo innumerabiles sunt figurae, verumetiam earum, quae figuram eandem habent, maxima varietas est; sic hominum inter se admirabilis est ac pene incredibilis dissimilitudo variaque pro locorum diversitate natura,"* and he accordingly sets himself the task:

"explicare, quae quibus populis leges congruant, quis cuique civitati status conveniat, quibusque rationibus gentium mores ac naturae percipiantur: ne aut formam civitatis a populi moribus alienam instituamus, aut naturae leges hominum arbitrio ac voluntati, repugnante natura, servire cogamus; quod plerique facere conati florentissima imperia funditus everterunt."[81]

And in other places: *"Principem ac legislatorem populi mores ac naturam regionis, in qua civitas est, nosse prius oportet, quam legum aut civitatis conversionem moliatur: cum de omnibus rerumpublicarum arcanis mullum majus sit, quam* ad varios gentium mores ac naturas civitatis cujusque leges ac formam congruentem accommodare."

"Peccatur ab iis, qui ab alienis civitatibus leges acceptas ad eam quae plane contraria ratione dirigatur rempublicam adhiberi putant oportere."[82]

4.

This insight, so clearly expressed by such prominent writers, into the significance of the study of history for the politician and the rela-

[78] *Disput.* (1643), Lib. I, Cap. II, p. 13.
[79] *Ibid.*, Lib. III, Cap. 1, p. 283.
[80] *De Rep.* (1591), Lib. V, Cap. 1, p. 750.
[81] *De Rep.* (1591), Lib. V, Cap. 1, p. 750.
[82] *Ibid.*, Lib. V, Cap. 1, p. 754 and Lib. IV, Cap. 3, p. 663.

tivity of political institutions has never again been completely lost, as we probably do not need to say, neither in general nor in respect to a particular branch of the political sciences. Even the writers of the Age of Enlightenment in France have been quite especially charged with lack of historical sense and the tendency toward "absolutism" in politics. Yet they by no means fail to recognize as fully as the historical school of German economists assumes the significance of the study of history for the statesman and the principle of the merely relative justification of political institutions.[83]

To be sure, historical studies could not gain for the social philosophers of the Enlightenment in general and the physiocrats in particular the significance which historians and even philosophers of history were inclined to attribute to them. Anyone who attacks existing institutions and is in favor of a new order of things understandably does not feel the call to investigate their historic origin and to follow their development with loving care. His first task is to show their harmfulness in respect to the present. Just as little can it reasonably be expected of writers who represent the intellectual movement of the French Revolution in the field of economy to emphasize the possible *former justification* of the institutions they are attacking. Nor can they be expected to emphasize the justification, which is only *relative* in respect to spatial and temporal conditions, of the institutions they are advocating. Such a thing is contrary to the practical-reformatory task of the physiocrats. It would mean, however, failure to recognize the significance of these writers who were under the recent impression of Voltaire's *Philosophy of History* or Montesquieu's *Spirit of Laws,* if one wanted to conclude from their not doing this that they had in general misunderstood the significance of the study of history for political science. One should not believe for this reason that they were in principle of the opinion that the same institutions which they recommended for France of the eighteenth century were suitable for all other nations and times, thus e.g., for the Tungus and the Kalmucks or the France of St. Louis.

Truly, only ignorance could assert that even A. Smith had not recognized the significance of the study of history for our science and the influence of spatial and temporal conditions on economic institutions.

The same thing holds true of A. Smith in his relation to the physiocrats that an excellent writer on the historical development of Greek philosophy

[83] *Quelles sont, suivant le temps, les lieux et les circonstances, les conclusions justement et clairement deduites de l'ordre politique?* This question turns up again and again in the writings of individual physiocrats (*Ephémérides du citoyen.* Program article by Baudeau [Paris, 1767], I, p. 5 ff.).

says of Aristotle in contrast to Plato. He says that the former was not only a splendid speculative thinker like the latter, but was also an indefatigable observer, that he had given his system a broad supporting basis of knowledge based on experience and had tried to establish his philosophical theses by an all-round consideration of actual data.

The gifted Sismondi remarks very correctly concerning the author of the *Inquiry into the Nature and Causes of the Wealth of Nations:*

"Adam Smith reconnut que la science du gouvernement ne pouvait se fonder que sur l'histoire des peuples divers et que c'était seulement d'une observation judicieuse des faits qu'on pouvait deduire les principes. Son immortel ouvrage, 'De la nature et des causes de la richesse des nations' . . . est en effet le resultat d'une étude philosophique de l'histoire du genre humain."[84]

Another thorough-going scholar, E. Baumstark, expresses himself on this as follows:

"The political part of our science particularly needs a *historical basis,* for without this it will go dangerously astray. With this I do not mean that a meager historical introduction be given with each doctrine. I mean, rather, that all of economics in its connections be placed upon historical bases instead of upon mere dogma and be developed as a result of research into the history of commerce, of culture, of the state, and of humanity in general. What vigor A. Smith and Ferguson have breathed into their immortal works in this way!"[85]

One may think as always about the results attained by A. Smith, one may declare them as ever so imperfect, yet one thing at any rate is refuted by the above two characterizations of Smith's work by two real experts on it. (That they are experts deserves special emphasis today when so many things are "read" but not much is read.) The refutation is better than any accumulation of citations from A. Smith's writings could be. It is refutation of the charge, which not even the founder of our science was spared, of underestimating the value of historical study for our science and of unhistorical absolutism in the previously mentioned meaning of the word.

Among A. Smith's followers Sismondi in particular emphasizes the study of history as the basis of research in the field of political economy and the idea of the relativity of all political institutions. He says:

"Ce n'est pas sur des calculs arides qu'elle (la science d'écon. pol.) est fondée, ce n'est pas non plus sur un enchaînement mathématique de

[84] Sismondi, *Nouv. Princ.* (Paris, 1827), I, p. 47 ff.

[85] Baumstark, *Kameralistische Encyclopädie* (Heidelberg, 1835), p. viii ff.

théorèmes déduits, d'axiomes obscurs, donnés pour des vérités incontestables. . . . L'économie politique est fondée sur l'étude de l'homme et des hommes; il faut connaître la nature humaine, l'état et le sort des sociétés en différents temps et en différents lieux, il faut consulter les historiens et les voyageurs etc. Une pareille étude . . . c'est la philosophie de l'histoire et des voyages."[86]

And in another place: *"On est tombé dans de graves erreurs, pour avoir toujours voulu généraliser tout ce qui rapporte aux sciences sociales . . . Il faut s'attacher tantôt à un temps, tantôt à un pays, tantôt à une profession, pour voir bien ce qu'est l'homme et comment les institutions agissent sur lui. Ceux au contraire qui l'ont voulu voir isolé du monde, ou plutôt qui ont considéré abstraitement les modifications de son existence, sont toujours arrivés à des conclusions démenties par l'experience."*[87]

We refrain from citing the long list of German writers, who obviously as a result of stimulation such as this have stressed the importance of history for political economy (its importance as a means for understanding the present and as an empirical basis for social research!). They have also stressed the relativity of economic institutions and laws, and were doing both in the first three decades of our century, that is, long before the founding of the "historical school of economists in Germany."[88] After all, it is more than sufficiently clear from the passages cited above, which, it scarcely needs be noted, could be increased and complemented without any trouble, that the principles under discussion here were never completely foreign either to the social sciences in general or—since it was established as a separate science—to political economy in particular. There has been no epoch in the development of our science when the leading principles of the historical school of German economists have not

[86] Sismondi, *De la Richesse commerciale* (Genève, 1803), I, p. xiv ff.; Storch, *Cours d'E. P.* (Paris, 1823), I, p. 36.

[87] Sismondi, *Etudes sur l'E. P.* (Paris, 1837), I, p. iv.

[88] Cf. especially K. H. Rau, *Lehrbuch der politischen Oekonomie* (Heidelberg, 1826), I, §18; G. F. Krause, *Versuch eines Systems der National- und Staatsökonomie mit vorzüglicher Berücksichtigung Deutschlands, aus dem Gang der Völkercultur etc. entwickelt* (Leipzig, 1830), II, p. vi; E. Baumstark, *Kameralistische Encyclopädie* (Heidelberg, 1835), p. iv ff. (where the author very decidedly attacks the derivation of economic principles from definitions instead of from history and life, and emphasizes the necessity of placing all of the theory of public economy in its historical connection on historical bases instead of on mere dogmatism, and of developing it as the result of research on the history of commerce, culture, the state, and humanity in general); J. Schön, *Die Staatswissenschaft, geschichtsphilosophisch begründet,* 1st ed. (Breslau, 1831), 2nd ed. (1840). (My work—says the author—is concerned with the task of letting politics shine forth as a philosophy of political history and to develop historical social laws in place of scattered rules, p. vii of the 2nd ed.).

been expressed in excellent writings of world-famous authors known and accessible to every educated person even today. There was truly no need of the discovery of the above truths in the middle of the nineteenth century or even of the establishment of a special school for their dissemination.

BOOK 4

CHAPTER 2

The Historical School of German Economists Has Failed to Recognize the Decisive Reform Thought of the Historical School of Jurists and Only Through Misunderstanding Considers Itself a Historical School in the Sense of the Latter

1.

What Adam Smith and even those of his followers who have most successfully developed political economy can actually be charged with is not the failure to recognize the obvious significance of the study of history for the politician. Nor is it failure to recognize the just as obvious principle that various economic institutions and governmental measures correspond to various temporal and spatial conditions of economy. It is their defective understanding of the unintentionally created social institutions and their significance for economy. It is the opinion appearing chiefly in their writings that the institutions of economy are always the intended product of the common will of society as such, results of expressed agreement of members of society or of positive legislation. In this one-sidedly pragmatic view of the nature of social institutions, the sphere of ideas of A. Smith and his closest followers comes into contact with that of the writers of the French Age of Enlightenment in general and of the French physiocrats in particular. Adam Smith, also, and his school predominantly strive for the *pragmatic* understanding of economy, even where such understanding is not adequate for the objective state of affairs. The result is that the broad realm of unintentionally created social structures remains closed to their theoretical comprehension.

This one-sidedness and these defects in the view of problems of economic policy on the part of A. Smith and his followers offered enough points of attack for a scientific reaction. However, one did not make itself felt in the field of political economy, at least not decisively. The scientific opponents of Smith attacked single theories and views of his, but not the above error in principle. And they could not keep the pragmatism of his theory from gradually attaining uncontested sway.

A reaction of a more principled nature was not to develop against Smith's theories from the ranks of the economists, but was to take place late enough through mechanical application of ideas and methods from other related fields of knowledge to economic policy. This was a process in which, moreover, many sorts of misunderstanding played no slight role.

2.

Pragmatism in the views of the nature and origin of middle-class society and its institutions has found outstanding opponents first in the field of constitutional law.

Burke was probably the first,[89] who, trained for it by the spirit of English jurisprudence, emphasized with full awareness the significance of the organic structures of social life and the partly unintended origin of these. He taught most convincingly that numerous institutions of his country, which were to a high degree of common benefit and filled every Briton with pride, were not the result of positive legislation or of the conscious common will of society directed toward establishing this, but the unintended result of historical development. He first taught that what existed and had stood the test, what had developed historically, was again to be respected, in contrast to the projects of immature desire for innovation. Herewith he made the first breach in the one-sided rationalism and pragmatism of the Anglo-French Age of Enlightenment.[90]

[89] Montesquieu already expresses the opinion that social and state institutions in their concrete form are not simply the result of arbitrary statutes (of positive legislation), but rather the consequence of natural and cultural conditions and of the historical evolution of nations: *"Les êtres particuliers intelligents*—he says *—peuvent avoir des lois qu'ils ont faites; mais ils en ont aussi qu'ils n'ont pas faites. . . . Avant qu'il y eût des lois faites, il y avait des rapports de justice possible. Dire qu'il n'y a rien de juste ni d'injuste que ce qu'ordonnent ou défendent les lois positives, c'est dire qu'avant qu'on eût tracé de cercle tous les rayons n'étaient pas égaux" (De l'esprit des lois* [1748] Liv. I, Chap. I). *"J'ai d'abord examiné les hommes, et j'ai cru que, dans cette infinie diversité de lois et de moeurs, ils n'étaient pas uniquement conduits par leurs fantaisies. J'ai posé les principes, et j'ai vu les cas particuliers s'y plier comme d'eux-mêmes, les histoires de toutes les nations n'en être que les suites et chaque loi particulière liée avec une autre loi ou dépendre d'une autre plus générale" (Ibid.,* pref.).

[90] Burke stresses the organic, *unintended genesis of English constitutional law* in the following way: *"From magna charta to the declaration of right, it has been*

3.

Burke's ideas became in Germany first of all the occasion for an attack on pragmatism in jurisprudence, which had one-sidedly come into play both in the treatment of positive law and in the philosophy of law. Hugo had also paved the way for the reaction against the pragmatic orientation by his studies in the field of the history of law. Savigny and Niebuhr with full awareness of the task took their places at the head of the movement. For them law is thought of only as a special aspect of the life of the people as a unit, inseparably connected with all its other aspects and expressions. For them law, like language, is at least originally not the product in general of an activity of public authorities aimed at pro-

---

the uniform policy of our constitution to claim and assert our liberties as an entailed inheritance derived to us from our forefathers, and to be transmitted to our posterity. . . . This policy appears to me to be the result of profound reflection, or rather the happy effect of following nature, which is wisdom without reflection and above it" (*Reflections on the Revol. in France. Works* [London, 1792], III, 58 ff.). One-sided rationalism he attacks with the following words, "*I cannot stand forward and give praise or blame to anything which relates to human actions and human concerns, on a simple view of the object, as it stands stripped of every relation, in all the nakedness and solitude of metaphysical abstraction. Circumstances (which with some gentlemen pass for nothing) give in reality to every political principle its distinguishing colour and discriminating effect. The circumstances are what render every political scheme beneficial or noxious to mankind*" (*Ibid.*, III, p. 28). And in another place: "*Old establishments are tried by their effects. If the people are happy, united, wealthy and powerful, we presume the rest. We conclude that to be good, from whence good is derived. In old establishments various correctives have been found for their aberrations from theory. Indeed they are the results of various necessities and experiences. They are not often constructed after any theory; theories are rather drawn from them. In them we often see the end best obtained, where the means seem not perfectly reconcileable to what we may fancy was the original scheme. The means taught by experience may be better suited to political ends than those contrived in the original project. They again react upon the primitive constitution and sometimes improve the design itself from which they seem to have departed*" (*Reflect. on the Revol. in France. Works*, III, 227 ff.). Necker writes in the same sense: "*On a consideré les principes comme une spiritualité qui trouvait place partout, et l'on n'a pas fait attention, que les conséquences de ces principes tenaient un espace réel. Les abstractions, sans doute, ont une application universelle, c'est un large compas qui s'ouvre à volonté et qui réunit figurativement les divers points de l'étendue; mais tout se touche en pratique, tout se meut terre à terre, et c'est alors qu'on fait l'épreuve des obstacles franchis en spéculation et des nombreuses difficultés dedaignées par la théorie*" (*Du pouvoir exécutif dans les grands états* [1792], s. 1. II, p. 72). Le Maistre's tracing back the existing authorities or rather the prerevolutionary authorities to divine appointment and Haller's conception of political powers from the point of view of properly obtained private rights likewise have a counter-revolutionary purpose. They nevertheless are so clearly based on false presuppositions that they can scarcely be considered beside Burke's expositions, which have an objective foundation, even if they are one-sided.

ducing it, nor in particular is it the product of positive legislation. It is, instead, the unintended result of a higher wisdom, of the historical development of the nations. Indeed, they deny to the pure abstract understanding either the competence for or—with special reference to their own time—the task of comprehensive construction of the law. The *further development* of law, too, they say, like that of language,[91] does not occur by arbitrary intention, but organically, by inner historical necessity, even if in the course of cultural development and for a variety of reasons legislation does enter in beneficially. Even in the latter case the lawgiver is to be regarded only as a representative of the people, as the representative of the true spirit of the people, and the continuity of law is to be respected by him.[92]

The essence of the school of jurists started by Savigny and Niebuhr[93]

[91] Wilhelm von Humboldt's writings have paved the way in Germany for similar efforts in the field of linguistics. He traced back the formation of language to a direct creative instinct, to an intellectual linguistic instinct of the human mind, and recognized in its structure a regularity which is analogous to that of organic nature. Savigny *(Vom Berufe unserer Zeit* [1814], p. 9) and his followers frequently appeal to the analogy of the genesis of law and language formation. Something similar is also found later in the economists of the historical school, especially in Hildebrand (cf. in this connection especially Humboldt, *Ueber die Verschiedenheit des menschlichen Sprachbaues und ihren Einfluss auf die geistige Entwickelung des Menschengeschlechtes* [Berlin, 1836]; Schasler's *Elemente der philos. Sprachwissenschaft W. v. Humboldt's* [Berlin, 1847], and Steinthal's *Der Ursprung der Sprache im Zusammenhange mit den letzten Fragen alles Wissens* [Berlin, 1852]).

[92] Cf. Savigny's three works, *Ueber den Beruf unserer Zeit zur Gesetzgebung* (Heidelberg, 1814), pp. 8-15, *Programmaufsatz* in the *Zeitschrift für geschichtliche Rechtswissenschaft* (1815), I, pp. 1-17 and III, pp. 1-52, *System,* I, pp. 13-21, 34-57; Eichhorn, *Deutsche Staats- und Rechtsgeschichte* (1808), preface and introduction, p. 1 ff. Of older writers cf. especially Hugo, *Encyclopädie,* 4th ed., §§21, 22, and *Naturrecht,* 1st ed. (1798), 3.A., §130, and in the *Civilistischen Magazin* (1813), IV, pp. 117-136. J. Möser is mentioned most honorably by Savigny in his *Beruf* (1st ed., p. 15) along with Hugo: "High honor is also due to the memory of J. Möser, who with magnificent intelligence tried to interpret history everywhere, often even in respect to civil law." Schelling's theory of the organic nature of political life has not been without influence on the development of the historical school of jurists. This is also true of his theory that the original development in all cultural realms is a subconscious one and that in general everything conscious has its presupposition and basis in a *subconscious* working of the human mind and the mind of the nation. *Plato,* moreover, has already said in a place (*Leges,* IV, 4) which as far as I know has remained unnoticed that no human being could (arbitrarily) create any law. All legal institutions, rather, were produced by many chance happenings and circumstances. . . . No mortal could make a law; all mortal dispositions are, rather, the result of conditions. To be sure, it would reasonably have to be granted that human ability is joined to this (cf. the passage from Montesquieu quoted on p. 173).

[93] "The essence of the historical school of jurists is a view of the *genesis* of law. Law is one aspect of the total life of a nation, inseparably connected with its other aspects and activities, like language, custom, art. Therefore, like these

is to be found in these views analogous to Burke's point of view in the field of state law, in contrast to pragmatism and rationalism in the field of jurisprudence, but not, for instance, in the principle of the relativity of law[94] nor in the significance, stressed long ago by French jurists, of historical studies for the understanding of law.

In what way now have the founders of the historical school of German economists realized their expressed intention of applying the basic thought of this school of jurists to political economy?

Adam Smith and his followers had by no means failed to recognize the significance of the study of history for political economy and the relativity of social institutions and their necessary differences (according to differences of temporary and local conditions). What they can justly be charged with, as already stated, is their pragmatism, which in the main had only an

---

it comes into being originally not by choice and reflection, but by an inherent sense and instinct, by a consciousness of necessity. . . . The basic doctrines of the historical school are accordingly: the involvement of law with the nation and national consciousness, its originally unintended genesis, the requirement of continuity in its further development" (Stahl, *Geschichte der Rechtsphilosophie,* 3rd ed. [Heidelberg, 1856], p. 572 ff.). Since the founding of the historical school the knowledge has again been gained that "law is not merely something presented from above," "but has grown out of the spirit of the nation, as its form." It is not something arbitrary that could be this way today and that way tomorrow. On the contrary, the past is closely connected with the present and future. It is not the result of chance, but of inner determination. "*This insight into the nature of positive law is the sole thing characteristic* for the historical school. Only from this point of view are its accomplishments to be judged, as well as the transformation which jurisprudence has since then undergone through them." (Thus Bluntschli, *Die neueren Rechtsschulen der deutschen Juristen,* 2nd ed. [Zürich, 1862], p. 18.) E. Kuntze characterizes the basic thought of the historical school of law by noting that "law was not devised, but was born; it is not a consciously arbitrary production of finite, limited understanding, but joined to the laws of all organic genesis and growth" (*Der Wendepunkt in der Rechtswissenschaft* [Leipzig, 1856], p. 53).

[94] How little the previously characterized mental sphere of the historical school of German economists agrees with that of Burke-Savigny can already be gathered from the fact that the representatives of the latter orientation designate it as an error that a state institution is excellent just because it suits the nature of the land and the people for which it is destined (cf. Gentz, *Politische Abhandlungen zu Burke's Betrachtungen über die französische Revolution* [Hohenzollern, 1794], II, p. 244). This emerges even more clearly from the battle which Savigny and Thibaut fought over the establishment of new law codes in Germany. The latter stresses ceaselessly that the civilian institutions are to be ordered *completely according to the needs of the subjects,* that they must in particular *correspond to the needs of the times (Ueber die Nothwendigkeit eines allgemeinen bürgerlichen Rechtes für Deutschland, Civilistiche Abhandlungen* (1814), p. 404 ff.). Nonetheless Savigny attacks him in his famous book *Vom Berufe unserer Zeit für Gesetzgebung und Rechtswissenschaft* because Thibaut did not recognize the organic genesis and development of law and thought that all law resulted from statutes, from express orders and prohibitions of legislative authority.

understanding for *positive* creations of public authorities. It, therefore, did not know how to value the significance of "organic" social structures for society in general and economy in particular and therefore was nowhere concerned to *preserve* them. What characterizes the theories of A. Smith and his followers is the one-sided rationalistic liberalism, the not infrequently impetuous effort to do away with what exists, with what is not always sufficiently understood, the just as impetuous urge to create something new in the realm of political institutions—often enough without sufficient knowledge and experience.

The organically developed institutions of economy had usually cared so wisely for the living, for things already existing, for what was close and immediate. Pragmatism in economy was concerned about the welfare of man in the abstract, about remote things, about things which did not yet exist, about future things. In this effort it only all too often overlooked the living, justified interests of the present.

Against these efforts of the Smithian school there was revealed to our science a vast realm of fruitful activity in the sense of the orientation of Burke-Savigny—not in the sense of simply maintaining what had organically developed as unassailable, as if it were the higher wisdom in human affairs as opposed to the intended ordering of social conditions. The aim of the efforts under discussion here had to be, on the contrary, the full understanding of existing social institutions in general and of organically created institutions in particular, the retention of what had proved its worth against the one-sidedly rationalistic mania for innovation in the field of economy. The object was to prevent the dissolution of the organically developed economy by means of a partially superficial pragmatism, a pragmatism that contrary to the intention of its representatives inexorably leads to socialism.

However, scarcely a trace of all that is found in the writings of the historical school of economists that arose in Germany in the 1840's—a belated straggler among the "historical" schools in other fields of the political sciences. And therefore it wrongly points to the historical school of jurists as its model; only wrongly does it call itself "historical" in the sense of the school of Burke and Savigny. It does not share the virtues of the latter, nor, to be sure, the one-sidedness and shortcomings. It has its own virtues, its very special one-sidedness, misunderstandings, and errors. As far as it has come to light in the works of its spokesmen, it is *essentially different* from the school treated above. It is, to be sure, *historical,* but in an entirely different sense from that of Burke-Savigny.

BOOK 4

CHAPTER 3

The Origin and Development of the Historical School of German Economists

1.

The historical school of German economists did not start from Burke and Savigny, nor from Niebuhr and W. v. Humboldt. It is really rooted mainly in the efforts of those German historians who toward the end of the last century and during the first four decades of ours taught history and incidentally politics at a few German universities, particularly Göttingen and Tübingen, as the result of the prevailing university arrangements. Accordingly, they found immediate occasion to utilize their historical knowledge for the science of politics and conversely their knowledge in the latter for their historical studies.

The desire to unite the study of politics with that of history first led the meritorious historians we are dealing with here to elucidate the political maxims set up by them with examples from history and to corroborate them by pointing to successes and failures of political measures. During the further course of development, however, it led to the attempt to place politics in general on historical bases and to present it as the outcome of reflective consideration, as a "philosophy" of history. It would be easy to follow these efforts back even farther. But for our purpose it is sufficient if we refer to Spittler, H. Luden, Pölitz, H. B. v. Weber, and Wächter, and furthermore to Dahlmann, Gervinus, and W. Roscher, to show that originally a "historical school" of political scientists arose in Germany and simultaneously a "political school" of historians.[95] From these there

[95] The majority of the above writers are just as intent on aiding historical research by the study of politics as conversely of aiding research in the field of politics through the study of history. They try, if this expression be allowed, to retain not only the historical point of view in politics, but also the "political"

gradually developed a historical school of economically oriented political scientists and—since economically oriented political science was frequently confused with political economy by the representatives of this general outlook—a historical school of political economy.

The general character of this group of "political scientists" and the close relationship of their typical ideas to those of our historical economists will best become clear from the following brief presentation of historical ideas. H. Luden characterizes the problem of politics with the following words: "I should like to write a book that presents a view of things that is in agreement with life and the eternal doctrines of history. . . . I should like as far as possible to verify everything with examples from history to make it felt that it is really history that is speaking."[96] Pölitz emphasizes the necessity of historical studies for the political scientist in the following characteristic manner: "If the statesmanship which belongs to the *real* life of nations and states were to be derived solely from pure reason without hearing the voice of history at the same time, it would become the dried skeleton of abstract concepts. It would not be applicable to the energetic proclamation of the state as a vigorous organization and it would not utilize the great truths which history offers during a period of several thousand years."[97] H. B. von Weber attacks the merely speculative orientation of politics as science:[98] historical experience, he says, presents the rules of good sense by which the most effective means for the purposes of the internal and external life of the state may be and ought to be applied.[99] Wächter, finally, in his introduction to Spittler's "Lectures on Politics" (given as long ago as 1796!) praises the consideration of the "individual." Spittler's political maxims, he says, are not absolute rules which have to be carried out everywhere and under all circumstances, but they are modified according to localities, temporal circumstances, geographical extent of land, constitution, character, and

point of view in history. For example, Luden says: "One must be in the clear about the principles which rulers have to follow in maintaining, increasing, governing and ruling states . . . to be able to understand the great events of life, the fates of nations and states (in brief, history!)" (*Politik* [Jena, 1811], p. iv). On the other hand he again considers history as the basis of politics (*ibid.*, p. vii). Similarly in respect to our science Th. Rogers (*A Manual of Pol. Econ.* [1869], p. v): "just as the historian, who is ignorant of the interpretations of political economy, is constantly mazed in a medley of unconnected and unintelligible facts, so the economist, who disdains the inductions of history, is sure to utter fallacies."

[96] H. Luden, *Handbuch der Staatsweisheit oder der Politik* (1811), p. vii ff.

[97] Pölitz, *Die Staatswissenschaft im Lichte unserer Zeit* (1823), I, p. 8 ff.

[98] H. B. von Weber, *Grundzüge der Politik oder philosophisch-geschichtliche Entwickelung der Hauptgrundsätze der innern und äussern Staatskunst* (1827), p. ix. (In Weber's *Politik* we find a few allusions to the mental sphere of the historical school of jurists. Cf. especially p. v.)

[99] *Ibid.*, p. 42.

mode of life of peoples. Furthermore Spittler always demands only a gradual course of reform and transitional stages.[100]

The initial trend of the orientation of research in the field of *politics* under discussion here is fully brought out in the above passages. What distinguishes it is the circumstance that, *in contrast to the one-sidedly speculative orientations of research workers in the political sciences who follow individual modern German schools of philosophy,* it acknowledges experience and particularly history as an essential basis, the most important basis of research in the field of politics. It tries to make the experiences of history useful for politics, even to build up the latter on the doctrines of history. It is the age-old reaction of *empiricism* in general and of *historical empiricism* in particular against a priori speculation in political matters which gives this peculiar character to the efforts of the above writers.

The basic thought of the historical schools of constitutional law and jurisprudence, the efforts which characterize the Burke-Savigny orientation and constitute the real center of their efforts, "the doctrine of the organic, unintended origin of a number of human phenomena" with all the consequences of that doctrine for legislation and administration—these are, on the contrary, secondary for the above political scientists, and are even quite alien to them. Their mental spheres hardly come into contact with those of the historical schools of constitutional law and jurisprudence. They are opponents of abstract speculation (even that of historizing philosophy), but not usually of the literature of the seventeenth and eighteenth century Enlightenment and of liberalism in politics. They are opponents of a priori construction in the political sciences and history, but not of one-sided pragmatism in the conception of social phenomena. On the contrary, the majority of the writers mentioned here belong to the liberal (even if not an abstract-liberal) orientation themselves. They try to support and substantiate its guiding ideas in their way, i.e., *by history,* as best they can.[101] What the above men, who were basically liberal on the whole, wanted, was a *method of research,* the utilization of their fine and solid knowledge in political history for the science of politics, and conversely of the latter for the former, but not conservatism in the sense of the great founders of the historical schools of constitutional law and jurisprudence.[102]

[100] F. v. Spittler, *Vorlesungen über Politik,* K. Wächter, ed. (1828), p. xix.

[101] Orientations in the political sciences which in particular respects are analogous to those of the historical school of constitutional law and jurisprudence are represented by: Justus Möser, D. G. Strube, Fr. K. v. Moser, Fr. Chr. J. Fischer, G. Sartorius, J. J. v. Görres, Fr. Gentz, Adam Müller, K. L. v. Haller, *et al.*

[102] Similar efforts in the field of political economy run parallel to the above

On the other hand they keep clear of those dispositions toward one-sidedness which we have characterized in Burke-Savigny's opposition to the rationalism and pragmatism of the French Age of Enlightenment. Nowhere, as they really were for the most part historians and political scientists at the same time, do they confuse politics with history. Nowhere do they, like Burke, defend what already exists, what has developed historically, simply in opposition to the reform efforts of their contemporaries. Nowhere, like Savigny,[103] do they think that the wisdom in

---

presented efforts to *base* politics *not on speculation,* but *on experience and history.*

L. H. v. Jacob, although an adherent of the Kantian philosophy, had already characterized history as the source of the fact "on which almost all political sciences must be built. Most of the principles of these must be proved from experience, by means of history. The study of history must therefore accompany the study of political sciences." (*Einleitung in das Studium der Staatswissenschaften* [Halle, 1819], p. 31). G. Fr. Krause wants to "develop the science of economics from the course of culture and industry" in his *Versuch eines Systems der National- und Staatsökonomie mit vorzüglicher Berücksichtigung Deutschlands, aus dem Gang der Völkercultur und aus dem praktischen Leben populär entwickelt,* I, p. v. Fr. List, in most respects opposed to the writers mentioned here, declares nevertheless "a sound system (of economy) must absolutely have a sound historical basis" (*Das nationale System,* I [1841], p. xxxi; cf. also *ibid.,* pp. xxxix and 170 ff.). H. Rau also ceaselessly stresses the significance of the study of history and statistics for political economy (cf. especially his *Pol. Oek.* [1826], 1, p. 13).

This trend appears even more clearly with E. Baumstark, Joh. Schön, and Fr. Schmitthenner. The first writes (*Kameralistische Encyclopädie* [Heidelberg, 1835], p. viii ff.): "The political part of our science particularly needs a historical basis, for without this it will go dangerously astray. By this I do not mean that in the case of every doctrine of the science of finance a meager historical introduction with dates and cold historical data should be given, but that *the whole doctrine of public economy in cohesion should be placed on historical bases instead of on dogmatism and be developed as a result of research in the history of commerce, of the culture of states and of humanity in general.*" Schön declares (*Die Staatswissenschaft, geschichtl.-philosophisch begründet,* 2nd ed. [Breslau, 1840], p. vii; 1st ed. [1831]) as the purpose of his book "*to bring out politics as a philosophy of political history* and to develop historical social laws in place of sporadic rules." According to him, it was a matter of a *historical-philosophical foundation for the political sciences* which now (1839!) would be more popular than when his book first appeared (1831!).

But the trend under discussion here appears most strikingly in the case of Fr. Schmitthenner. He writes (*Zwölf Bücher v. Staate* [1845], III, p. 15 ff.), turning directly against the abuses of purely speculative philosophy in the realm of the social sciences in Germany: "A philosophy which sees an organic system in the state cannot allow the claim that it is possible to recognize its nature *merely logically,* i.e., from the relationship of concepts or from the rational development of concepts. It can only admit the full significance of the logical element where the premises are given to it *by historical knowledge.*" "*For the historical-organic method it is a question of discovering the law of the organic development of mankind.*"

[103] In the field of jurisprudence also, the historical orientation of the Savigny-Eichhorn school, one-sided in many respects, meets an opposition that is no longer

organically created social structures is a priori and without sufficient proof higher than human wisdom, i.e., higher than the judgment of the present. Just as little do the majority of them, with all acknowledgment of the significance of the study of history for politics, become the victims of another error so natural for "historical political scientists"—that of one-sided empiricism or even of one-sided overestimation of historical development. Pölitz says:[104] "Statesmanship (politics) is a mixed science (i.e., of philosophical principles and historical facts, equally). If one wanted merely to reduce it to rules borrowed from experience and history, it would not merely lack that firm basis which depends primarily on principles of reason. It would not even be without inner contradictions, because not infrequently one can set up examples from history for mutually opposed political views and assertions." We have already pointed out above[105] that Pölitz just as little wants politics derived one-sidedly from reason. Weber expresses himself similarly.[106] He says: "Politics is neither a purely philosophical nor a purely historical science. It is a *mixed* one insofar as it is simultaneously formed from philosophical principles and from historical facts.[107] There may be many objections to the above view,

---

sporadic by any means, and particularly the theoretical aspect of law is recently being emphasized more strongly. This is clear from the writings of G. Beseler, Leist, Bluntschli, Kierulff, Rein. Schmidt, Ihering, Brinz, Ahrens, Kuntze, Lenz, *et al.* After all, Savigny himself in the evening of his life declared in the preface to his *System des heutigen römischen Rechtes* (1840) that the historical orientation of research in the field of jurisprudence was *fulfilled.* He pointed out that the science had to return to subsequently neglected paths. He writes: "All success in our science depends on the collaboration of different intellectual activities. *Earlier* others and I unsuspectingly used the expression *historical* school to characterize in its peculiarity one of these activities and the scientific orientation chiefly coming from it. At that time this side of the science was not stressed particularly in order to deny or diminish the value of other activities and orientations. It was because that activity had long been neglected by others; thus it *temporarily* needed vigorous support more than others to regain its natural due" (*op. cit.*, I, p. xiii). Outstanding representatives of the historical school of jurisprudence at the moment no longer designate their method as a specifically *historical* one, but as a *historical-philosophical* one. Cf. J. Unger's *System* (1876), I, p. i.

[104] *Op. cit.*, p. 7 ff.

[105] See p. 179.

[106] *Op. cit.*, p. 42.

[107] In a similar vein the economists mentioned above (note 102). H. Rau still writes (*Pol. Oek.* [1863], I, §24): "History presents the opportunity to recognize the influence of fluctuating circumstances on the shaping of economy, and again the influence of economic conditions on the events in political life. Furthermore, it offers . . . an abundance of most useful experiences by way of favorable or unfavorable results of the procedures selected by governments in respect to economic affairs. The instruction is to be valued so much the more highly because in general one can rarely set up experiments in state administration without endangering the welfare of the state, and one must therefore be instructed by consideration of previous cases. . . . Historical consideration of economic affairs,

especially to the designation of politics as a "partly philosophical" science. Also in the above arguments on the untenability of pure empiricism or of pure historicism in politics, allusion to many obvious objections may be missed. One-sided overestimation of historical development still is not to be found in the presentations of the above-mentioned writers.

2.

Movement toward this kind of one-sidedness—actually a backward movement far behind the position of J. Bodin!—was first undertaken in the thirties of our century, and by an excellent Göttingen historian at that. He had been planning all his life to write a *Politik,* but had never carried out the idea. He therefore did not experience the clarifying influence which ordinarily is exerted on one-sided scientific ideas by the process of working them out. We refer here to Gervinus, a writer who exerted considerable influence on the young minds of the Göttingen historical school and by a rare concatenation of events was to become of decisive importance for the conception of methodological problems held by German economists.

Dahlmann in his *Politics* (1835) had stressed the organic view of the origin and formation of social institutions and the inadequacy of the one-sidedly pragmatic position in explaining them. He did this more vigorously and with incomparably greater depth than his predecessors. The mental sphere of the historical school of jurists had made more than superficial contact with him. Nor does he miss any opportunity to stress the importance of experience in general and the study of history in particular for the science of politics. He is protected, on the other hand, against the error of one-sided overestimation of historical development by his insight into the nature of politics as a *practical* science with the shaping of life as its aim.[108]

He assigns to politics "the worthy task of distinguishing, with a perspective sharpened by a comparison of the ages, necessary new formations from innovations which are insatiably invented, whether through exuberance or through bad temper."

In a review of this work, which was first published in 1836, Gervinus now developed the following views on a "purely scientific political science," which he planned, but never finished. "He (the author) would have gone over and taken up for this work the realm of history in all its

---

however, will not do away with general economic laws, but will make their functioning understandable under the most varied conditions."

[108] *Politik* (1835), p. 236 (cf. also p. 83 ff.).

extent. He would have tried to retain what was regular and general out of the vast total of experience, out of what is impermanent, fleeting, recurrent, particular. He would have tried to guess the unfinished history of humanity from the finished histories of nations, and to explain the parts from the whole as well as the whole from the parts, the state from the states. . . . He would have tried to take up in his picture only what proves to be necessary and according to the law of nature in the development of nations and states. His political science would have become equivalent to a history of the state, his history of the state equivalent to a *philosophy of history,* and that would have become the most necessary foundation stone for a philosophy of mankind or, what is the same thing, of man. For purely scientific politics should be nothing but a philosophy of the political part of history, just as esthetics should be the philosophy of the history of literature. . . . With this method politics would correspond to *physiology,* or to that part of it which has recently been derived from the history of life." Gervinus, however, thinks that he retreated from these high plans because the historical material "was far from adequate for one to be able to think of such a work, and the childish attempts that had been made here and there simply shrank from such undertakings. A science (political) which was to be based entirely on empiricism would best be developed only after a certain termination of experiences. . . . The writings of Plato and Aristotle were incontestably the prime basis for such a philosophical political science."[109]

This plan of work by the distinguished Göttingen scholar, which is magnificent at least in its own way and has opened up a really endless field of activity for the industry of the scholarly world, did not fall on barren soil in Germany. Its execution after all did not demand direct insight into political life or into the goals and means of governmental activity, nor did it call for that great mass of experience and knowledge which only the direct examination of governmental activities and participation in political affairs ordinarily give. Nor did it demand that very difficult judgment in matters of state which in an immediately original way chooses the aims of political activity and the means for achieving them from the consideration of political life. What the above program required was a careful, comprehensive study of historical works and sources and an understanding that abstracted the general from the particular.[110] These were prerequisites which could be fulfilled so much the more easily in German scholarly circles, as even individual details offered a praiseworthy

[109] Gervinus, *Historische Schriften* (Karlsruhe), VII, p. 595 ff. (The above review appeared first in 1836 in the *Litterarische Untersuchungsblätter.*)

[110] Cf. note 43.

contribution to the problem in its entirety. Furthermore, considering the defective character of preliminary historical works, even less perfect accomplishments could count on a friendly and considerate reception by fellow aspirants. The problem offered much that was appealing in every respect. To a high degree it was in tune with the peculiar genius of the vast majority of specialists in the field of the social sciences in Germany.

To this was added the fact that the above plan of work met the need of the scholarly world and the reading public for *positive* knowledge, a need which was stimulated most keenly by the rank speculation of modern German schools of philosophy, and was even stimulated one-sidedly for the sake of contrast to the latter. The scholarly world and reading public, after the excesses of philosophic speculation, were really languishing for experience and history and seemed inclined to value scientific systems the more highly the more these outbid each other in emphasizing empiricism and historical empiricism in particular.

Gervinus with his program had not brought the previous historical orientation of politics any closer to that of the historical schools of jurisprudence and constitutional law. He had, rather, moved considerably farther away from their mental sphere. However, his "program for the reform of politics" was at any rate as historical as the nature of the science under discussion here permitted.

But with this we find ourselves at the starting point of that school of German economists which at present is called the "historical."

3.

When the twenty-one-year-old *studiosus historicarum politicarumque literarum* in Göttingen, Wilhelm Roscher, who subsequently attained such great significance for the school of German economists under discussion here, published his doctoral dissertation on certain doctrines of the Sophists,[111] he already took the opportunity to present his views on the relationship of *politics* (certainly not of *political economy*!) to history. In this little work Roscher unreservedly assumes the position of the Göttingen historical school of the time. And in particular the overestimation of historical development which Gervinus brings out in his view of politics seems not to have remained without decisive influence on him. For him history is the exclusive empirical basis of politics, and the latter is merely the result of a universal consideration of history, of a comparison of different national developments. The best politics is that which is the result of considering the golden ages of the history of nations. Any-

[111] *De historiae doctrinae apud Sophistas majoris vestigiis* (Göttingen, 1838).

one who possessed a universal knowledge of history would at the same time be in possession of the whole *objective* truth in politics, a truth which, as Roscher seems still to have assumed at that time, would correspond not only to certain historical epochs, but to man in *abstracto*.[112]

Four years later Roscher still says: "I consider *politics* as the theory of the laws of the development of the state. I consider state economy and *statistics* (?) as especially important branches and aspects of *politics* (?) which are therefore worked out in special detail. I think I will find those laws of development by comparing the national histories known to me. . . . My political science is certainly based on universal-historical preliminary studies."[113]

Only in his *Grundriss zu Vorlesungen über die Staatswirthschaft nach geschichtlicher Methode* (1843) does Roscher declare that he is an adherent of the *"historical method"*[114] and with it "wants to attain for *state economy* something similar to what the Savigny-Eichhorn method attained for jurisprudence."[115] He characterizes the nature of this method by his statement that he will endeavor "to bring together as a law of development what is homogeneous in various national developments,"[116] "to find in the great mass of phenomena what is essential, what is regular, for what purpose all nations that one can get hold of are to be compared with each other in the economic respect."[117]

But with this there begins a series of misunderstandings about the nature and method of our science which have become detrimental to the development of scientific economics in Germany and have not yet been straightened out. Roscher wants to attain for political science something similar to what the Savigny-Eichhorn method did for jurisprudence.[118] But what he has designated as the nature of his method has scarcely a remote similarity to the Savigny-Eichhorn orientation. Neither Savigny nor Eichhorn designates as the main task of his research, nor in general as a major problem, the setting up of laws of the development of law itself, on the basis of comparison of the legal evolution of nations insofar as he can grasp it. And neither seeks to attain to a juridical science of "*objective* truth" in this way. What they seek is the *historical* understanding of concrete law codes, the proof that these are the unintended results

[112] *Op. cit.*, p. 54 ff.

[113] *Leben, Werke und Zeitalter des Thukydides* (Göttingen, 1842), p. vii ff.

[114] *Grundriss*, p. i.

[115] *Ibid.*, p. v.

[116] *Ibid.*, p. 2.

[117] *Ibid.*, p. iv.

[118] Roscher still speaks here of *state* economy, not *national* economy, but does not distinguish theoretical economics from the practical sciences of national economy.

of organic developments and as such not the objects of arbitrary transformation and the mania for innovation, that they are above human wisdom. The idea of a philosophy of law, or a *philosophy of the history of law,* for instance in Roscher's sense, is far from being the object of their scientific endeavors; it is partly in direct contrast to these. What Roscher wants is the treatment of political economy in the sense that Bodin thought he was treating political science, as Gervinus thought he was treating politics. But he does not want the historical orientation of research in the economic field in the spirit of historical jurisprudence.[119]

The vagueness about the nature of political economy and of its subdivisions; the lack of any really strict distinction of the historical, the theoretical, and the practical point of view in research in the economic field;[120] the confusion of individual orientations of theoretical research and of the philosophy of economic history in particular with theoretical economics and with political economy at large; the vagueness about the nature of the exact orientation of theoretical research and its relationship to the empirical-realistic orientation; the opinion that the historical-philosophical orientation is the only one justified in political economy and is

[119] If we wanted to parallel completely the orientation of research characterized above with the same kind of orientation in jurisprudence, we would have the *comparative science of law,* that is, something like the orientation of a Feuerbach, a Bernhöft (the editor of the *Revue de droit international et de legislation comparée*), etc. "Why," Feuerbach writes in the preface to Unterholzner's *Jurist. Abhandl.*, p. xi ff., "does the anatomist have his comparative anatomy, but the jurist as yet no comparative jurisprudence?" . . . Just as the philosophy of language, the true science of language comes from the comparison of language, in the same way *universal jurisprudence,* the science of law, comes from the comparison of laws and legal customs of the most closely related nations as well as of the most heterogeneous ones of all times and countries," etc. Fr. Bernhöft ("Ueber Zweck und Mittel der vergleichenden Rechtswissenschaft" in the *Zeitschrift für vergleichende Rechtswissenschaft* [1878], I, p. 3) and even before him J. Unger (*System* [1876], I, p. 4, note 12) and others demand of the *philosophy of law* that it obtain "its results from research into the ideas present in the history of mankind" and thus also obtain a strictly scientific basis. However, it occurs to none of the jurists mentioned to recognize the nature of *historical jurisprudence* in general, or even of Savigny's method, in this orientation of research. Nor are they satisfied to expect from the *scientific philosophy of law*—for they have this in mind—the establishment of parallelisms of the history of law, for instance. Their intention is aimed rather at finding new bases for the understanding and the reform of the law of the present by comparing the various solutions which have been found for the practical problems of jurisprudence in prescriptive law and in the legislation of the various nations. The laws of the development of law, in the sense of Roscher's "laws of the development of economy," could at best be designated as the research goal of a secondary branch of comparative jurisprudence. A comparative science in the sense of the above jurists would, moreover, in our estimation, be of incomparably greater significance in the field of economy than would the determination of all imaginable "parallelisms of economic history."

[120] *System,* I, §§22 and 26, etc.

analogous to historical jurisprudence; the failure to recognize the true nature of the historical point of view in our science, especially as regards its theoretical aspects; the exaggerated importance which is attributed to the so-called historical method; the vagueness about the nature of the organic approach in economy and about the problems resulting therefrom for social research—all these methodological errors and one-sided emphases appearing already to no small extent in Roscher's youthful writings are also found in his later writings, in which, to be sure, he is more and more frequently likely to designate his method as "historical or (!) physiological."[121]

To this is added the fact that with Roscher as with most of his followers the presentation of political economy by no means corresponds to the above theoretical principles. His system of political economy, as every unprejudiced person must admit, is in truth not at all a philosophy of economic history in the sense he himself characterized, but mainly a compilation of theoretical and practical knowledge from "historical" treatments of political economy; usually, however, from "unhistorical" ones. It is a compilation, the historical element of which on the whole does not consist in the special character of the range of *theoretical* and *practical* knoweldge of economy it reveals, but in adventitious historical and statistical pronouncements and historical and historical-philosophical digressions about individual economic matters. His political economy is in its foundations not a history of economy according to the *"historical method."*

[121] Roscher in several places in his writings (cf. especially *Deutsche Vierteljahrsschrift* [1849], 1st section) makes a start toward distinguishing the theoretical and practical problems of political economy. Thus, for example, he writes (*op. cit.*, p. 182): "Previously I have already called attention to two essentially different classes of questions which arise in any economic investigation, and in any investigation in political science: the questions, namely, *What is?* and *What is supposed to be?"* With this statement not elaborated further Roscher characterizes, however, only the contrast between the *"realistic"* and the *"practical"* problems of research in the field of economy. For historical research in the field of economy, also, is concerned with the *what is.* This contrast thus in no way characterizes the relationship of the theoretical to the practical economic sciences. To be sure, Roscher speaks in the same treatise (p. 180) of laws also, indeed even of *"laws of nature,* by which nations satisfy their material needs," of *laws of nature* especially "by which these needs affect the state and in turn are influenced by the state." Indeed, he characterizes the investigation of such laws as the task of economics. However, by these "laws of nature" Roscher understands exclusively the parallelisms of economic history (*ibid.*, p. 181): "The simple, but of course far-reaching way to become acquainted with those laws of nature is to compare as many and as different national developments as possible. What appears consistently is set up as a rule, what does not is to be explained as an exception." Here, too, "theoretical economics'" is taken over and absorbed in the "philosophy of economic history" in the case of Roscher.

The virtues of the scientific personality of the learned Leipzig scholar; his outstanding merits and his advancement of the historical understanding of a number of important economic phenomena; the incomparable stimulation which his studies in the literature of our science have given to all younger colleagues; the judgment pronounced by the educated reading public of Germany on the art of his presentation and on his fine understanding for the literary needs of his circle of readers—all this does not come into question at this point, as scarcely needs to be said. What is to be made clear here are the methodological errors of the founder of the historical school of German economists, errors which have become pernicious to the development of our science and particularly of its theoretical side.

4.

Among the representatives of the historical school of German economists B. Hildebrand is to be mentioned among the very first. To be sure, in his first short work (1845) of partially methodological content[122] he merely stresses *collectivism* in the consideration of economy in contrast to the "individualism" of Adam Smith and the majority of his followers.[123] But just three years later Hildebrand[124] declares that he wants to clear the way for a basic historical orientation and method in the field of economy and to change this science to a *doctrine of the economic laws of development of nations.* He proposes a reform of the knowledge of the economic aspect of the life of nations such as the science of language has experienced in this century. Smith and his school, he says, had tried to construct an economic theory whose laws were to be absolutely valid for

[122] *Xenophontis et Aristotelis de oecon. pub. doctrinae illustrantur Partic.* (Marburgi, 1845), I.

[123] "quae est inde ab Adami Smithii aetate per Europam divulgata doctrina, ea quidem haud immerito in reprehensionem incurrit propterea, quod solis suis quemque consulere rationibus jubet quodque, cum summam de lucro contendendi licentiam poscat, si ipsam constanter persequantur omnes, omnem tollat honestatem singulorumque in singulos excitet bellum necesse est" (l. c., p. 3). Hildebrand thinks now that the study of the economic writings of the ancients permeated by a common spirit will contribute to correcting this error of the Smithian school. Hildebrand has also in his later writings adhered to the above view directed against "individualism" in economy (cf. especially his *Nationalökonomie der Gegenwart und Zukunft* [1848], pp. vi and 29 ff.). He thus (and already before him Schütz, *Tüb. Zeitschrift für die Staatsw.* [1844], p. 133 ff.) contributed appreciably to establishing the "ethical" orientation of economic research in Germany, and in part to establishing the "social-political" orientation probably to be distinguished from the other. This, to be sure, was long after Sismonde de Sismondi had undertaken to solve the same problems in France (cf. in this connection Appendix IX: "The So-Called Ethical Orientation of Political Economy").

[124] *Die Nationalökonomie der Gegenwart und Zukunft* (1848), pp. v and 324.

all times and nations (and thus without considering the various stages of development and the distinctive dispositions of nations). These were to be applied to all states and nations equally and be above time and space. In Germany as in England the laws and rules of economic science had been called "economic laws of nature" and timelessness ascribed to them as to other laws of nature. He plans to oppose this orientation.[125]

Fifteen years later Hildebrand writes:

The science of economy does not have the task of dealing with laws of nature as do the physiology of the animal organism or other branches of natural science . . . but it has to detect the progress of the human species in the fluctuation of economic experiences and the perfection of the species in the economic life of mankind. Its task is to investigate the course of economic development of both individual nations and of all humanity step by step. It must recognize in this way the foundations and the structure of present-day economic culture as well as mark the task, the solution of which is reserved for the work of the living generation . . . that is to say it must note the link which the work of the present generation is supposed to add to the chain of social development. The history of economic culture in connection with the history of all political and juridical development of nations and statistics is the only sure basis on which a successful development of economic science seems possible.[126]

Hildebrand's attitude toward the theoretical problems dealt with here, and particularly his relationship to Roscher's methodological position, is sufficiently characterized by these statements. He separates theoretical economics from the practical sciences of economy. If he deals almost exclusively with the method of economic theory, the problem of the historical treatment of the practical economic sciences with each other does not grow hazy for him, as it does for Roscher. Hildebrand does not, like Roscher, find the realization of the historical method in the *physiological* conception of economic problems. He is against "laws of nature" in economy in general, and, if I may say so, he is against an economic physiology as well as against an economic physics. Rather he looks for the nature of the historical method exclusively in the collectivistic consideration of phenomena of the life of the nation and in the determination of the laws of national economic development. Here, in the partly insufficient separation of history and theory of economy and in his lack of understanding for the exact orientation of theoretical research, his views in the main meet certain of Roscher's statements. But Hildebrand has nowhere expressed himself in detail about the *nature* of the laws of development which Roscher comprehends in the sense of parallelisms of the economic history of nations. He twice (1848 and 1863) made starts toward doing this and

[125] *Ibid.*, pp. 27 ff. and 34.

[126] *Jahrbücher für Nationalökonomie und Statistik* (1863), I, pp. 3 ff. and 145 ff.

toward the solution of the real problems of historical methodology. But both works were broken off at the decisive points and left as fragments.

5.

To a higher degree than the two previously mentioned writers Karl Knies has helped in the solution of the theoretical problems of the historical orientation of our science. With him we do not find that vagueness about the concept of political economy and the nature of its subdivisions which we find in Roscher; we do not find that limitation of the historical point of view in our science to its theoretical problems, as with Hildebrand, nor to its practical aspect, as with many others. His methodological investigations are not a juxtaposition of disconnected or even of contradictory remarks about the nature of our science, its paths to knowledge, or its methods. Rather, they form a unit borne by homogeneous ideas, substantively even if not always formally. He also has the clear feeling that nothing is accomplished with mere postulates and affirmations in reference to the "historical method," nor with the demand, kept to very general terms, for a science of "laws of economic development," if what is written does not in fact agree with those fine postulates which treat economic problems in such fashion as to retain theoretically desirable principles.

But neither did Knies attain full clarity about the nature and problems of the historical orientation of political economy and its subdivisions. He looked now to the historical understanding of economic phenomena, now to an interpretation of the literary history of our science that should do justice to alternating historical conditions, now to a philosophy of economic history, and now to the relativity of results of economic research. The main flaw in his methodological position consists, however, in his one-sided tendency toward realism and collectivism in the view of theoretical economic problems. No writer before him so completely developed the methodological postulates of the realistic orientation of research in the economic field. But also, no one else so completely failed to recognize the independent meaning of the exact orientation of theoretical research in the economic realm, or to recognize the nature of exact economic laws or even of economic laws in general. His position in theoretical economics actually leads to a science of "empirical economic laws" (observed regularities in succession) differing according to time and place. Indeed, it leads ultimately to an acknowledgment of specifically historical research as the solely justified orientation of the striving for cognition in the field of economy.

Knies is a scholar true to his convictions, one who goes thoroughly into the methodological problems of the "historical school" and who draws the logical conclusions from its one-sided premises with relentless love of truth, and thereby to a certain extent completes the sphere of ideas of the above school in respect to the methodology of political economy. Whatever in the way of new results has been brought to light after him by investigation into the methodological problems of historical economics we have taken into consideration in the appropriate place. On the whole, however, it was at least already hinted at by Knies. Even the comprehensive investigations by J. Kautz[127] into the historical method of our science and the works, pertinent in many respects, by Dietzel, Held, Schmoller, H. v. Scheel, and Schönberg do not constitute an exception to this as far as the methodology of the historical school of political economy comes into question. We will refrain completely from mentioning numerous Italian and individual English and French adepts of the historical orientation who, not yet completely sobered by their own experience, still expect results from that orientation in the field of our theoretical-practical science which shall be similar to those which modern German jurisprudence and linguistic research have achieved.

What remained to be accomplished in the above field of research after Knies was the clarification of the methodological errors and one-sidedness of the "historical school" of our science and the building up of a theory of knowledge which takes into consideration all justified orientations of research in the economic field.

[127] K. Knies and J. Kautz, in contrast to W. Roscher, have taken the "historical method" seriously not only in the theory of research, but also in its practice. They have, in fact, written "political economies according to the historical method," which, however, are not really presentations of political economy.

APPENDIX I

The Nature of National Economy

Not only individuals separated from any human contact, but also the members of a nation can exhibit the phenomenon of isolated economies,[128] that is, to the extent that they have no traffic in goods with each other, whatever their relations to one another may be otherwise. It scarcely needs to be stated that under such circumstances no "national economy" in the *common* sense of this word would be present. At any rate, the term "national economy," if permissible in this case at all, would designate only the *summation* of individual economies in a nation, in contrast to individual economies as such.

Wherever, on the contrary, members of a nation come into economic communication with each other, the concept of "national economy" already gains a significantly different meaning. To be sure, even here we cannot speak of national economy in the *true,* strict sense of the word. Such a sense would be present if (as e.g., in the planned institutions of many socialists) its goal were *really* the greatest completeness possible in the economic situation of satisfaction of the needs of the *nation thought of as a unit.* It would be present if the *nation in its totality* (whether directly, or indirectly by means of its functionaries) were really the economic subject; and finally, if the goods available were actually at the disposal of the *nation, thought of as a unit.* But these are conditions, as scarcely needs to be said, which are not found in present-day national economy. For under our present social conditions the nation is simply not *the* economic subject (nor are its functionaries). The leaders of the individual and common economies are really the economic subjects. The goal of the latter is on

[128] The concept of *economy* is taken in too broad a sense by a number of writers on national economy. Some of them conceive of every activity aimed at the satisfaction of human needs (body movement! looking at works of art! etc.) as an economic act; others so conceive the *consumption* of goods, along with production and distribution as such. In truth only the premeditative activity of humans aimed at the indirect or direct satisfaction of their material needs is to be considered as economic, while the acts of the actual consumption of goods do not in themselves come under this concept.

the whole not the meeting of the material needs of the nation in its totality, but the meeting of *their* material needs or of those of other definite actual or potential persons. Finally, the economic means at hand do not serve to secure the needs of the nation as a unit, but merely those of actual or potential people. What the national economists designate with the expression "national economy," national economy in the common sense of the word, is *by no means a juxtaposition of isolated individual economies.* The latter, rather, are closely tied together by traffic with one another. But just as little is what they so designate a *national economy* in the above strict sense, or per se *one economy* at all. It is really, on the contrary, a complex, or, if one wishes, an *organism of economies* (of singular and common economies), but, we repeat, it is not itself an economy. To make use of a popular image, there is here the same relationship as e.g. in a chain which presents a unit consisting of links, without, however, being a link itself. It is the same as in a machine which presents a unit made up of wheels, and so on, without being a wheel itself.[129]

The beneficial influence which governments in most countries exert or think they exert on economic affairs, also, cannot change this fact in any way. The benefit of the economic efforts of third parties is by no means to

[129] The majority of contemporary economists differentiate very sharply between "private economy" and "national economy." Their error is thus by no means based on a confusion of these two phenomena. It is to be found, rather, in the fact that "national economy" is not to be viewed as a *complex of individual economies,* but is to be viewed *itself as a large individual economy* in which the "nation" is to represent the needing, economic, and consuming subject.

But in this an evident error is present. Because several persons who have up to now been isolated economically and continue to pursue their *individual* economic aims and efforts start trafficking in goods with each other (and thus really only undertake to pursue their *individual* interests more suitably than before), their previous isolated economies do not change into *one* common economy, nor is a new one added to these. Rather, the previously isolated economies hereby merely undergo organization. They do sacrifice their character as *isolated* economies but not their character as singular *economies.* The latter would be the case only if each economic subject gave up *his* individual economic aims and efforts, *his* economy, that is, and if the fullest possible satisfaction of the needs of all members of society were to become the common goal of all economic subjects. Only in this event would the individual economies under discussion here disappear and a common economy take their place. On the other hand, a new economy, and, indeed, a common economy would be added to the previous individual economies if the economic subjects were to organize just a part of their economic effort in the previously mentioned fashion of a common economy and their singular economy were to remain in respect to the rest of their effort. Moreover, it is self-evident that, within the circle of persons under discussion, only some portion of such persons can construct comprehensive common economies. What at present is called *national economy* is an organizing of individual and common economies of the most varied kinds, but is not a national economy in the true sense of the word, nor is it, in its totality, *one* economy (cf. on this E. Cohn, "Gemeinbedürfniss und Gemeinwirtschaft" in the *Tübinger Zeitschr.* [1881], p. 478 ff.).

be considered per se as an independent economy. The circumstance that individual economies or a *complex* of them are fostered and benefited by any power, of whatever conceivable kind it may be, does not change these into a *unitary* economy. The beneficial activity which state governments exert on the economy of the state subjects can thus not be considered a national economy itself, nor can it change a mere complex of individual economies into a national economy in the strict meaning of the word. Moreover, it is, of course, obvious that the beneficial influence of state governments does not have as its aim the protection of the needs of the nation, thought of as an individual economic unit, but only the welfare of that complex of individual economies which is not a national economy in the strict sense of the word.

The activity of state governments aimed at the protection of their *own* needs (public finance) is without doubt an independent economy. State governments are, in fact, economic. However, the financial economy is always just one member of that complex of individual economies, the totality of which is commonly designated with "national economy," but is never itself a national economy.

Let us sum up what has been said. The fact that the individual economies in a nation have traffic with each other cannot change the individual economies in a nation into an undivided economy of the nation, into a national economy in the true meaning of the word. Nor can the fact that the rulers in a nation develop an activity aimed at the benefit of the individual economies in their totality. Nor, finally, can the existence of a genuine financial economy in a state. That phenomenon, which is commonly designated by "national economy," always presents itself to us, rather, merely as an organized complex of individual economies, as a multiplicity of economies joined together into a higher unity which is nevertheless not an economy itself in the strict meaning of the word.

We have already stressed in another place[130] how important the above distinction is for the proper understanding of economic phenomena. It is one thing if the economic phenomena of socially organized humans are considered in a way completely inadequate to reality, as a result of the unitary activity of the nation as such, and as a result of application of its disposable means—and are interpreted in the light of this fiction. It is another thing if these same phenomena, in accordance with reality, are construed as the result of numerous individual efforts, as the outcome of the endeavors of economic agents (actual or potential) bound together by their commerce. For in the first case the phenomena of human economy in its present-day social form will, to be sure, present themselves to us

[130] See p. 93 ff.

under the extremely simple image of phenomena of an individual economy, and their interpretation in this view will offer no sort of noteworthy difficulties. In the latter case, however, we will be confronted with a social structure, differing from the individual economy, and just as involved as it is hard to interpret. In the first case, namely, we have before us a familiar phenomenon which is essentially analogous to the individual economy and hence very clear to our understanding. In the latter case the incomparably more complicated and more difficult goal of economic research is *"the explanation of the complicated phenomena of human economy in their present-day social form through the efforts and relationships of the individual economies connected by their commerce with each other."*

It is clear, however, that the above simplification deprives our science of any true value, because it is based on a thoroughly inadmissible fiction. And scholars in the field of political economy will be compelled of necessity to comprehend and solve the problems of the science in that complexity in which they are actually offered to us by experience. *Natura rerum subtilis* can also be said of human economy in its social form. But how foolish to want to simplify the science in contrast to the nature of things by an inadmissible fiction, to want to view a complex of economies as a large individual economy. How foolish to do this, instead of examining the real phenomena of human economy in their actual complication, i.e., instead of reducing them to their factors of individual economy and thus striving for understanding of them—an understanding which, to be sure, is not easy. Certainly, the problems of science can thus be simplified extraordinarily—but only at the price of complete success.

Adam Smith and his school have neglected to reduce the complicated phenomena of human economy in general, and in particular of its social form, "national economy," to the efforts of individual economies, as would be in accordance with the real state of affairs. They have neglected to teach us to understand them theoretically as the result of individual efforts. Their endeavors have been aimed, rather, and, to be sure, subconsciously for the most part, at making us understand them theoretically from the point of view of the "national economy" fiction. On the other hand, the historical school of German economists follows this erroneous conception consciously. It is even inclined to see in it an incomparable deepening of our science. It is clear, however, that under the sway of the fiction discussed here a theoretical understanding of the phenomena of "national economy" adequate to reality is not attainable. Also, the slight value of the prevailing theories of economics finds its explanation in no small measure in the above erroneous basic view of the nature of the present-day social form of human economy.

APPENDIX II

The Concepts of Theoretical Economics and the Nature of Its Laws

The definition of a science has to contain three elements: (1) the exact designation of the science to be defined; (2) the object that research is related to (e.g., the animal world or plant world, the state, national economy, etc., or specific realms of these); and (3) the formal point of view from which the object is to be examined (e.g., the historical, the theoretical, etc.). Thus a correct definition of theoretical economics not only has to designate this science and its object, national economy; it also has to determine the formal point of view from which the above science concerned with national economy has to investigate economic reality (as opposed to other sciences, which are concerned with the same objects, e.g., history, statistics of national economy, economic policy, etc.).

The definition of a science, and thus of theoretical economics, may accordingly suffer from three fundamental weaknesses. *In the first place,* it may not characterize clearly enough the science which is to be defined. This is the case with all those definitions of theoretical economics which do not expressly indicate what is to be included: whether political economy in general (theoretical economics, economic policy, and the science of finance in their entirety), or merely the first two subdivisions of political economy mentioned, or else, finally, only the theoretical portion. In fact, they even leave us in doubt occasionally whether it is not political or social sciences in general which are in question.

In the second place, the object to which the science concerned refers may not be designated precisely. This is the case with all those definitions of theoretical economics which leave us in the dark concerning the object of research in this science; or else designate as this object at one time social phenomena in general, at another only specific fields or aspects of national economy.[131] Both the conception of theoretical economics in

[131] Many present-day economists try less in the definitions of economics to define the latter than to define the concept of *"national economy"*; they try to define not

the sense of a general theoretical social science and also the conception of it in the sense of a mere catallactics, a philosophy of the history of national economy, etc., are errors of this kind.

In the third place—and here the chief weakness of most definitions of theoretical economics is to be looked for—the formal point of view from which economic science investigates the phenomena of national economy may not be precisely indicated. For the majority of definitions leave us in doubt whether economics investigates national economy from the historical, the theoretical, or the practical point of view. Or, in other words, we are in doubt whether it is a historical, a theoretical, or a practical science dealing with national economy. In fact, definitions usually jumble up inextricably these three absolutely different points of view in research.

However, even those who do not fundamentally fail to recognize the formal character of theoretical economics succumb almost without exception to certain errors concerning it. Theoretical economics has the task of presenting not merely the *"laws"* of economic phenomena to us, but also their *"general nature."*[132] A presentation of the above science, for example, which would, to be sure, enlighten us on the laws, but not the *nature,* of goods, of value and the various forms in which value appears, of economy, of price, of ground rent, of income on capital, of speculative gains, of money, etc., would at any rate have to be designated as incomplete. The definition of theoretical economics (not to mention that of political economy in general) as a "science of the laws of national economy" is thus in any case too restricted.

This definition seems even less suitable if the concept of "laws" is viewed in any arbitrarily chosen sense characterizing only a definite type of "law." If by "laws" of phenomena we understand, as Rümelin does in

---

the science but the *object* of research. They endeavor to incorporate their special views about the nature of the latter into the definition of the science, instead of first taking account of the object by a separate investigation and going on to the definition of economics after the solution of the pertinent preliminary question. This is a procedure which finds its explanation, moreover, in the immense vagueness about the true field (the object) of research which political economy has to deal with.

[132] Herbert Spencer has undertaken an interesting venture in this regard in his *Descriptive Sociology, or Groups of Sociological Facts* (London, 1873). In the magnificently planned work which he is publishing together with a group of collaborators, Spencer intends to present in tabular form which facilitates comparison the social empirical forms of individual peoples (referred to political, religious, intellectual, economic life, etc.) at the various stages of their development. This is an undertaking which cannot, as Spencer thinks, offer the summation of all the empirical material necessary for theoretical research in the field of the social sciences. However, when completed it will prove to be of unquestioned value for this orientation of the striving for knowledge, especially for the different branches of the empirical-realistic orientation of theoretical research in the field of the social sciences.

his investigation of the concept of a social law, only the so-called *"laws of nature"* in contrast to so-called *"empirical laws,"*[133] then the definition of theoretical economics as a science of the "laws" of national economy proves to be so restricted that it really does not apply to the greater part of the knowledge which commonly is included in the presentations of theoretical economics. The same holds true of the definition of theoretical economics (or even of political economy!) as a "science of the laws of development of national economy," as a "philosophy of economic history," and other such things.

Here we append the views of a few modern German economists about the nature of our science.[134] The criticism to be made of these views will be directly clear from what is said.

H. Rau, in the last edition of his *Politische Oekonomie* which he himself supervised (1868, I, §9), defines: "Economics[k] (the first theoretical main part of political economy) is the science which shows the nature of national economy or which shows how a nation is constantly provided with material goods through the economic efforts of its members." L. v. Stein (*Lehrbuch der Volkswirthschaft,* 1858, p. 2): "The scientific presentation of national economy constitutes economics" (cf. in addition the 2nd ed., 1878, p. 564 ff.). W. Roscher characterizes (*System,* I, §16) economics as "the science of the laws of development of national economy, of the economic life of the nation." So also does H. v. Mangoldt (*Grundriss der Volkswirthschaft,* 1871, p. 11). Br. Hildebrand (*Jahrbücher für Nationalökonomie u. Statistik,* 1863, I, 3) writes: "The science of the economy of nations . . . has the task of investigating the historical course of development of individual nations as well as of all humanity step by step, and in this way of recognizing the link which the work of the present generation is to add to the chain of social development." With respect to Knies' views, that were never brought together in one place, compare his *Politische Oekonomie vom Standpunkte der geschichtlichen Methode,* 1853, pp. 17 and 32 ff. and especially the 2nd ed., 1881, p. 1 ff. J. Kautz (*Theorie und Geschichte der Nationalökonomie,* 1858, I, 288) says: "Economics is the science of the bases, the means, and the laws of development of the welfare of the nation." J. C. Glaser (*Handbuch der Politischen Oekonomie,* 1858, I, 10 ff.): "The science of economy is the presentation of the activity of man aimed at the acquisition and use of

[133] *Reden und Aufsätze* (1875), I, p. 5 ff. (cf. also J. St. Mill, *Logic,* Book III, Chap. IV).

[134] Some of the older literature in J. Kautz, *Theorie und Geschichte der Nationalökonomie,* I, p. 288 ff.

[k] Rau uses *Volkswirthschaftslehre oder Nationalökonomie.* F.J.N.

wealth, or, what is the same, aimed at the utilization of nature and its forces for the satisfaction of his needs." After this he distinguishes three different ways of looking at economic conditions, "so to speak, three types of the theory of economy," namely: the technical, the real, and the ethical (cf. on this *op. cit.*, p. 12). K. Umpfenbach (*Die Volkswirthschaftslehre,* 1867, p. 12): "Economics is the systematic establishment of the laws by which the contingent nature of human populations is brought about by their means of livelihood in the struggle for existence." Schäffle (*System,* 3rd ed., I, 46) defines economics "as the science of the phenomenon of the economic principle in human society," while Ad. Wagner (*Politische Oekonomie,* 1876, I, 59) views "economics or political economy"[1] as "the science of national economy, the organism of the individual economies of politically organized nations" and remarks in opposition to Schäffle that the problem of economics is in the presentation of the *realization* of the principle of economic reality in national economy. M. Wirth (*Grundzüge der Nationalökonomie,* 1861, I, 3) sees in "the science of economics or national economy the science of those laws of development of nature, under the influence of which the production and distribution of goods in human society take place; in the observation of which nations thrive, and in the violation of which they suffer and perish."

G. Schönberg (*Die Volkswirthschaft der Gegenwart,* 1869, p. 38) says: "'The subject of our science is the economic life of the nation, which, as a special phenomenon of the spirit of the nation and progressing step by step in closest causal connection with the cultural development, forms an increasingly higher organism. To recognize it as such in its appearance in the laws and regulations which emerge in it, and starting with this recognition, which also discovers the problems which the work of our generation has to solve, to engage in this work to bring economic life closer and closer to its high, ethical goal—this is, briefly, the problem of our science" (cf. also his *Volkswirthschaftslehre* 1873, p. 3 ff.). F. J. Neumann (*Tübinger Zeitschrift für die gesammte Staatswissenschaft,* 1872, p. 267) recognizes in our science "the science of the relation of the individual economies to each other and to the state unit," while H. v. Scheel (in Schönberg's *Handbuch der Politischen Oekonomie,* 1882, I, 57) designates as the problem of political economy "the presentation of the connection of private economies with each other and their connection with the larger economic communities (state, municipality, etc.) according to origin and quality, and the establishment of rules for the most suitable arrangement corresponding to the demands of the cultural stage that is

[1] Wagner here uses three terms: *Volkswirthschaftlehre, Nationalökonomik, oder Politische Oekonomie.* F.J.N.

attained and is to be attained." G. Cohn (*Ueber die Bedeutung der Nationalökonomie,* 1869, p. 3) defines economics "as the science of the economic human, i.e., of that activity which is directed toward acquiring the external means which we need to reach our diverse life goals."

The above definitions of our science reflect quite clearly the low status of theoretical investigations in the realm of political economy in Germany. We learn from them—needlessly[135]—for the most part the special views of the authors concerned on the nature of economy, of national economy, even of society. But no unprejudiced person will deny that these—quite aside from the question of their correctness—do not even satisfy the formal presuppositions of a suitable definition of a science.

In connection with a few pertinent questions *about the nature of social laws* broached by Rümelin for the social science literature in Germany, the following remarks may be in place here: The "laws of phenomena" (in contrast to normative laws!) can be classified according to the empirical realm to which they refer (according to objects!) or else according to their formal nature. In the first connection we distinguish laws of nature in general and of inorganic and organic nature in particular, laws of psychic life, laws of social phenomena in general and of economic phenomena in particular, etc. In the formal connection we distinguish laws of succession and coexistence, exact and empirical laws, and again within the above categories "laws of development," "laws of great numbers," etc. Accordingly, that not unusual means of expression is confusing and superfluous which refers to the *laws of nature* of social phenomena in general and of national economy in particular, whereas laws of nature can really refer only to natural phenomena. In the above case one should speak of *exact* laws of social phenomena and of national economy in contrast to the merely *empirical* laws.

The view of the so-called "'laws of nature" of phenomena as the "expression for the elementary, constant mode of action recognizable as the basic form in all individual cases" can still, with J. St. Mill and Rümelin, be considered valid. For it characterizes the contrast between the "empirical" and the "exact" laws of phenomena and prevents the confusion of these two kinds of scientific knowledge. Rümelin has earned decided merit in connection with the methodology of the social sciences in Germany by trying to make the methodological achievements of modern English logic comprehensible to German scholars in the social sciences, and by trying to put an end to the thoughtless confusion of the exact laws of phenomena with theoretical knowledge obtained in a realistic-empirical

[135] See note 131.

way. For theoretical economics, however, his concept of "law" is much too narrow. For this science, according to the present-day conception of it, as already stressed elsewhere (p. 67), has to investigate and describe not only exact laws, but also the empirical ones; indeed, many kinds of the latter. And it has to investigate and describe not only the *elementary* regularities in the general connection of economic phenomena, but also the derived ones.

APPENDIX III

The Relationship of the Practical Sciences of National Economy to Economic Practice and to Theoretical Economics

For anyone in any way experienced in the general theory of knowledge the remark is scarcely needed that the so-called practical sciences (the technologies) in general and those of national economy in particular (economic policy and the science of finance) are themselves capable of practical application and that accordingly a strict distinction must be made between the practical sciences of national economy on the one hand and their practical application on the other. The first teach us the general principles, the maxims by which national economy can be benefited, according to different circumstances, and by which state finances can most suitably be instituted. The practical application of these sciences, on the contrary, appears in the form of concrete legislative acts, administrative measures, etc. The relationship of the theoretical sciences to the practical ones and of both to the practice of national economy is thus the following: Theoretical economics has to describe for us the general nature and the general connection (the laws) of economic phenomena, whereas economic policy and the science of finance teach us the maxims by which, according to the particularity of conditions, national economy can best be advanced and state finances can most suitably be instituted. The *practice* of national economy, however, consists in the application of the practical sciences of national economy on the part of the public authorities according to the particularity of the conditions of individual countries and nations. The relationship of theoretical economics to economic policy and the science of finance and of both categories of sciences to the practice of the workers in economic policy and of men in finance is thus the same as, for instance, that of theoretical chemistry to chemical technology on the one hand and of both to the activity of the practical chemist on the other. Or it is the same as that of anatomy and physiology to surgery and therapy and of both groups of sciences to the practical activity of scientifically trained physicians.

It is a sign of the slight philosophical sense of the workers in our science that even among the more outstanding economists so much vagueness and conflict of opinion appears concerning the above really most elementary questions of the theory of knowledge. Cf. J. B. Say, *Cours complet d'E. P.* (Paris, 1852), I, 24 ff., and especially his note on Storch's *Cours* (Paris, 1823-24), I, 4. Here Say wants to grant the validity only of a *practical application* of political economy, but not a *practical science* of national economy, an opinion which innumerable followers of Say have to a great extent followed. *Roscher,* too, is inclined to think that political economy breaks down into a general portion and particular portions, but not into a theoretical and a practical portion. Actually political economy breaks down into a theoretical science and a series of practical sciences of national economy. Each one of these sciences, however (both theoretical economics and also each practical economic science) exhibits again a general portion and particular portions in an orderly presentation. (Cf. also A. Wagner's *Allgemeine oder theoretische Nationalökonomie,* 1876, Part I, p. xii and *passim;* H. v. Scheel in G. Schönberg's *Handbuch der Politischen Oekonomie,* 1882, I, 57; and F. J. Neumann, *ibid.,* p. 115 ff.).

It is true that theoretical economics appeared as an independent science later than the two practical subdivisions of political economy. However, the assumption is false that it came into being through the circumstance that *common elements* were taken from the latter two portions and joined together (F. J. Neumann, *op. cit.*). Theoretical economics arose from the need for a theoretical establishment of the practical sciences of national economy. Discussions of this type—investigations into the general nature and the general connection, the *laws* of the phenomena of national economy—are found scattered in the oldest writings on the art of government, later in those on economic policy and on finance. They are, however, fundamentally different from the "general" aspect of these sciences, which by its formal nature, as is obvious, is likewise practical. That is, it comprises *general practical* truths in respect to furthering national economy and the conduct of finance, but it does not comprise *theoretical* knowledge in national economy. Theoretical national economy came into being as a science when a few German scholars (first Jacob, Hufeland, Soden, *et al.*) collected, completed, and systematically arranged theoretical discussions scattered in the practical sciences of national economy, and in the general as well as in the special portions thereof. These had already found a broad range with the *physiocrats*, especially, however, with A. Smith and J. B.

Say. The previously mentioned view obviously has as a basis the erroneous presupposition that the *general* aspect of a science and the *theoretical* aspect are identical.

A failure to recognize the true relationship of theoretical and practical economics is particularly inherent in the opinion that the former has to develop "the laws of economic life of the nation *without consideration of the interference of the public authorities* in it," while the latter, on the contrary, has to consider the principles of this interference. This is a view which frequently comes to light in the economic literature in Germany (cf. Pölitz, *Staatswissenschaften im Lichte unserer Zeit,* II, 3; Lötz, *Handbuch,* 1837, I, §6; Rau, *Politische Oekonomie,* I, §9, etc.). This conception of the nature of theoretical economics is thus incorrect simply because the latter also includes among its problems research into the general nature and laws of the *real* phenomena of national economy, and thus, at any rate, the phenomena influenced by the state. It is incorrect because an abstraction of economic life of the nation from political influence is really inconceivable, at least in respect to the *empirical orientation* of theoretical research. Therefore L. H. v. Jacob (*Grundsätze,* 3rd ed., §5), Rotteck (*Vernunftrecht,* 1835, IV, B, 23 ff.), and recently Roscher, Knies, Scheel, Wagner, and others justifiably reject this conception of theoretical economics. However, it is a misunderstanding when Wagner (*Politische Oekonomie,* I, §9) thinks that the division of economics into a theoretical and a practical aspect is ultimately based on the notion that "national economy is to be considered first *without* the state and only then *with* it," for this division has no conceivable relation to the idea discussed here. L. H. v. Jacob (*Grundsätze,* 3rd ed., §5 ff.) deals entirely correctly with the relationship of the theoretical and practical sciences, and this author justly may claim the merit of having completed the above important separation of the two main fields of political economy.

APPENDIX **IV**

The Terminology and the Classification of the Economic Sciences

We have already spoken in another place[136] about the nature of *"political economy"* and of its subdivisions, and the terminology which has come into usage for designating the latter. Only the question might still arise whether this expression is apt for the designation of the totality of the theoretical-practical sciences of national economy brought together under that heading, and whether the expressions "theoretical economics," "economic policy," and "science of finance" are apt for the individual subdivisions of "political economy." This is a question which, to be sure, offers only a secondary, terminological interest with regard to the previously mentioned investigations into the sciences discussed here. Still, because of the fundamental character of the problems that lie at its foundation, it is not completely without importance.

The desire to establish satisfactorily the terminology of a science, particularly in consideration of its main categories, to harmonize the nature and designation of these categories, to harmonize objects and concepts in the sciences, appears to us under all circumstances to be highly praiseworthy. For a correct terminology not only prevents countless confusions in the investigation and reception of scientific knowledge. It really affords a lodestar for that large number of fellow scientists, whom experience shows always to predominate, whose attention is really directed less toward things than toward words.

The terminological problem which concerns us here first offers, moreover, very particular difficulties. These explain the most varied attempts, continued into the present, to change the terminology referring to the designation of political economy and its subdivisions in contrast to the terminology which has become prevalent.[137] These are difficulties, the

[136] See p. 38 ff.

[137] A survey of these attempts in J. Kautz, *Theorie und Geschichte der Nationalökonomie,* I, p. 285 ff.; cf. also *ibid.,* p. 288 ff.

ultimate reason for which is probably to be found mainly in the fact that political economy according to its present conception comprises sciences of very different formal nature, and that the problem of a thoroughly adequate designation of them according to their character offers formal difficulties not easy to overcome.

Here one question seems to us above all to be worthy of consideration, because it touches the very *nature* of political economy and its subdivisions. It is the question whether political economy is to be included in the *political sciences* or the *social sciences*. We should not like to avoid it completely because, as is well known, it has really become basic for the terminological attempts under discussion.

If, as is the intention of the majority of those who characterize political economy as a social science, the concept of *society* is viewed as a contrast to that of the *state* and political economy is designated nevertheless as *social-economy* (*économie sociale,* etc.), the point is overlooked that economic policy and the science of finance are political sciences in the truest sense. This designation, with the above presupposition, thus seems at least to be unsuitable for presentations of our science which include the latter elements. Conversely the expression "*science of state economy*" used with preference for political economy by older German authors (still by Lotz, Fr. B. W. Hermann, and even by Roscher in his first writings!) again produces many doubts about the designation of "theoretical economics" as such (cf. L. v. Stein, *Die Volkswirthschaftslehre,* 1878, p. 571 ff.).

The expression "*economics*"[m] seems less dubious as the designation of the totality of theoretical-practical sciences which are included in common under the concept of political economy. If the concept "*national economy*" is correctly understood, i.e., in the sense of a complex of all the economies in a nation (also economy of finance!), as an "organism" of economies from which with advancing culture a political activity (cultivation of national economy!) aimed at benefiting it seems less inseparable,[138] then the above expression actually appears to be a not wholly unsuitable designation for the group of sciences in question here. Also the division of "economics" into a theoretical and a practical portion and of the latter into an "economic policy" and a "science of finance" flows rather easily from these reflections. If nevertheless a large number of German and the vast majority of foreign economists cling to the expression "political economy" which is just as indefinite as inexact, this obviously is done because of the

[138] See Appendix VI.

[m] Again, in a single sentence, Menger writes of *Volkswirthschaftslehre,* of *Nationalökonomie,* and of *Politische Oekonomie.* For simplicity's sake no translation has been given of *Nationalökonomie.* L.S.

international currency of the term. That is, it is done for a reason which in questions of terminology is of great significance, usually even of decisive significance. But perhaps it is done partly just because of its indefinite nature, which expediently cloaks the vagueness of the concept which it designates.

Incomparably greater interest, but, to be sure, incomparably greater difficulties are offered by the problem of a satisfactory terminology of our science if we do not look upon this problem merely in respect to political economy in the present-day conception of it, but in consideration of the *science of human economy in general.* A terminology adequate for the nature of the latter can only be the result of full insight into the nature of the various tasks which research in the realm of economic phenomena has to fulfill. It has as its presupposition a satisfactory solution of the comprehensive problem of *classifying the economic sciences.*

It scarcely needs to be stressed how far removed from this goal the theory of the human sciences in general and of the social sciences in particular still is. After all, the analogous problem in the realm of the natural sciences is still far from solved. And, as the most recent experiments show, the related theory is still controversial even in the most essential points. And yet, how much higher the development of the natural sciences has gone, and the epistemology related to it, than that of the human sciences! The latter will need a long development before the various aims of scientific research in the realm of human phenomena are completely clarified and thereby the basis gained for a complete classification and terminology of social science in general and of the economic sciences in particular. Until then the following intimations about a few of the main points bearing on the pertinent problems may help prepare for the solution of these problems.

The totality of the sciences related to human economy, *economic science*[n] in this broadest sense of the word, breaks down into three large groups, corresponding to the three main tasks which the human mind may set for itself in the investigation of economic phenomena: I. the historical, II. the theoretical, III. the practical.

I. The *historical* economic sciences have to examine and describe the individual[139] nature and the individual connection of economic phenomena. According to whether they undertake to solve their problem from the

[139] See p. 38 ff. and especially notes 6 and 7, where we also have characterized the problems of scientific statistics and the various orientations of statistical research. Cf. on this especially M. Block, *Traité théoretique et pratique de Statistique* (1878), where also the very valuable modern German literature on the nature and concept of statistics finds careful consideration.

[n] Here Menger's term is *Wirthschaftswissenschaft.* L.S.

point of view of condition or development they break down into the *statistics* and the *history* of human economy. The historical sciences can respond to their task in universal fashion only under the presupposition of *collective* consideration of human phenomena and the historical economic sciences only under the presupposition of collective consideration of economic phenomena. This evidently must be the case if we consider the vast number of individual phenomena of human life[140] or economy and the exigencies of the technique of scientific presentation. The historical economic sciences are just because of their universal-scientific task necessarily *presentations of human economy from the point of view of a collective outlook, i.e., of national economy* in the just-mentioned sense of the word.[141]

[140] This circumstance, extremely significant for the methodology of the historical sciences in general, does not exclude the presentation of the condition and the development of individual economic phenomena of human economy, as is obvious. However, it does explain how the *universal* problem of the *historical* economic sciences necessarily leads to the collectivist view of economic phenomena—to the history and statistics of *"national economy."*

Here also the basis for solving a problem frequently concerning historical research is to be sought: which phenomena of human life is it the task of the historical sciences to lift out of the vastness and to present? These disciplines really have the task of presenting the individual phenomena of human life from the point of view of collective considerations, and of presenting the individual phenomenon only insofar as it is per se significant for the *collective image of human life*. Only in this way can they satisfy their particular task *universally*.

What is called the *artistic problem of writing history* is also sufficiently explained in the above conception of the nature of history and its relationship to the individual phenomena of human life. The real art of the historian (also of the statistician!) consists chiefly in the ability to make us aware of the immense number of individual phenomena of human life from the point of view of a collective outlook. It consists in the ability to offer us a collective picture of the development and of the condition of human phenomena in their totality. (Cf. on this the attempts made repeatedly since Humboldt to explain the nature of the so-called "historical art," in Gervinus, *Grundzüge der Historik*, p. 13 ff.; J. G. Droysen, *Historik* [1875], p. 75 ff.; O. Lorenz, *Fr. Chr. Schlosser, Sitzungsbericht der Wiener Akademie der Wissenschaften*, vol. 88, p. 136 ff.).

Here also appears with special clarity the contrast between the *historical* and the *theoretical* sciences. The latter do not have to do with the presentation of the "individual," but of the "general," of "phenomenal forms," and "laws of phenomena." They do not have the task of making us aware of the vast number of *individual phenomena*, but only of the incomparably narrower sphere of *phenomenal forms* and their *typical relationships*. The *collectivist* point of view, quite inseparable from the idea of historical sciences, can be dispensed with by the theoretical sciences. Indeed, we have seen that it is quite inadequate for them (cf. on this the pertinent discussions in Book II, Chap. 2, p. 117 ff.).

[141] Those who undertook to put the *"historical method"* in place of the previous methods of social research characterized as unsatisfactory have one thing in common with the adherents of the so-called *"organic view"* of social phenomena. They labor under an intensive delusion about the present state of the methods concerned. We have already stressed elsewhere (cf. p. 137) that the explanation of

II. The *theoretical* sciences of human economy have to examine and describe the general nature and the general connection (the laws) of economic phenomena. In their totality they form the *theory of national economy,* while singly they correspond to the various orientations of theoretical research in the field of national economy. In the latter we have become acquainted with and learned how to distinguish the *exact* and the *empirical* orientation of theoretical research, and in the empirical orientation the *historical-philosophical,* the *theoretical-statistical,* the "physiological-anatomical" orientations, etc. Yet at first glance it is clear that even with this the totality of the various justified orientations of theoretical research in the field of national economy is by no means exhausted. It is clear that the development of our science can, rather, again and again bring to light new orientations of theoretical striving for knowledge. At present, with the slight development of the social sciences, the results of all orientations of theoretical research in the field of national economy are grouped together suitably into one science, "theoretical economics," into a discipline which, incidentally, just for this reason necessarily lacks strict formal unity in the knowledge it presents and thus lacks a strict systematic approach also. However, in our estimation there is no obstacle to its gradually splitting into various branches with progressive development, as this has already happened in the field of research in natural science, partly for logical reasons for division, partly for factual reasons. Each one of these branches will exhibit a certain, at least relative, independence. Until then what has been said may serve to clarify the theoretical problem in the field of national economy and to explain the peculiar difficulties which a strict systematic approach in theoretical economics encounters.

III. The *practical economic sciences* finally are supposed to instruct us on the basic principles according to which the economic designs of people (according to conditions) can be most suitably fulfilled. These are:

---

social phenomena by analogies to organic structures is really an interpretation of what is little known by what is known still less, but also the *historical method,* with which some of our economists operate with such naive assuredness, as if they had fully explored its depths or as if not the least doubt existed about the nature of this method, does not seem to be anywhere nearly as clear to the true historians themselves as to the just-mentioned economists. Concerning this cf. Droysen (*Historik* [1875], p. 3): "If the historical studies are questioned about their scientific justification and their relationship to other forms of human knowledge, if they are questioned about the establishment of their procedure and the connection of their problems, they are not able to give a satisfactory answer." Cf. O. Lorenz (*Fr. Chr. Schlosser und über einige Aufgaben und Principien der Geschichtsschreibung, Berichte der Wiener Akademie der Wissenschaften,* vol. 88, p. 133): "It must be admitted that even today we have no thoroughgoing principle, no acknowledged historiographic orientation, not even a historical style of any uniformity."

1. *Economic policy,* the science of the basic principles for suitable advancement (appropriate to conditions) of "national economy" on the part of the public authorities.

2. The *practical doctrine of individual economy,* the science of the basic principles according to which the economic aims of individual economies (according to conditions) can be realized most completely.

The latter breaks down further into:

(a) the *science of finance,* the science of the basic principles for the suitable institution, according to conditions, of the largest individual economy in the nation, of the government budget, and of other economic subjects endowed with financial power,[142] and

(b) the practical *science of private economy,* the science of the basic principles according to which private people (living in our present-day social circumstances!) can best institute their economy (according to conditions).[143]

These economic sciences refer altogether to human economy in its pres-

[142] The budget of economic subjects endowed with financial power has a variety of peculiarities which form the basis of the distinction of the practical science from the suitable institution thereof. By its nature, however, it is an individual economy and the science of finance thus falls under the more general category of the *"practical sciences of individual economy"* together with the practical science of private economy.

[143] From the above it is clear at the same time that the opinion of those who recognize a contrast in principle between the practical science of *private* economy and practical *economics* is quite erroneous. For the practical science of private economy also refers to the economy of socially organized people and it also has its theoretical basis not in a special theoretical science of private economy but in theoretical economics. The stockbroker, the banker, the speculator in stocks and in grain, etc., in their private economic operations, rely upon the theory of price, of capital income, of ground rent, etc., that is, on the sciences of theoretical *economics,* just as someone engaged in economic policy does, or as an organ of the administration of finances in its public activity does. Theoretical *economics* is the theoretical basis of the practical science of private economy just as well as it is of the science of finance and economic policy. Victims of error also are those who, like J. St. Mill (*Essays on Some Unsettled Question,* p. 125), do not *at all* acknowledge *private economy to be the subject of science,* but merely of *art.* For, as is obvious, theoretical and practical knowledge is at the basis of private economy, too.

All practical sciences of economy thus depend on the theoretical science of economy. But it would be erroneous to assume that the latter forms their sole theoretical basis. For the practical sciences, of whatever kind they may be, are not at all rooted exclusively in individual theoretical sciences. Rather, there is even usually a majority of these which form the theoretical basis of the former. Not only anatomy, but also physiology, physics, mechanics, chemistry, etc., are, for example, the theoretical bases of surgery and therapy. Theoretical chemistry is not the sole theoretical basis of chemical technology, but physics, even mechanics and mathematics, provide foundations for it as well. The same thing holds true of the practical sciences of economy. To be sure, they are thoroughly, but not exclusively, rooted in the theoretical science of economy.

ent organization, i.e., to "national economy" in the present-day figurative meaning of the word. But with a strict socialistic organization of society they would, like economy itself, assume a considerably different form.

In a community ordered thus there would in the main exist neither private individual economies along with the community economy nor a special cultivation of national economy and administration of finance. Thus the practical sciences concerned with these would cease. There would then be only one economy, a national economy in the real sense of the word.[o] Its economic subject would be the nation (or the representatives of it); its aim would be the fullest possible satisfaction of the needs of all members of society. There would thus be only one practical economic science, the science of the basic principles by which the community economy, according to conditions, could be most suitably instituted and conducted. What in our day are designated with extreme inaccuracy as "socialistic *theories*" are the beginnings of this *practical* science, and its nature and place in the system of economic sciences are thus clear.

This practical economics in the true, socialistic sense of the word would, like all other practical sciences, need a theoretical basis. This is just as clear as the fact that it could find one only in a science which would make us aware of the general nature and the general connection of the phenomena of the community economy. *Theoretical economics* in this true sense of the word would by no means coincide with that same science in the present-day sense, but just as little would it of necessity have to be absolutely different from it. The psychological basis for the most general economic phenomena, the theory of human needs and the means available to us for satisfying them, the theory of the nature and quantity of needs and goods (of need and the available quantity of goods!), of use value and its measure, of the nature of economy and abstract economic reality, etc., would all be common to the theoretical science of economy in both cases. It is true that in respect to the general nature and the general connection of complicated economic phenomena this theoretical science would in turn exhibit differences in the two cases, corresponding to the differences of the real phenomena.

Thus the systematic approach of the social sciences in the socialist state would in no way be identical with that of the present-day social sciences. For in the first situation "economic policy" and the "science of finance," and in the main the "practical science of private economy" also, would cease. "Economic science"[p] in the most universal meaning of this word

[o] Here, and in the next paragraph, when referring to "the real sense of the word" or "the true sense of the word," Menger uses *Volkswirthschaft,* which evidently has a special appropriateness given the "collectivistic" meaning he wishes to convey. L.S.

[p] Here Menger reverts to *Wirthschaftswissenschaft.* L.S.

would then merely be divided into the "historical sciences" of national economy, into a "theoretical" and a "practical" science of the economy. These, too, in accordance with the changed object of research, would exhibit different features compared to the analogous social sciences of the present.

APPENDIX V

In the Realm of Human Phenomena Exact Laws (So-Called "Laws of Nature") Can Be Established Under the Same Formal Presuppositions as in the Realm of Natural Phenomena

No opinion is more widespread among social philosophers than that exact laws (so-called laws of nature) prevail in the realm of natural phenomena, but not in that of human phenomena, and that exact theories can be established in the former, but not in the latter. This opinion is based on the one hand on the fact that strictly typical phenomena can be observed in the realm of nature (e.g., the simplest elements of chemistry, the most elementary agencies of physics, etc.), but in the realm of human phenomena the complexity of phenomena (completely disregarding the factor of their development!) excludes a strictly typical character and thus the possibility of exact laws applying to them. On the other hand it is based on the fact that the phenomena of nature follow forces that act only mechanically, while in human phenomena the factor of will plays a decisive rôle.

But in this line of argument there are a number of fundamental errors. We admit quite unreservedly that *real* human phenomena are not strictly typical. We admit that just for this reason, and also as a result of the freedom of the human will—and we, of course, have no intention of denying this as a practical category—*empirical laws of absolute strictness* are out of the question in the realm of the phenomena of human activity. What we do attack, however, is the opinion that natural phenomena are strictly typical *in their full empirical reality,* or else that laws of natural phenomena of absolute strictness can be established by way of the empirical-realistic orientation of theoretical research in nature.[144] From the stand-

[144] Every exact law of nature, for whatever realm of the empirical world it may claim validity, is based on two unempirical assumptions. First, that all con-

point of empirical realism exact laws of nature are just as unattainable as exact laws of social phenomena. The exact laws of nature, also, in the true meaning of this word, are not the result of empirical-realistic research in nature, but of exact research. But this, by its basic character, is analogous to exact research in the realm of social phenomena.[145]

The error of the social philosophers consists in the fact that they try to arrive at exact social laws by means of empirical research, and thus in a way in which exact laws of phenomena cannot be established at all, neither exact social laws nor exact natural laws.

The opinion predominating with the social philosophers that the strict laws of physics, chemistry, etc., are the result of the empirical orientation of theoretical research has had the consequence of causing some of them to try to attain *exact* laws of social phenomena in an "empirical" way, that is, not in an *exact* way. But it induces others of them to apply the standards of *exact* research to the results of empirical research in the realm of the social sciences and conversely the standards of empirical research to the results of exact social research. These are two errors which have had an equally pernicious effect on the development of the social sciences. We must attribute to them the greater part of the misunderstandings which dominate theoretical social research in its present-day form and in its present endeavors (cf. concerning this chapters 4, 5, and 7 of Book I).

---

crete phenomena of any definite type (e.g., all oxygen, all hydrogen, all iron, etc., in the sense that the law of nature concerned conceives of these things) are qualitatively identical, and second, that they can be measured in an exact way. In *reality*, however, the above phenomena are neither strictly typical, nor can they be measured in an exact way (cf. p. 85 ff.).

[145] It is a peculiarity of the exact social sciences that exact research in the realm of the phenomena of human activity starts with the assumption of a definite volitional orientation of the active subjects. This does not, however, establish an essential distinction between exact research in nature and exact social research, for the former starts with presuppositions which exhibit a formal analogy to the one under discussion here.

APPENDIX VI

The Starting Point and the Goal of All Human Economy Are Strictly Determined

Particularly with advanced economic civilization, we do not have need only for *consumers' goods,* i.e., for goods which serve directly for the preservation of our life and well being. We also have need, on the one hand, for *means of production*[146] (e.g., for raw materials, auxiliary materials, machines for technical production, for technical efficiency of labor, etc.) and, on the other, for *means of exchange* (e.g., for money, or other wares meant for exchange). These are needs which could be designated as *indirect,* in contrast to the first-mentioned, the *direct* ones. Our need for means of production and means of exchange is limited, however, by our need for consumers' goods[147] and the *ultimate* goal of all human economy is thus to cover our direct material needs, to assure the satisfaction of our direct needs. However comprehensive the economic measures which we take to attain this goal, and even if we strive first for the satisfaction of our indirect need and consider this in concrete cases as the first goal of our economic activity—the *ultimate goal* is always, as said, the meeting of our direct material needs.

The starting point of every economy, however, is the goods *directly* available to economic subjects. In respect to future times, or periods, we also have goods available in an *indirect* way (through the means of production or exchange in our possession). The goods which we have available in this way (the pertinent products and materials) are, however, limited quantitatively and qualitatively by the goods that we have directly availa-

[146] See my *Grundsätze der Volkswirthschaftslehre,* I, p. 4. The expression "goods of the first order" which I use to designate consumers' goods and the designation of the levels of means of production, varying in respect to consumers' goods as goods of the second, third, fourth, and higher orders, seem to me not only suitable per se. The classification of goods at the basis of this terminology seems really indispensable for the exact understanding of the phenomena of value and price.

[147] Cf. for the whole following investigation my *Güterlehre,* p. 35 ff.

ble. The most obvious starting point of our economy is always the latter only.

We understand by economy premeditative activity aimed at satisfying our material needs. If we sum up what has previously been said together with this characterization of the nature of economy, it is clear that "economy" ultimately means that activity by which we satisfy our direct material needs with the directly available goods (the directly available means of production, means of exchange, and consumers' goods, and, indeed, by way of production, commerce, and management). Economy is really nothing else than the way which we travel from the previously indicated starting point of human activity to the previously indicated goal.

The direct needs of each economic subject are given in each case by his individual nature and previous development (by his individuality). The goods directly available to him are strictly given by the economic situation of the moment. Our direct need and the immediately available goods are in respect to any present moment given facts that are not within our discretion. Thus *the starting point and the goal of every concrete human economy are ultimately determined strictly by the economic situation of the moment.*

What lies between the two above limits of all human economy, the economic activity of people, may at first glance seem ever so complicated, irregular and arbitrary. Our ultimate goal is always to assure the satisfaction of the *direct* needs strictly determined by our nature and previous development. It is always the *directly* available goods strictly determined by the state of things at the moment which form the most obvious starting point for us. What we can do to maintain our life and well being, what in this respect depends on our power and volition, is to travel the road from a strictly determined starting point to a just as strictly determined goal in as *suitable* a way as possible, i.e., in our case, in as *economic* a way as possible.

There is scarcely need to allude particularly to the significance of these circumstances for the solution of the theoretical problems of our science from the point of view of exact research. However, it comes to light much more clearly still if the following fact is considered.

If the starting point and the goal of a human endeavor are given, of whatever conceivable type this endeavor may be, the way which can really be taken or actually will be taken by human agents for attaining the desired goal is by no means strictly determined a priori. Volition, error, and other influences can, on the contrary, and actually do, bring it about that human agents take different roads from a strictly set starting point to a just as strictly determined goal of their action. On the other hand, it is certain that under the above presuppositions only *one* road can be the *most suitable*.

Of course, this also holds true of human economy. If it is correct that the starting point and the goal are given in each concrete case by the economic situation, there can in each such case be only one most suitable road, only one *economic* road to the pertinent goal. In other words, if economic humans under given conditions want to assure the satisfaction of their needs as completely as possible, only *one* road prescribed exactly by the economic situation leads from the strictly determined starting point to the just as strictly determined goal of economy. This road, or what is the same thing, the economic activity of people, is thus determined *economically* even if, to be sure, not *de facto*, since the above conditions apply in each concrete case. In every concrete economy innumerable orientations of the action of the economic subjects are conceivable. However, it is certain that only *one* orientation of economic conduct can be the most suitable, can be the *economic* one, if we disregard economically irrelevant differences. In other words, in every economy innumerable uneconomic forms of enterprise are conceivable; however, disregarding economically irrelevant differences, only *one* form of enterprise is conceivable, namely, that in which a strictly determined *economic* orientation prevails.

It is not hard to recognize the importance of this result of our investigation for the methodology of our science, especially, however, for the understanding of the nature of the exact orientation of research in the economic field and its relationship to the empirical-realistic orientation. The *real* phenomena of human economy, as paradoxical as it may sound at first, are to no small extent of an uneconomic nature, and as a result of this fact are by no means strictly determined phenomena, viewed from the standpoint of economic reality. The *realistic* orientation of theoretical research in the field of economy cannot, however, and just for the reason given, lead to "exact laws," but only to more or less strict "regularities" in the coexistence and succession of the real phenomena of human economy. The *exact* orientation of theoretical research in the above field, on the contrary, examines the phenomena of *abstract economic reality*, phenomena which are strictly determined, as we saw. It thus, to be sure, does not arrive at exact laws of the *real*, in part extremely uneconomic, phenomena of human economy but it does arrive at exact laws of economic reality.

The high value of these laws for the theoretical understanding of the economic aspect of social phenomena has already been stressed by us repeatedly,[148] as well as the fact that their formal nature is no different from

[148] See especially p. 62.

that of the laws of all other exact sciences and of the exact natural sciences particularly.[149] Also, the charge that these laws show an unempirical nature and all those objections which the one-sided adherents of the empirical-realistic orientation of theoretical social research make against them only show by how much the social philosophers who make the objections fail to recognize the true nature of exact research in the realm of social phenomena.

[149] Appendix V, pp. 214-215.

APPENDIX VII

The Opinion Ascribed to Aristotle that the State Is an Original Phenomenon Given Simultaneously with the Existence of Man

We have already (p. 149 ff.) demonstrated that the opinion that the state was an original phenomenon, given simultaneously with the existence of man, is untenable and even absurd. Such nonsense was of course completely foreign to Aristotle, no matter how often he has been called the creator of this theory. But to clarify the interesting question of the great philosopher's conception of the origin of the state, we will first cite the pertinent passages from his writings, since some of them have given at least superficial cause for misunderstanding.

Aristotle (*Polit.,* I, 1) expresses himself as follows on the nature and origin of the state: "One cannot better ascertain the nature of a thing than if one sees it come into existence before one's eyes. Let us adopt this method therefore in respect to our subject (the determination of the nature of the state!). For this purpose we must first bring those two humans together who are absolutely indispensable to each other, namely man and wife. For their destiny is the propagation of their race. Their coming together, however, is *not a work of their intention* and of reason, but of instinct. . . . The second of the simplest unions is that between master and servant, between the one giving orders and the one who obeys. . . . This union also is natural. . . . From these two unions, the marital and that of master and servant, there develops first a home, a family. . . . The *natural* origin of a locality, however, is to be derived from the fact that the first family sent colonists forth from its bosom. . . . Thus from families there arose cities and tribes, and in the family the monarchical form of government existed. The oldest man of a family was of course the head of it. This method of rule then spread easily to the families which developed from the first and settled down beside it in separate homes. The almost complete and self-sufficient society resulting from the union of several localities is a state, or a community of citizens. . . . Now if those simple unions of homes and locality are *natural,* then the community of citizens is also something *natural.* . . . From this it is evident that the society of citizens, the state in its first and simple form, is to be accounted one of the *works of nature,* and man is a creature naturally destined and adapted to lead the life of a citizen (a ζῷον πολιτικόν)."

In the preceding (for the purpose of explaining the nature of the state) Aristotle describes the process by which the state develops from individuals or families. He shows that this process is by no means the result of men's intention directed toward forming a state, but is a result of their natural instincts. He shows that the process is a *natural* one and the state itself is thus a natural product in the above sense. He then continues as follows:

"Although the family consists of individual people and the state of several families, still one can *in a certain sense* say that the state or the community *is the first and original thing* and that the family and the individual are only beings *limited* by this (dependent upon it). For the whole is necessarily the basis for the parts and must therefore be considered as the more independent and more original. As soon as the whole body dies the hand and foot are also dead. At least, they exist only in external form and in name, just as a form made of stone is called a hand. . . . If, therefore, man cannot exist without civilian society and is not self-sufficient when separated from it, his relationship to society is no different from that of any part to the whole. But the whole is the independent and original entity, the part the limited and derivative. Thus the state also is the first entity, the individual last."

The frequently misunderstood meaning of the above Aristotelian description of the nature and origin of the state, which in part seems contradictory, is thus the following: The state is an organism in which each part is limited by the whole. (Civilized) man is inconceivable without the state. Therefore the state, in respect to *civilized humans,* is the more original, and the civilized human is the later, the limited entity. However, Aristotle by no means asserts that *uncivilized* man also cannot be conceived of without the state and that therefore the appearance of the state is as old as that of man in general. On the contrary, he states (*Pol.,* I, 1 toward the end): "Among the Cyclops, as Homer describes them, the families lived separated from each other. *This manner of living was general in older times,"* and he even, as we saw above, describes in detail the process by which states developed from families (the essential difference of these from states he expressly emphasizes: *Pol.,* I, 1 at the beginning).

He needlessly declares quite expressly (*Nic. Eth.*, V, 14) that man is by nature *even more* of a creation intended for family ties than for state union, *since the family is older and more necessary than the state.*

Aristotle even acknowledges the possibility that civilized man might live "by chance circumstances outside the boundaries of civilian society" (*Polit.*, I, 2). Only of those people who "*by virtue of their nature*" live beyond society, in whom, therefore, the natural *instinct* for associating with others is not present, does he say in true Greek fashion that they must be either more or less than humans. He by no means denies the possibility of existence to the uncivilized human who has this instinct, but has not yet reached the point of forming a state. The often quoted Aristotelian "*ἄνθρωπος ζῷον πολιτικόν*" thus does not mean that man has always lived in a state and that the latter is as old as man himself. It means only that the instincts inherent in man impel him toward associating with others and toward forming a state and that man in the "*Greek*" sense, civilized man, cannot be older than the state. And this view—if a single passage taken out of context is not exclusively taken into consideration—corresponds to the words of the great philosopher. Not only that, it corresponds to the dictates of common sense, which tell us that a complicated whole cannot be just as old as the elements to which it necessarily owes its existence.[q]

[q] I have translated the author's translation, for it is more important to show what he thought Aristotle said than to find possible errors in his translation or interpretation. F.J.N.

APPENDIX VIII

The "Organic" Origin of Law and the Exact Understanding Thereof

Law, to the extent that it is presented as the result of positive legislation, is a social phenomenon, the explanation of which, as such and not in any particular orientation, leads to special difficulties. Law as the intended result of the will of an organized national community or of its rulers is a phenomenon which does not challenge the sagacity of the scholar unduly either in respect to its general nature or its origin. But the case is different with law wherever it appears not as the result of positive legislation (of the *intended* common will), but as the result of an "organic process." For here, as above in the case of money, we are met with a social structure which in the most outstanding sense benefits the common welfare. Indeed, it really conditions it and yet does not appear as the result of a will of society directed toward this. An unintended product of social development which conditions and advances the welfare of society, and this perhaps to a higher degree than any social institution which is the work of human intention and calculation—the explanation of this remarkable phenomenon is the difficult problem which social science has to solve.

There is scarcely need to remark that the problem under discussion here cannot really be solved with the mere allusion to the organic origin, the "primeval nature," the "originality" of law, etc.[150] These attempts at explanation are mere figures, analogies between the genesis of natural organisms and that of law. Moreover, they are analogies which, as already set forth in another place,[151] are thoroughly superficial. If the theory of the

[150] Just as little is the above problem solved by allusion to the origin of law in the *national mind.* For even if a national mind differing from the mind of human individuals were to be acknowledged as a real existence with consciousness and desires differing from those of individuals in social intercourse, the question would still have to be asked how the idea of law is actually formed in a mind so conceived and gains its special form in the concrete case. The problem under discussion here is only obscured, not solved, by the above fiction. Cf. Ahrens, *Philosophie des Rechtes* (1870), I, p. 175 ff.

[151] See p. 133 ff.

"organic origin" of law is to be more than an empty phrase, if the above problem is really to be solved, if we are actually to become clearly aware of the "organic origin" of law as opposed to its social-pragmatic genesis, then, on the contrary, it is necessary for us to examine its nature. It is necessary to examine the course of the process by which law appears without positive legislation, that process which one can always call "organic."

The examination of how law *actually* developed originally in individual concrete cases, and the compilation of parallelisms of this historical development in various nations, would undoubtedly be a very useful and reliable methodological procedure for establishing the origin of law and its various possible forms. Yet it is just as unquestionable that this goal cannot be reached in the way just described. Law came into being in periods of human development which are far before those of documented history. What the historians can report about this process is based therefore only on inferences, not on attested empirical knowledge. Even the most careful utilization of history could not offer us a sufficient empirical basis for the solution of a problem in which laws of prehistorical development come into question. Certainly theoretical research will have to utilize history and ethnology most carefully in this undertaking. However, the attempt to solve the problem under discussion here exclusively in a historical-empirical way would be scarcely less permissible than if a natural scientist wanted to find out the first origin of natural organisms only by way of historical-empirical investigation.

The mere allusion to the "organic origin" of law, to its "primeval nature" and to similar analogies, is completely worthless. The striving for the specifically historical solution of the above problem is hopeless.

There can be only one way to reach the theoretical understanding of that "organic" process to which law owes its first origin. That is to examine what tendencies of general human nature and what external conditions are apt to lead to the phenomenon common to all nations which we call law. We must examine how law was able to arise from these general tendencies and conditions and according to the measure of their difference to come to understand its particular empirical forms.

The knowledge thus obtained is not historical in the empirical-realistic sense of this word. However, it is knowledge which, in contrast to the phrases "originality," "primeval nature," "organic origin" of law, etc., indicates at any rate a significant advance in the theoretical understanding of that process by which law came into being in its most original form. Indeed it has the advantage of offering us not only the superficial picture of the development under discussion, but also of revealing the motivating forces which led to the genesis of law with the growing insight of man into his interests.

There is scarcely need to remark that law usually comes into being and develops in an advanced community by way of legislation, or by way of an express agreement of the members of society directed toward establishing it, that is, predominantly in a pragmatic manner. Accordingly, it must also be interpreted predominantly in a pragmatic manner, through the intentions of the lawgivers and the conditions determining these. It was otherwise at the first beginnings of civilization, in epochs when the intercourse of people inhabiting a definite territory was slight, when their integration was not strong, when the awareness of integration was, furthermore, imperfect. In such times therefore we cannot yet properly speak of law as the expression of the organized *total will* of a nation. Here, at any rate, the genesis of law is not pragmatic in the above meaning of the word, and the question of what it actually is becomes inevitable.

The same external situation in which family heads of a territory find themselves under the most primitive conditions plus the insecurity, common to all, of the products of their *individual* efforts, cause the oppression of the individual to be felt most keenly by all others, too. It is human nature to feel the continued threat of evils almost more acutely than the threatened evils themselves. Each individual, even if not directly harmed, feels threatened most seriously in *his* interests by acts of violence, especially the weak individual, who is always in the majority compared to the strong one.

Under such circumstances are formed convictions of the necessity of certain limits to despotism, which are to be discussed below. Probably this occurs initially only in the minds of the wisest in the nation, namely, of those who can recognize their permanent interest beyond the shortsighted interest of the moment. But with increasing insight it gradually occurs in the minds of all those who find an advantage in the limitation of individual despotism. Among these are even the strong individuals, whose interest requires the conservation of what their power has achieved.

The conviction of the necessity of such limits of despotism was not, therefore, originally realized in the nation thought of as an organized unit. Still much less was it realized as the result of the reflection of an individual, or even of a national council, aimed at the welfare of all. It arose, rather, *in the minds of individual members of the population* with the increasing awareness of *their interest, the individuals' interest*. What benefits all, or at least the far greater majority, gradually is realized by all.

The form in which the population becomes aware of convictions of the above type is, according to the nature of the matter, that of *rules for action,* but first and directly it is not at all of necessity a form that is agreed upon among all the people of the nation. Only the contents of the rules, and not their form, will show agreement at first, until gradually chance or talent brings forward an especially fortunate form of those rules which especially suits the perceptive faculty of less civilized people. This form is then fixed in the minds of the population without contract or particular agreement. Such principles are characteristic of all nations, even the most barbaric.

With this, with the genesis of certain rules for the action of the people of the nation, of whose suitability in respect to their welfare the members of the population have become aware, the concept of *law* is, however, not yet completed. For this to be the case another factor must be added which is already given implicitly, to be sure, with the situation we described above.

Everybody in the beginnings of society is directly aware of the significance of the rules for his own well being. Every individual recognizes that he is benefited in *his* interests by their observation on the part of the members of society and that he is threatened in *his* interests by their violation.

The protection of what everyone recognizes as *his* interest becomes the interest of every individual. There thus develops in the population the awareness that adherence to rules in the concrete case is not at the discretion of the individual, but must be assured. With this the contrast between *law* and *morals* is established. But at the same time the concept of national law in its original form is completed. It is the essence of the rules which are supported by national conviction and limit the individual arbitrariness of the people of the nation, the adherence to which is not left to the free discretion of individuals according to the will of the population.

That law is actually enforced in all cases, that what has been violated is actually expiated, or can be, that in particular a coercive power meant for this is actually present and functions duly—all this is on the contrary foreign to the concept of law in its most original form.[152] But without doubt the genesis of a coercive power is a natural consequence of the conditions described above.

[152] It is an error that, since Thomasius, a long line of philosophers of law look for the difference between *law* and *morals* in the addition of a coercive power, or even in the actual enforceability of what is presented by the rule of law. For law obviously remains law even if it is not enforced (e.g., against the cleverer or stronger, or even as a result of injustice), or if the violated law cannot be expiated. Indeed, this is true even if a relevant coercive power is not present at all (as e.g., in many cases of international intercourse). Law differs from morals rather through the fact that the rule of law in the consciousness of the populace, or according to the intention of the lawgiver, is a rule compliance with which *is not to be* left to the free discretion of the individual. This, however, is by no means the case with the rules of morality. The actual existence of a compulsive power and the actual expiation of the violated law are, to be sure, natural and regularly occurring results of the situation described above, but they are by no means necessary presuppositions or attributes of law.

In those beginnings of civilization in which national law arises every member of the nation is not only convinced of the purposefulness of the rules of law and of the necessity of not leaving the adherence to them to the free discretion of the individual; he also feels the impulse to defend the threatened law, or to have the violated law expiated, since no power outside the power of the individual is competent to protect it. Law in its most original form arises and lives only in the mind of the population, but its realization is also exclusively the affair of the latter. It is actually expressed in "self-help" and in "national justice." It is affirmed in tradition and in the custom of even-handed dealing. The less developed a nation is, the greater the force of the conditions portrayed here. In all nations whose legal life is still in its childhood, self-help and national justice play a prominent part. Even in periods of higher development we can still recognize in law the traces of these most original forms of its protection.

In the minds of the population the idea of a closer solidarity, the awareness of national community, and an organization bringing together all people of the nation into a higher unity develop only gradually. They develop through like external destinies, through the community of history, of kinship, of language, of religious feelings, and to no very small extent also by means of community of convictions pertaining to law (and of rules of law) and of the action directed toward realizing them.

Only from then on does law, which up to then was alive only in the minds of individuals and *found its guarantees in the energy of the individuals (of those participating and those of the same conviction),* become the expression of the uniformly organized national will. Only then does its realization become an affair of the population of a territory or of a state, a population which has become an organized unit.

National law in its most original form is thus, to be sure, not the result of a contract or of reflection aiming at the assurance of the common welfare. Nor is it, indeed, given with the nation, as the historical school asserts. Rather, it is older than the appearance of the latter. Indeed, it is one of the strongest ties by which the population of a territory becomes a nation and achieves state organization.

When the population becomes aware of the idea of community, when it gradually begins to feel that it is one, then the sphere of its interests expands and with it that of its rules of law. They cease to be the mere result of the efforts of the people of the nation directed toward protection of the *individual interest.* Also the *common interest,* or what is considered that, enters the mental sphere of the population and with it the awareness of the necessity for protecting this interest against individual despotism. To law which results from the effort of individuals to assure their individual achievements is added law which is the result of efforts directed toward the protection of the community. But this is not necessarily the fruit of common counsel, either, of an agreement, of a contract, or of positive legislation. Its origin is analogous to that of national law in general.

In the first beginnings of civilization man may have become aware of the idea of law as if a new light were dawning. Later generations, however, which did not experience the original formation of law per se, but had inherited it in its basic features from their forefathers, may have become aware of it as an inspiration of a higher divine wisdom, for all nations have connected the idea of law with the loftiest presentiments in very early periods of their development. The rules of law have become the subject of national belief, of a sanctified tradition handed down from generation to generation, and they have become an important subject of religious education. What each individual experienced in himself and created from himself at the beginnings of civilization had thus in the opinion of the nation gradually become something *objective,* something divine standing above human wisdom and human interest. And the gradually awakening insight into the common usefulness of law has affirmed this pious error.

The above process was certainly completed only gradually, almost imperceptibly, because of its nature. Also, in itself it scarcely influenced the contents of law. However, the nature of the latter has by no means remained uninfluenced by it.

In place of the living insight into the connection between the interests of the people of the nation and law as the result of the appreciation of those interests by the people there gradually developed law as the object of belief in authority—the belief in the sanctity and higher origin of law. At least, in terms of its core idea and in its basic determination, it no longer appears before the minds of the population as something they experienced, as the expression of *their* insight and *their* conviction, as something *subjective.* Rather, it appears as something independent, offered to them from outside, something *objective.*

The special contents that law assumes in a concrete case, before legislation begins to shape them, depend on the particular conditions of the population from whose mind law originated. Directed in its original form toward assuring the most important and most general individual interests of the people of the nation, it broadens and deepens gradually with increasing intercourse and the growing insight of individuals into their interests. It is affirmed by custom and is shaken and finally altered by the change of those conditions to which it owes its origin. Certain conditions resulting from general human nature and thus appearing everywhere produce similar institutions of law everywhere by their nature, while tribal differences and variety of external conditions and mental spheres result in differences in law. What is considered law and justice in one nation may in part not appear so to another. With the change of conditions the same phenomenon may appear in the same nation in different eras of its development. Everywhere law is set in the current of time and of human conditions and only in respect to these does it have its special existence.[153]

However, law can also come into being, and even under the most original conditions, in another way essentially different from the above: by *authority*. The man in power or intellectually superior can set certain limits to the discretion of the weak men subject to him or of those mentally inferior. The victor can set certain limits for the vanquished. He can impose on them certain rules for their action to which they have to submit, without considering their free conviction: from fear. These rules, however similar they appear on the surface to those of national law, are both by origin and by the guarantees of their realization essentially different from the law which grows out of the convictions of the population and the realization of which was also originally an affair of the nation. Indeed, they can be in direct contrast to national law; they are really *statute,* not *law*. But the strong man has an interest in calling them "'law," in cloaking them with the sanctity of law, in connecting them with religious traditions, in elevating them so that they become the objects of religious and ethical education. This is the case until the habit of obedience and the sense of subjection developed by them recognize in them something analogous to law and until this habit and sense scarcely distinguish any longer those rules limiting the discretion of the individual which are produced by the convictions of the nation from those which power prescribes for the weak. If the latter have existed for generations and merged with national law in eras when written history does not exist, then even science can scarcely recognize them any more. The amalgamation of national law and the statutes of power advances, however, so much the more easily, the more national law itself has become the object of a belief in authority and is no longer supported by convictions based on the insight into individuals' interests, from which it originally developed. All institutions which sanctify law, even the philosophical systems which "objectify" it

[153] Schmoller (*Ueber einige Grundfragen des Rechts und der Volkswirthschaft* [1875], p. 25 ff.) justly attacks the opinion that the ethical ideas of marriage, of private property, etc., always remain the same, and he shows (p. 29 ff.) that the ethical element is not to be found in the constancy of an institution. Cf. also his "Gerechtigkeit in der Volkswirthschaft" (*Jahrbuch für Gesetzgebung, Verwaltung und Volkswirthschaft* [1881], p. 29 ff.).

or describe it as something "above human wisdom," always benefit power.[154]

Law arose originally from the conviction of the members of the nation or by force. As soon as the conditions of a nation and therewith its law assumed such a complicated character with the advance of civilization that knowledge of the law could no longer be the affair of all people, the necessity for the division of labor led to a special class of people here, too. This class, the class of jurists, is concerned with the study, application, and development of law. On the other hand, the advance of state organization causes law to be recognized more and more as the expression of the uniformly organized common will and the protection of it as a matter for the state authority. In individual spheres of existence, or where state law leaves a gap, law may still develop in its original form and there may arise a common law based on the persuasions of certain elements of a population and even a peculiar legal persuasion antagonistic to statute law. On the whole, however, development of law, administration of law,

[154] Legal order is a condition of all relatively progressive intercourse; the latter in turn is a condition of all higher human welfare; the desire for welfare, however, is in general human nature. Thus law is *not a chance affair,* but, both in terms of its essential idea and its particular content, it is something *implicitly given* essentially by human nature and the particularity of conditions. With this, however, law is not already *something real* either in terms of idea or particular content. For it really to appear, those factors which determine it must be recognized and considered and *law must be created by a mental process.* If one does not want to assume that people became aware of law by way of external or inner revelation, in a word, if one wants to operate only with scientifically admissible means, then that mental process by which law, only *postulated* by human nature and the other pertinent conditions, became *something real* can in any case have taken place only in human minds. *It is the task of science to give us clarity concerning this process,* a task which is by no means solved by the phrases "originality," "primeval nature," or "organic origin." By attacking the solution of the above problem relevantly, we have at the same time shown that law in its *objective reality* is not contained a priori in the human mind in general or in the national mind in particular, nor is it revealed by an intelligence external to the human race. Rather, as far as it is presented to us not as a product of power or of positive legislation, *it is the result of reflective consideration and judgment of needy human nature and the conditions that environ the members of a nation.* Law is thus not an *end in itself.* It is so definitely not this that it would disappear at once and become just as useless as burdensome a limitation of human freedom if those barriers to individual discretion which we call the legal order were to become superfluous in a certain state of society, or if law were to become detrimental to human welfare. Everyone would then recognize by himself that it is neither "external" nor "native to the human breast," nor "divine," but an institution sprung from human intelligence and serving human interests. What was misunderstood frequently enough before the appearance of the historical school of law in Germany is the fact that law is not always the result of an (intended) *common will* directed toward establishing it and toward the furthering of human well-being. Originally it was not this at all. This is a fact which, however, by no means excludes the genesis of law as the result of human intelligence.

and the realization of law in the course of cultural development become in general the affair of state authority and the jurist class. They become the condition of any universal knowledge of law and its practice and of any higher technical perfection thereof. They become the tool of which the practice of law makes use.

The process indicated here was also, as is obvious, completed only gradually and by no means as a matter of necessity, in contrast to the original national law. State authority did not usually do away with common law, but recognized and perfected it technically. Also the jurist class with its professional skill only gradually began its function of developing and administering law. But with this was given the possibility of a contrast between the law convictions of the members of the nation, of the jurist class and statutes.

In this, national law by no means proved inferior in all details when examined more closely. In detail it could show gaps, contradictions, inexact features, and technical flaws of other kinds. On the whole it could not always correspond to the momentary views of the rulers on the purposes of the state and its law order. Above all, it could not follow the mobility of political and social conditions fast enough. All these weaknesses, as soon as a special class began to concern itself professionally with the study of law, could not help coming directly to their attention. This occurred to so much the greater degree the more the ability of the jurists to see such weaknesses had been sharpened by the study of the developed law of other nations. In respect to content, the national law organically developed from the most individual conditions of life without reflection on the common welfare could not always be equal to a test of its suitability for common usefulness.

Thus the jurist class, usually in the service of the state authorities, completed everywhere a thorough-going reform of national law, not, to be sure, without succumbing to individual errors arising from the very nature of the whole matter.

National law had developed from the needs and convictions, from the basic character of the population, and through centuries of constant practice had taken on form corresponding to concrete conditions. As the result of old, tested national wisdom it lived on in the hearts of the population, who clung to it instinctively. They clung to it even where they had long since lost insight into the connection between the rules of law and the particular conditions from which these came. There was a good part of wisdom in national law which the people now only felt and were no longer clearly aware of.

This important factor the learned jurist class has misunderstood for centuries, and, indeed, the more completely, the more they turned away from the study of their own national character and one-sidedly moved in the mental spheres of the developed law of other nations and of abstract law theories. They lacked not only *understanding* of the unintended wisdom in national law, but also *feeling* for it.

There were those who recognized in the state and state institutions and in society and social institutions only the result of the purposeful activity of the inhabitants of a territory or of their rulers. They naturally were inclined from the start to consider all social institutions of organic origin or influenced by organic powers, as far as they did not understand these in their significance for the preservation and development of society, as abuses and social evils. They were inclined to strive for a reform of these in the sense of a policy which not infrequently appeared the more utterly arbitrary the more defective the insight behind it was. The *"intuitive wisdom"* in organically developed social institutions (not completely unlike the "suitability" which in natural organisms strikes the admiring attention of the expert natural scientist, but is easily missed by the bungler!) was in general overlooked by the representatives of this orientation. The fruit of this in the field of practical politics was an immature criticism of existing social institutions, to which were joined no less immature reform efforts.

Theoretical one-sidedness and erroneous desire for innovation have thus spoiled the law of a nation often enough where those who applied the reformer's hand thought they were acting for the common good. But how much worse it was when the rulers and the jurists joined hands to replace the common law which arose *from* the nation and *for* the nation with one which was to serve the rulers!

It was an undeniable merit of the historical school of jurists to have restrained those immature and precipitate reform efforts in the field of legislation and to have pointed out again the organic origin of common law and the unintended wisdom in it. This was a merit which is worthy to be joined to that which the same school gained for itself by comprehensive research in the field of legal history and by broadening the specifically historical understanding of our law.

What the above school can be blamed for, on the other hand, is a series of errors and omissions which we cannot avoid indicating here briefly.

The historical school of jurists has, to be sure, emphasized the "organic origin" of common law, its "primeval nature" and "originality," its genesis in the national mind, etc. But it has stopped here, as if the problem of the origin of common law were in some way solved by the above partly figurative, partly meaningless phrases. It has neglected to make us understand theoretically the nature and the course of that process, the result of which is common law.

Also, only very little was gained by mere allusion to the *"higher wisdom"* of unintentionally created common law. In part, a new error was even brought into the sphere of scientific considerations. The meaning of the allusion can rationally be only that common law, in spite of its not turning out to be the result of a social will aimed consciously at the common good, benefits the latter nonetheless to a higher degree than a corresponding positive legislation could. This assertion is, however, erroneous in every conceivable respect. For common law has also proved harmful to the common good often enough, and on the contrary, legislation has just as often changed common law in a way benefiting the common good. The above theory contradicts experience.

If it nonetheless keeps recurring in the methodological writings of the historical school of jurists, as it obviously does, with all conceivable reservations, the cause for this lies in the vagueness which exists concerning the nature of the *"organic process,"* the result of which is designated common law. Natural organisms, to be sure, exhibit a quite incomparable suitability, one which justly arouses the admiration of the expert scholar. But what is proved by that for common law and its suitability *in respect to benefiting human welfare?* Common law can above all be designated only in a figurative sense as an "organic structure." What is true of natural organisms cannot thus be simply applied to the law. This is so much less the case as common law is, indeed, not the intended result of the common will aimed at the common good but, as we have seen, an outcome of *individual human efforts,* and thus not in direct contrast to human wisdom.[155]

But even if the above image were strictly apt, if common law were actually a structure completely analogous to natural organisms, would it follow that legislation has to refrain from any interference in the development of this organism, or even any interference required by particular situations?

A statesman who would hesitate to change the law with regard to the common good just because it is really or supposedly of "organic origin" would be comparable to a farmer, a technologist, or a physician who would avoid any interference in the course of natural organic processes out of veneration for the high wisdom which is manifest in nature. And are there not even absolutely noxious organisms?

The theory of the "higher wisdom" of common law thus not only contradicts experience but is at the same time rooted in a vague feeling, in a

[155] Cf. p. 225 ff.

misunderstanding. It is an exaggeration, carried to the point of distortion, of the true statement that positive legislation has upon occasion not comprehended the unintended wisdom in common law, and, in trying to change the latter in the sense of the common good, has not infrequently produced the opposite result.

If the historical school of jurists had not stopped with phrases such as organic nature and the higher wisdom of common law, if they had gone deeper to the core of the actual conditions under discussion here, they could not be in doubt for a moment about their attitude toward this problem. If the rules and institutions of common law not infrequently prove to be highly suitable in respect to the common good, it was the task of science to make us understand this advantage. That suitability of common law, which is the unintended result of an "organic process," had to come to the notice of jurists and lawgivers to make the thus gained new insight useful for positive legislation. If individual eras have failed to recognize the peculiar worth of common law and changed the law by immature or hasty reforms, instead of bettering it, it was the duty of the historical school of jurists to avoid a similar procedure for the future—not by proclaiming the higher wisdom of common law, but by teaching the proper evaluation of the insight they had gained in legislation. The fruit of their view was not to be the avoidance in principle of positive law development, however well stipulated. It had to be the purification of the latter by new insight gained from the thoughtful consideration of common law. As the farmer, the technologist, and the physician investigate nature and the laws of its motion in order to shape things for their purposes on the basis of the thus gained insight, so, too, the historical school of jurists had to make us understand the previously uncomprehended advantages of common law. They had to do this to offer to the lawgiver new ways and means to practice his high profession through the thus expanded knowledge. But never, and this is the essential point in the matter under review, may science dispense with testing for their suitability those institutions which have come about "organically." It must, when careful investigation so requires, change and better them according to the measure of scientific insight and the practical experience at hand. No era may renounce this "calling."

APPENDIX IX

The So-Called Ethical Orientation of Political Economy

Different from the "historical orientation" and yet closely connected with its methodology is the so-called *"ethical orientation"* of our science. As its main representatives in German economics we can designate C. W. Ch. Schütz, B. Hildebrand, K. Dietzel, the Hungarian J. Kautz, *et al.* As its chief adherents, however, we can designate the majority of the historical economists of Germany.

We have already made it clear in principle in Book I[156] that in respect to the *theoretical* portion of "political economy" this orientation means a methodological misunderstanding, a failure to recognize the true nature of theoretical research in the field of national economy and its special problems. What we should like to stress here particularly is the fact that we cannot rationally speak of an *ethical* orientation of *theoretical* economics either in respect to the exact orientation of theoretical research or to the empirical-realistic orientation.

Exact theories have in principle the task of making us understand theoretically[157] *individual aspects of the real world.* Exact economics has the task of making us understand the *economic aspect* of national life. An "ethical orientation of exact economics" can thus by no means have the sense of aspiring to reveal to us at the same time the exact understanding of the ethical aspect of national life *and* of the economic aspect, that is, aspiring to unite the tasks of ethics and economics. The requirement of an ethical orientation of exact economics could only mean that this science must render to us exact understanding not simply of economic phenomena but of those influenced by ethical tendencies or even of those conformable to the demands of ethics. This is a postulate of research which,

[156] See Chapters 6 and 7 of Book I.
[157] See p. 75 ff.

however, as scarcely needs to be noted, simply contradicts the nature of the exact orientation of theoretical research.[158]

Just as inappropriate is the idea of an ethical orientation of the empirical-realistic theory of national economy. For in this the consideration of ethical influences on national economy, as far as they are real in the phenomena of the latter, is involved in the very nature of the pertinent striving for cognition. Indeed, it is inevitable. It is impossible to attain laws of the phenomena of national economy in a realistic-empirical way without taking into consideration possible ethical influences on the phenomena. Thus we cannot imagine what sort of task an ethical orientation of empirical-realistic economics should really have.

The idea of an "ethical orientation" is in respect to the *theoretical* aspect of our science a vague postulate of research devoid of any deeper content.

A similar vagueness underlies the so-called "ethical orientation" in respect to the *practical* economic sciences. Certainly everyone is subject to the moral code in his economic activity, of whatever conceivable kind it may be. The scholar in the field of the practical sciences of economy will thus not be able to get rid of the influence of this fact, either. The basic principles of the economic action of people, as they are developed in the practical economic sciences, will have to be confined to the limits presented by law and custom.

However, this is a property of all practical sciences of whatever nature, even of politics, pedagogy, therapy, military science, even of technology. If the "ethical orientation" in the practical sciences of national economy were viewed in this sense, then there would be no practical sciences of

[158] Many writers on national economy look for the ethical orientation of theoretical economics in considering the phenomena of national economy from the point of view of morality; thus, e.g., in investigating which goods might be acknowledged as such from the standpoint of the latter, that is, might be acknowledged as "true" goods; in investigating which prices, incomes on capital, etc., are to be designated as morally objectionable. In this, however, as scarcely needs to be noted, there is no ethical orientation of research in *economics*, but a *moral* judgment on single phenomena of national economy. This judgment in no way can touch the results of theoretical research in the field of national economy. An ever so "untrue" or "immoral" item of goods is subject to the economic laws of value, of price, etc., and is thus from the economic standpoint an "item of goods" whose value, price, etc., must be interpreted theoretically just as well as the value or price of goods serving the highest purposes. Or should an "ethical" theory of national economy perhaps reject in principle the interpretation of *economic* phenomena to be observed in connection with goods which serve immoral purposes? Is it to limit itself to the theoretical interpretation of that part of economic phenomena which are in harmony with the principles of ethics or a certain ethical orientation? What science, then, would have the task of giving us theoretical understanding of the laws of "not true" goods, or of the "not ethical" phenomena of national economy?

any other but the ethical orientation, for all human endeavors, not just economic ones, are under the moral code.

Only practical sciences of economy in which ethical considerations beyond the above-characterized limits were fundamentally acknowledged as decisive for the economic activity of people, practical sciences in which economic considerations were fundamentally subordinated to those of morality—only those sciences could claim to have a distinctively ethical orientation. Presentations of this type, however, would not really be "practical sciences of economy," but *moral* writings about human economy.

The so-called "ethical orientation" of political economy is thus a vague postulate devoid of any deeper meaning both in respect to the theoretical and the practical problems of the latter, a confusion in thought. We can, indeed, imagine a justified orientation of the desire for knowledge which establishes the *relationship* between law, morals, etc., on the one hand and economy on the other, or between ethics and economics. But the notion of an *ethical orientation of economics* has no greater justification than, for instance, that of an economic orientation of ethics.

Truly, this whole idea is rooted on the one hand in a failure to recognize the nature and peculiar problems of the theoretical and the practical sciences of national economy. On the other hand, it is rooted in the underestimation of the economic aspect of national life in relation to other more highly esteemed aspects and in the consequent effort of a number of our economists to ennoble by an "ethical orientation" of research an object of investigation which they do not regard highly. As if the worth of a science were dependent on its object, and the worth of those who profess it were dependent on the nature of the object, and not rather on the importance, depth, and originality of the results of their investigations! The desire for an ethical orientation of our science is in part a residue of a philosophy that comes from antiquity, and, in a different sense, of medieval-ascetic philosophy. In good part, however, it is a lamentable crutch for scientific insufficiency, just as in its day the ethical orientation of historical writing was. It is an almost typical sign of those who show insufficient ability for the solution of the problems of *their* science to want to get satisfactory solutions in their own field of research by bringing in the results of other sciences and utilizing them mechanically.